DEVELOPMENT IN PAKISTAN

ANNUAL REVIEW
2000

Rs 395.00

SOCIAL DEVELOPMENT IN PAKISTAN

ANNUAL REVIEW
2000

SPDC
SOCIAL POLICY AND
DEVELOPMENT CENTRE
KARACHI

OXFORD
UNIVERSITY PRESS

OXFORD
UNIVERSITY PRESS

Great Clarendon Street, Oxford OX2 6DP

Oxford University Press is a department of the University of Oxford.
It furthers the University's objective of excellence in research, scholarship,
and education by publishing worldwide in

Oxford New York
Athens Auckland Bangkok Bogota Buneos Aires Calcutta
Cape Town Chennai Dar es Salaam Delhi Florence Hong Kong Istanbul
Karachi Kuala Lumpur Madrid Melbourne Mexico City Mumbai
Nairobi Paris Sao Paulo Singapore Taipei Tokyo Toronto Warsaw

with associated companies in Berlin Ibadan

Oxford is a registered trade mark of Oxford University Press
in the UK and in certain other countries

© Social Policy and Development Centre, 2001

First published by the Social Policy and Development Centre,
and Oxford University Press, 2001

All rights reserved. No part of this publication may be reproduced,
stored in a retrieval system, or transmitted, in any form or by any means,
without the prior permission in writing of Oxford University Press.
Enquiries concerning reproduction should be sent to
Oxford University Press at the address below.

This book is sold subject to the condition that it shall not,
by way of trade or otherwise, be lent, re-sold, hired out or otherwise
circulated without the publisher's prior consent in any form of binding or cover
other than that in which it is published and without a similar condition
including this condition being imposed on the subsequent purchaser.

ISBN 0 19 579609 8

Photographs by Mr. Akhtar Soomro
Designed by Publications Unit, Social Policy and Development Centre, Karachi
Printed in Pakistan at Hamdard Press (Pvt) Limited, Karachi

Published by
Social Policy and Development Centre
15 Maqbool Co-operative Housing Society
Block 7 & 8, P.O. Box 13037, Karachi-75350, Pakistan
Tel: 111-113-113, Fax: 4534285, e-mail: spdc@cyber.net.pk
Website: www.spdc-pak.com
and
Ameena Saiyid, Oxford University Press
5-Bangalore Town, Sharae Faisal
P.O. Box 13033, Karachi-75350, Pakistan.

FOREWORD

The return of rapidly increasing poverty in Pakistan has emerged as the principal problem requiring public attention. Today, one in every three families is poor. The spread of poverty has to be restricted if a large-scale social breakdown is to be averted, with its concomitant implications on law and order. However, given its intensity and complexity, it needs to be properly understood. Who are the poor? Why is poverty on the rise? How best to tackle it? These are some of the critical questions.

The theme of SPDC's Annual Review of 2000 on *Social Development in Pakistan* is *Towards Poverty Reduction*, deals with these issues. It presents a comprehensive poverty reduction strategy which goes considerably beyond the poverty alleviation programme recently announced by the government. Chapter 1 provides an overview of the report, summarizing the principal findings and key recommendations. Chapter 2 identifies the nature, extent and profile of poverty in Pakistan. The findings highlight the structural dimensions of poverty and indicate that the poverty reduction strategy will have to be comprehensive and multidimensional in character. Chapter 3 explores the role of the informal economy in mitigating poverty, both as the residual employer and through a household or community based welfare and support system of intra- and interhousehold transfers to the poor.

Given the trend of rising poverty and the increasing inability of the people to organize and provide for themselves in the fight against it, it is clear that the government has to step in now through the implementation of a national poverty reduction strategy. Chapters 4 to 8 deal with different elements of such a strategy consisting of, first, increased economic opportunities for the poor, second, their empowerment, and third, access to welfare and support through the development of appropriate social safety nets. Chapter 4 focuses on improvements in macroeconomic policy to achieve faster growth in income and employment. Chapter 5 proposes pro-poor economic reforms, including land reform, as a prime instrument for eliminating rural poverty, along with fiscal reforms which orient public expenditure towards the poor and reduce the tax burden on them.

The relationship between governance and poverty is examined in chapter 6. Chapter 7 focuses on the key element of augmenting human capital endowments through improved access to social services. Chapter 8 analyses the role of social safety nets. The government has announced four direct anti-poverty interventions: the integrated small public works programme, establishment of a microfinance bank, the food support programme, and improvements in the *Zakat* system. We evaluate these initiatives in terms of their scale, design features, implementation modalities and their likely impact on poverty.

This review has been prepared as part of an effort to heighten general awareness, promote debate and improve policy effectiveness in the area of poverty reduction. Government, donors, civil society and people at large will all have to work together with great determination and commitment to prevent a deterioration in the situation. *Towards Poverty Reduction* is SPDC's humble contribution in this regard.

Moeen Qureshi
Chairman

Hafiz A. Pasha
Managing Director

TEAM FOR THE PREPARATION OF THE REPORT

The SPDC Team

Hafiz A. Pasha
Aisha Ghaus-Pasha
Zafar H. Ismail
Sajjad Akhtar
Haroon Jamal
Kaiser Bengali
Ejaz Rasheed
Nadeem Ahmed
Nazia Bano
Sumaira Jafarey
Hari Ram Lohano
Abu Nasar
Sehar Rizvi
Muhammad Sabir
Naveed Aamir
Naeem Ahmed
Mansoor Ahmed
Aisha Bano
Kalim Hyder
Naeema Kazmi
Fauzia Mukarram
Imran Ashraf Toor
Kamran Shaikh

Editing Team

Sheila Riordon
Sehar Rizvi
Mukarram Farooqi
Rizwanullah Khan
Niels Kristian Skou

THE SOCIAL POLICY AND DEVELOPMENT CENTRE

Established in 1995, the Social Policy and Development Centre (SPDC) is a private sector research organization that serves as a focal point for policy-relevant research on social sector development. Using a multidisciplinary approach, the Centre assists both public and private sector institutions and non-governmental organizations to plan, design, finance, execute and manage social sector programmes in a cost-effective manner. The results of its research are made available to policy makers, interested groups and the general public to promote informed discussion and action on vital social sector issues.

SPDC is independent and non-partisan and cooperates with a wide range of organizations working in related areas, within Pakistan and internationally. It determines its own pace-setting research agenda within the parameters of its mandate and objectives, and maintains autonomy, flexibility and balance between responsive and proactive social sector research. Key activities include research and policy analysis; social sector government database support; pilot project monitoring and evaluation; training of government, private sector and non-governmental organizations; and information dissemination through publications, conferences, seminars and workshops.

SPDC has core funding from the Canadian International Development Agency (CIDA). The Canadian Advisory Agency (CAA) provides advisory services and support to strengthen SPDC and help it achieve its mandate. In addition, SPDC undertakes a significant component of self-financing.

The SPDC Board of Directors consists of eminent personalities selected for their commitment to social sector development and their belief that the use of analytical tools in developing public policy is necessary to ensure sustainable social sector development. It includes:

Moeen Qureshi, Chairman
Sartaj Aziz, Vice Chairman
Hafiz A. Pasha, Managing Director
Rafiq A. Akhund
S. Babar Ali
Quratul Ain Bakhtiari
Munawwar Hamid
Javed Jabbar
Saeed A. Qureshi

Social Policy and Development Centre
15-Maqbool Co-operative Housing Society
Block 7 & 8, Karachi 75350, Pakistan
Tel: (92-21) 111-113-113
Fax: (92-21) 4534285
E-mail: spdc@cyber.net.pk

CONTENTS

Foreword	V
Team	VII
The Social Policy and Development Centre	IX
Acronyms	XVII
Views of a leading social sector personality	XXI

CHAPTER 1

Towards poverty reduction

The poor	2
The poverty reduction strategy	5
Opportunities	5
Empowerment	9
Welfare	15

CHAPTER 2

The poor

Per capita income	24
Income inequality	25
Measuring income poverty	27
Incidence of poverty	29
Understanding the poor	32
Poverty of opportunity	39

CHAPTER 3

Is the informal sector a poverty cushion?

Measuring the informal economy	44
Is the informal economy counter-cyclical or pro-cyclical?	50
Level of informal transfers	54
Impact of informal transfers	57

CHAPTER 4

Promoting economic opportunities for the poor

Macroeconomic explanations of poverty	64
Constraints to economic revival	71
Macro elements of a revival strategy	78
Micro elements of a revival strategy	86

CHAPTER 5

Economic reforms and poverty

Public expenditure reform	96
Tax reform	103
Land reform	113

CHAPTER 6

Governance and poverty

Democracy	120
Rule of law	125
Economic governance	128
Corruption	131
Institutional capacity	134
Decentralization and devolution	136

CHAPTER 7

Providing services to the poor

Pro-poor services	142
Levels of coverage	145
Public expenditure on services	151
The Social Action Programme	155
Role of NGOs and the private sector	159

CHAPTER 8

Targeting the poor

Types of social safety nets	166
Public works programme	168
Microfinance	173
Food support programme	181
Zakat	185
Overall evaluation	189
Role of donors	192

APPENDICES

A.1	Chronology of key events in the social sectors - 1999	198
A.2	Extent and depth of poverty: Analytical framework	206
A.3	The poverty of opportunity index (POPI)	207
A.4	Integrated social policy and macroeconomic (ISPM) model	208
A.5	SPDC publications	212

SELECTED SOCIAL DEVELOPMENT INDICATORS

Demographic profile	220
Labour force and employment	222
Education	225
Health	229

	Shelter	230
	Public finance	231
Bibliography		232

B O X E S

Box 2.1	Approaches to determination of the poverty line	28
Box 2.2	What causes the feminization of poverty?	35
Box 2.3	A poultry vendor dreams of social reform	36
Box 2.4	Human development and economic growth	40
Box 3.1	The informal sector of Pakistan: Some stylized facts	45
Box 4.1	Economic growth and rate of poverty reduction	65
Box 4.2	What is happening in the labour market?	67
Box 4.3	Determinants of growth of Pakistan's economy	72
Box 4.4	Why is the Indian economy performing better?	74
Box 4.5	What is happening to total factor productivity?	74
Box 4.6	A chronicle of revival strategies	83
Box 4.7	Employment generation capacity of different sectors	93
Box 5.1	Subsidies add up to 5% of the GDP	97
Box 5.2	Comparative fiscal effort of Pakistan	104
Box 5.3	The size of Pakistan's black economy	105
Box 6.1	Legal aid for the poor	127
Box 6.2	Fighting crime	128
Box 6.3	How corruption affects the poor	132
Box 6.4	Salient features of local government in the devolution plan	137
Box 7.1	Which services are pro-poor?	144
Box 7.2	What determines primary level enrolment?	146
Box 7.3	Cost-effectiveness in public education and health	154
Box 7.4	School Management Committees (SMCs) in the Punjab	160
Box 7.5	A public-private partnership in the health sector	161
Box 8.1	Public works in practice	170
Box 8.2	HBL-NRSP: A key microcredit initiative	178
Box 8.3	Food support programmes in selected countries	183

Box 8.4	Widow turns to *Zakat* for assistance	187
Box 8.5	*Zakat* at the local level: Insights from the field	188
Box 8.6	*Zakat* helps handicapped achieve better lifestyle	189
Box 8.7	Suicide as an escape from poverty	195
Box A1.1	Oxfam International education report, 1999	198
Box A1.2	National health survey of Pakistan	200
Box A1.3	Pakistan Poverty Alleviation Fund	202
Box A1.4	State of Human Rights in Pakistan, 1999	203
Box A1.5	UNICEF report, 2000	204
Box A1.6	Human Development Centre's report, 1999	205

CHARTS

Chart 1.1	Elements of the poverty reduction strategy	4
Chart 2.1	The ladder of poverty reduction	38
Chart 2.2	Comparison of income poverty and poverty of opportunity	41
Chart 3.1	Relationship between growth rates of the formal and informal economies	51
Chart 4.1	Policy evaluation matrix of instruments for revival	80
Chart A4.1	Basic structure of the ISPM model	209

TABLES

Table 2.1	Per capita income by province (rural and urban)	25
Table 2.2	Average per capita income by income quintile	25
Table 2.3	Gini coefficients for per capita income	26
Table 2.4	Calorie consumption	28
Table 2.5	Sources of calories for poor households	29
Table 2.6	Poverty line estimates	29
Table 2.7	Income poverty in Pakistan	30
Table 2.8	Spatial distribution of poverty in Pakistan	31
Table 2.9	Relationship between incidence of poverty, per capita income, income inequality and poverty line	32
Table 2.10	Incidence and depth of poverty by type of household	34
Table 2.11	Incidence of chronic poverty	39

Table 2.12	Indicators of education, health and income deprivation	40
Table 2.13	Poverty of opportunity index	41
Table 3.1	Shares of GDP in, and growth rates of, agriculture, informal and formal economies	47
Table 3.2	Ratio of currency in circulation to demand deposits	48
Table 3.3	Reported and estimated size of the informal economy	49
Table 3.4	Annual growth rates of the informal and formal economies	49
Table 3.5	Shares of employment in, and growth rates of, agriculture, informal and formal economies	52
Table 3.6	Real gross value added per worker in the informal and formal economies	53
Table 3.7	Level of informal transfers	55
Table 3.8	Composition of informal transfers	56
Table 3.9	Provincial distribution of total transfers	56
Table 3.10	Targeting efficiency of transfers	57
Table 3.11	Coverage of transfers	58
Table 3.12	Provincial coverage of transfers	59
Table 3.13	Adequacy of support of transfers	60
Table 3.14	Provincial adequacy of support of transfers	60
Table 4.1	Trend in poverty: Headcount	64
Table 4.2	Trend in macroeconomic indicators and incidence of poverty	66
Table 4.3	Elasticity of incidence of poverty with respect to different poverty determinants	69
Table 4.4	Contribution of factors to change in incidence of poverty	69
Table 4.5	Level of investment and savings	72
Table 4.6	Efficiency of investment	73
Table 4.7	Sectoral growth pattern	75
Table 4.8	The *base* macroeconomic scenario	77
Table 4.9	Number of poor in the *base* scenario	78
Table 4.10	The *best case* macroeconomic scenario	84
Table 4.11	Number of poor in the *best case* scenario	85
Table 4.12	Comparison of macroeconomic magnitudes in different scenarios	85
Table 4.13	Evaluation of candidates for leading sector	88

Table 4.14	Ranking of leading sectors for the process of economic revival	90
Table 5.1	Tax-to-GDP ratio and share of indirect taxes	103
Table 5.2	Factors contributing to change in tax-to-GDP ratio	104
Table 5.3	Tax expenditure in Pakistan	106
Table 5.4	Burden of general sales tax as a percentage of income	108
Table 5.5	Index of prices of petroleum products	112
Table 5.6	Overall tax content in prices of petroleum products	112
Table 5.7	Impact on cost of living of households due to a doubling of petroleum prices	113
Table 5.8	Level of, and trend in, rural income inequality in Pakistan	114
Table 5.9	Farm size distribution in Pakistan	114
Table 6.1	Performance by military and democratic governments in Pakistan	122
Table 7.1	School attendance by income level of household	145
Table 7.2	Dropout rate in primary education	147
Table 7.3	Coverage of curative health facilities and personnel	148
Table 7.4	Coverage of immunization by income level of household	149
Table 7.5	Use of family planning methods by income level of household	149
Table 7.6	Expansion in coverage of electricity	150
Table 7.7	Public expenditure on social sectors	151
Table 7.8	Real per capita expenditure on social sectors	152
Table 7.9	Rate of expansion in pro-poor services in the '90s	153
Table 7.10	Priority to social sectors	154
Table 7.11	SAP expenditures	156
Table 7.12	Share of private schools in primary enrolment	162
Table 8.1	Characteristics of selected leading microfinance programmes	175
Table 8.2	Key characteristics of PPAF and Khushali (microfinance) bank	180
Table 8.3	Total value of transfers under different schemes	190
Table-A4.1	Integrated Social Policy and Macroeconomic (ISPM) Model	209

ACRONYMS

ADB	Asian Development Bank
ADBP	Agricultural Development Bank of Pakistan
ADP	Annual Development Programme
AIT	Agricultural Income Tax
AKRSP	Aga Khan Rural Support Programme
APTMA	All Pakistan Textile Manufacturers' Association
ARV	Assessed Rental Values
ASS	*Atta* Subsidy Scheme
BHU	Basic Health Unit
BOP	Balance of Payments
BPS	Basic Pay Scale
CBR	Central Board of Revenue
CCB	Citizens' Community Board
CCF	Calorie Consumption Function
CPI	Consumer Price Index
CPLC	Citizens-Police Liaison Committee
CTI	Common Taxpayer Identifier
DCO	District Coordination Officer
DFID	Department for International Development
DHH	District Headquarter's Hospital
EFF	Extended Fund Facility
EOBI	Employees' Old Age Benefits Institution
EPI	Education Performance Index
ESAF	Enhanced Structural Adjustment Facility
FATA	Federally Administrated Tribal Areas
FBS	Federal Bureau of Statistics
FCA	Foreign Currency Account
FDI	Foreign Direct Investment
FEBC	Foreign Exchange Bearer Certificates
FER	Foreign Exchange Reserves
FIR	First Information Reports
FMC	Frontier Medical College
FPAP	Family Planning Association of Pakistan
FSP	Food Support Programme
FSS	Food Subsidy Scheme
GDI	Gender Development Index
GDP	Gross Domestic Product
GEM	Gender Empowerment Measure
GER	Gross Enrolment Ratio
GNP	Gross National Product
GOP	Government of Pakistan
GST	General Sales Tax
GVA	Gross Value Added
HBFC	House Building Finance Corporation
HBL	Habib Bank Limited
HDC	Human Development Centre
HDI	Human Development Index
HGI	Humane Governance Index

HIES	Household Income and Expenditure Survey (changed in 1996-97 to Household Integrated Economic Survey)
HSD	High Speed Diesel (oil)
HUBCO	Hub Power Company
IBA	Institute of Business Administration
IHS	Integrated Health Services
IMF	International Monetary Fund
IMR	Infant Mortality Rate
IPP	Independent Power Producer
ISPM	Integrated Social Policy and Macroeconomic (model)
ISPWP	Integrated Small Public Works Programme
IT	Information Technology
ITO	Income Tax Ordinance
KB	Khushali Bank
KESC	Karachi Electric Supply Corporation
KMC	Karachi Metropolitan Corporation
LHRLA	Lawyers for Human Rights and Legal Aid
LPG	Liquified Petroleum Gas
LZC	Local *Zakat* Committee
MEGS	Maharashtra Employment Guarantee Scheme
MFB	Microfinance Bank
MFI	Microfinance Institution
MLR	Martial Law Regulation
MSDP	Microfinance Sector Development Programme
NEP	National Education Policy
NFBE	Non-Formal Basic Education
NFC	National Finance Commission
NGO	Non-Governmental Organization
NIPA	National Income and Product Accounts
NRB	National Reconstruction Bureau
NRSP	National Rural Support Programme
NWFP	North-West Frontier Province
OECD	Organization for Economic Cooperation and Development
O&M	Operations and Management
OPP	Orangi Pilot Project
PAP	Poverty Alleviation Programme
PARC	Pakistan Agricultural Research Council
PDP	Participatory Development Programme
PDS	Pakistan Demographic Survey
PIHS	Pakistan Integrated Household Survey
PML	Pakistan Muslim League
PO	Partner Organizations
POPI	Poverty of Opportunity Index
PPAF	Pakistan Poverty Alleviation Fund
PPP	Pakistan People's Party
PSDP	Public Sector Development Programme
PWA	Progressive Women's Association
PWD	Public Works Department
RHC	Rural Health Centre
R&M	Repairs and Maintenance
Rs.	Rupees
RWSS	Rural Water Supply and Sanitation

SAP	Social Action Programme
SBFC	Small Business Finance Corporation
SBP	State Bank of Pakistan
SEMIS	Sindh Education Management Information System
SHMI	Small-Scale Household Manufacturing Industires
SKAA	Sindh *Katchi Abadis* Authority
SMC	School Management Committee
SMEs	Small and Medium Enterprises
SMEDA	Small and Medium Enterprises Development Authority
SPDC	Social Policy and Development Centre
SPO	Strengthening Participatory Organization
SROs	Statutory Rules and Orders
TFP	Total Factor Productivity
TMO	*Tehsil* Municipal Officer
TO	*Tehsil* Officer
TOR	Terms of Reference
UN	United Nations
UNDP	United Nations Development Programme
UNESCAP	Unitod Nations Economic and Social Commission for Asia and the Pacific
UNFPA	United Nations Fund for Population Activities
UNICEF	United Nations Children's Fund
UPE	Universal Primary Education
VAT	Value Added Tax
WAPDA	Water and Power Development Authority
WASA	Water and Sanitation Agency
WB	World Bank
WFP	World Food Programme
WHO	World Health Organization
WPI	Wholesale Price Index
WTO	World Trade Organization
ZC	*Zakat* Committee

Views of a Leading Social Sector Personality

"Go to the people, live with them, learn from them, love them, and start with what they have."

– Tasneem Ahmad Siddiqui

Tasneem Ahmad Siddiqui is an unassuming person. He describes himself as a civil servant who is a realist and an optimist. But in the words of his colleagues and admirers, he has a passion for innovation and is known for his ability to transform the system from within--characteristics that place him outside the standard mould of the Pakistani bureaucrat. It is these characteristics, along with his moral devotion to learning from communities, that make Mr. Siddiqui an internationally respected proponent of government reform.

Mr. Siddiqui's commitment to people-responsive governance began at the elite Civil Service Academy of Pakistan where, in the 1960s, he first encountered Dr. Akhtar Hameed Khan, founder of the Comilla project and the quintessential role model for development through self-help. As a career civil servant, Mr. Siddiqui has served in a diversity of positions in the country's federal and provincial governments. In the late 1980s, as Director General of the Hyderabad Development Authority, he, with a team of dedicated young workers, designed the Khuda ki Basti: a land and shelter project that imitates the way illegal squatters provide housing for themselves. Mr. Siddiqui managed to persevere for over four years despite a smear campaign against him which eventually forced his removal. Not a stranger to bureaucratic reprisals for his innovative efforts to reform governance, Mr. Siddiqui opted instead to spend most of the next year apprenticing under Dr. Akhtar Hameed Khan. From there, he proceeded to resurrect the Sindh Katchi Abadis Authority (SKAA) to the dynamic, people-responsive, transparent, and self-financing institution that it is today. Mr. Siddiqui currently serves as Director General of SKAA.

In a recent interview, SPDC asked Mr. Siddiqui to share his views on social issues in Pakistan. Following is a paraphrased version of his observations; a web of inspiration based on his years of firsthand experience.

In my opinion, the most important social issue in Pakistan is that we lack a vision of development. I see everything on two levels: the government and society. In Pakistan, the structure of society is not well understood, nor is it empathized with. We do not take into consideration what the different segments of society are thinking and doing, and what methods and strategies they are using. Only by going through the process of incorporating the ground reality of society–by finding out people's thoughts, approaches, problems and economic status–will we *know where we need to go and what our necessities and priorities should be. Only then will we have a vision for development.*

As a nation, we also lack vision about the sequence of development. Since the beginning, we have felt that Pakistan can achieve development through rapid industrialization. We ignored the importance of our agrarian roots, and instead tried to emulate the West, without recognizing the historical process and transition through which Western countries have passed. We must comprehend that without vision, direction, understanding, and historical process, our planning and development paradigm would remain distorted.

First, it is necessary to understand history; second, to learn from it. History enables us to understand people's complex attitudes towards their personal, social and societal development. As a consequence of the 200-year colonization of the subcontinent by the British Raj, the Pakistani people have remained subjugated and developed an attitude of servitude and dependency. It is the social responsibility of the few privileged, educated and enlightened members of our society to change this through social engineering. However, they will not deliver because, in Pakistan, there is no genuine middle class. The historical experiences of other countries have shown that a middle class develops its own ethical and moral principles of diligence, discipline, competence, integrity and commitment for social change. But in our case, influenced by the darbari culture of their past, the Pakistani middle class lacks the characteristics of the genuine middle class[1].

Educated people must stop thinking fatalistically of Pakistan as a poor country, and recognize that we have ample resources: land, water, good weather, other physical resources, as well as a wealth of good human material. Our country is surviving, in fact, due to the ingenuity, hard work and creativity of eighty per cent of the population. While the majority of the population lacks formal schooling, they are nevertheless endowed with natural talent and an inborn ability to absorb skills that should be tapped to its fullest. But whereas developed countries have historically supported small- and medium-size businesses, in Pakistan these people get no support from the professional classes or government. Thus there is a pressing need to overhaul the existing system through social change.

---

[1] In the period of the Mughal Emperors, Delhi was the centre and prosperous people belonged to the Darbar. Access to the Darbar was gained through supplication, and according to Mr. Siddiqui, today's educated Pakistanis still have a Darbari mentality.

These are the issues we must keep in mind if we want real social development. The most important reason for the success of the Khuda ki Basti project, for example, is that we studied the ground reality and accepted it. We saw what people needed, what their problems were, and why government housing projects were not able to deliver. In most cases, plots in housing schemes were lying vacant while, on the other hand, people were going to the land grabbers to get a piece of land. We realized that the State was not properly addressing the people's needs but, surprisingly, the informal sector was--because it understood the dynamics of society and took into consideration people's priorities. So we tried to learn from them. They start with targeting, affordability, and immediate delivery, whereas government ignored these important aspects. As a matter of fact, we formalized the informal sector. Many eminent economists do not give due importance to the informal sector, and some don't even accept its existence. But they fail to understand that the informal economy is simply the result of the dysfunctional and deficient formal sector, and plays a major role, especially in the urban centres.

It is universally known that ninety per cent of the issues of the people are at the local level, yet in Pakistan local government hardly finds any mention in the constitution. Most of the power is concentrated at the federal level, and to a lesser extent at the provincial level. We must accept the importance of local government. Decentralization, or devolution of power, is required so that local government has constitutional protection, duties, powers, resources, managerial and technical skills, as well as fiscal independence; elections on a continual basis; and the assurance that it will not be easily dismissed. It also requires the authority to spend the collected money by mutual consensus with the people. In this way, there will be both participation and empowerment of the people.

Success can only be achieved when the community or beneficiaries are involved at each stage—from identification to prioritization of schemes, followed by all issues of planning, design, cost estimation, implementation and maintenance. What we need is a paradigm shift in the planning and development process from top-down to bottom-up. If you involve the community in the entire process, from inception to completion, they will eventually own the project. The way in which a project is designed is of utmost importance. If the above factors are built into the design of the project, it will not go awry. In every aspect of Pakistani society, whether it be the economy, science, or social sectors, planning and development needs reforms and innovation.

We must also think innovatively with regard to poverty alleviation. We must look for the root cause, rather than the symptoms. We have been experimenting unsuccessfully with various approaches since the mid-1950s, the Social Action Programme (SAP) being the latest in the series. Recently we created the Pakistan Poverty Alleviation Fund (PPAF), but so far it has had no impact on poverty. Pakistan's significant increase in poverty is due mainly to the fact that the planning and development has been deeply flawed; we do ad hoc planning instead of research-oriented long-term planning, and fail to adopt a participatory approach. Therefore, in spite of a six per cent average growth rate, the human development index figures are dismal and poverty is increasing. The answer, as has been suggested in independent evaluations of SAP and other multidimensional infrastructure development projects, lies in true institutional reforms and adopting a pro-people approach.

Acting on the belief that the ground reality must be accounted for at all levels, Mr. Siddiqui synthesizes his approach towards planning, development and social change in Pakistan with a Chinese saying: "Go to the people, live with them, learn from them, love them, and start with what they have." He concludes by commending the people of Pakistan, and expects that the day is not far off when they will be given a fair chance to use their capabilities, and their true potential will be realized.

Mr. Siddiqui has received both national and international recognition for his work, having been conferred the Aga Khan Award for Architecture in 1995, the Ramon Magsaysay Award for Government Service in 1999, and the Sitar-e-Imtiaz (Medal of the Order of Merit) by the Government of Pakistan in March 2000. Mr. Siddiqui's approach and achievements are an inspiration to SPDC, which strives to emulate and reinforce the forward thinking of such notable citizens.

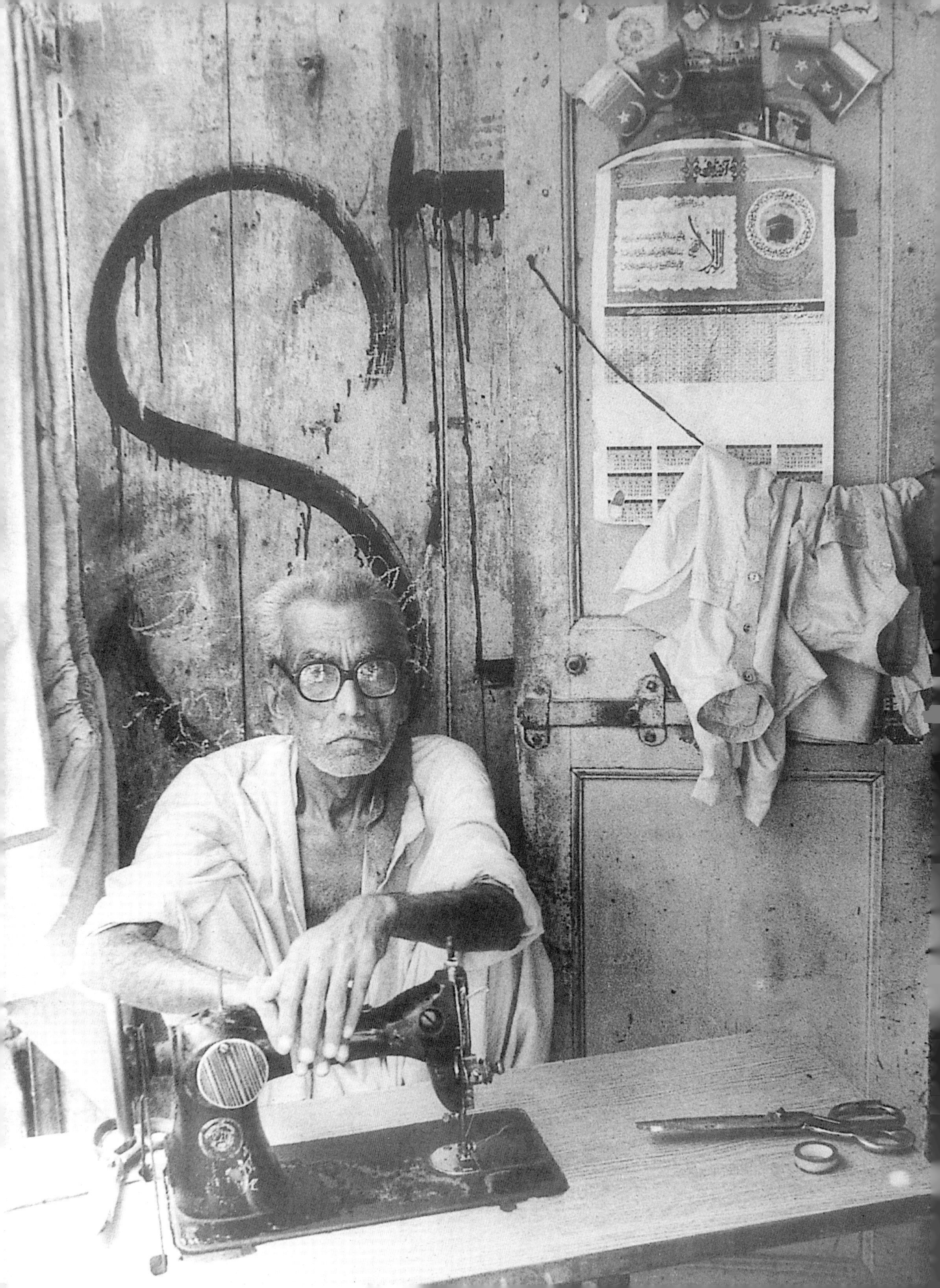

TOWARDS POVERTY REDUCTION

1

"A national poverty reduction strategy must focus on increased economic opportunities for the poor, their empowerment, and access to welfare."

TOWARDS POVERTY REDUCTION

The return of (rapidly increasing) poverty in Pakistan during the 1990s is increasingly being recognized by government and civil society at large as the principal problem requiring urgent attention if a large-scale social breakdown is to be averted, with its concomitant implications on law and order. The objective of this SPDC report on *Towards Poverty Reduction* is to present a comprehensive poverty reduction strategy that goes considerably beyond the poverty alleviation programme recently announced by the government. This chapter presents an overview of the key elements of such a strategy.

■ THE POOR

The report first identifies the extent, nature and profile of poverty in Pakistan **(see chapter 2)**. Principal findings include the following:

- Today, almost one third of the population is poor. This translates into 46 million people currently living below the poverty line.[1]

- The incidence of poverty increased sharply during the 1990s. Whereas one in five families was living in poverty at the beginning of the decade, the proportion is now one in three.

- The incidence of poverty varies substantially within Pakistan, being significantly higher in rural areas. Pockets of extreme poverty, in which as much as half the population lives in poverty, exist in rural Sindh and Balochistan.

- Poverty tends to be concentrated in large families that have few earners and high dependency ratios; households in which the head of the household is illiterate or has a primary level education, and is under- or unemployed; female-headed households; and households that either do not own assets (e.g., property, land, livestock) or have no access to transfers.

- In rural areas, ownership of land or livestock is the single greatest factor contributing to poverty alleviation; in urban areas, access to employment and the acquisition of skills/education make the greatest contributions.

- Much of Pakistan's poverty is chronic, with almost 70 per cent of the country's poor households headed by someone who is either illiterate, elderly, or female.

- Overall poverty of opportunity, measured in terms of access to basic education and health services, is even more pronounced than income poverty.

---

[1] The poverty line is currently estimated at between Rs. 2,800 and Rs. 4,700 per month for a household of six members, depending upon location. These estimates have been arrived at by increasing the poverty line estimates for 1996-97 in accordance with the cumulative increase in the consumer price index (CPI) between in 1996-97 and 1999-2000.

At the beginning of the decade, one in five families was poor; it is now one in three families

Such an innovative initiative cannot hope to succeed unless supported by a friendly policy environment.

These findings highlight the structural dimensions of poverty in Pakistan and indicate that the poverty reduction strategy will have to be comprehensive and multidimensional in character.

Chapter 3 explores the poverty-mitigating role played by Pakistan's informal economy; that is, the extent to which the informal economy acts as a residual employer and provides sufficient income-earning opportunities, especially to unskilled and illiterate workers. While there is evidence that employment growth in the informal economy is counter-cyclical with respect to economic growth in the formal economy, it appears that growth of both incomes and value added is pro-cyclical. This finding implies that during periods of economic recession (e.g., the late nineties), while the level of employment remains stagnant or decreases in the formal economy, it increases relatively rapidly in the informal economy; however, it does so at the cost of falling labour productivity and incomes, which ultimately causes higher poverty. Therefore, there are no grounds for complacency and optimism about the growth-preserving and poverty-reducing role of the informal economy.

This chapter also asks to what extent people are able to cope with poverty through an informal household or community-based welfare and support system of intra- and interhousehold transfers to the poor.

SPDC's research on informal transfers leads to the following conclusions:

- Informal transfers are indeed sizeable (currently estimated at Rs. 100 billion),[2] and almost two thirds reach poor families. Aggregating to over 3 per cent of the gross domestic product (GDP), they represent more than five times the total amount of public transfers.

- The bulk of these transfers are in the form of remittances, either from within or from outside Pakistan.

- Almost three million households receive transfers in one form or another, at a monthly average of about Rs. 2,500 per household. Half of these households are able to rise above the poverty line as a result of the transfers.

---
[2] Based on extrapolation of estimates for 1996-97 to 1999-2000.

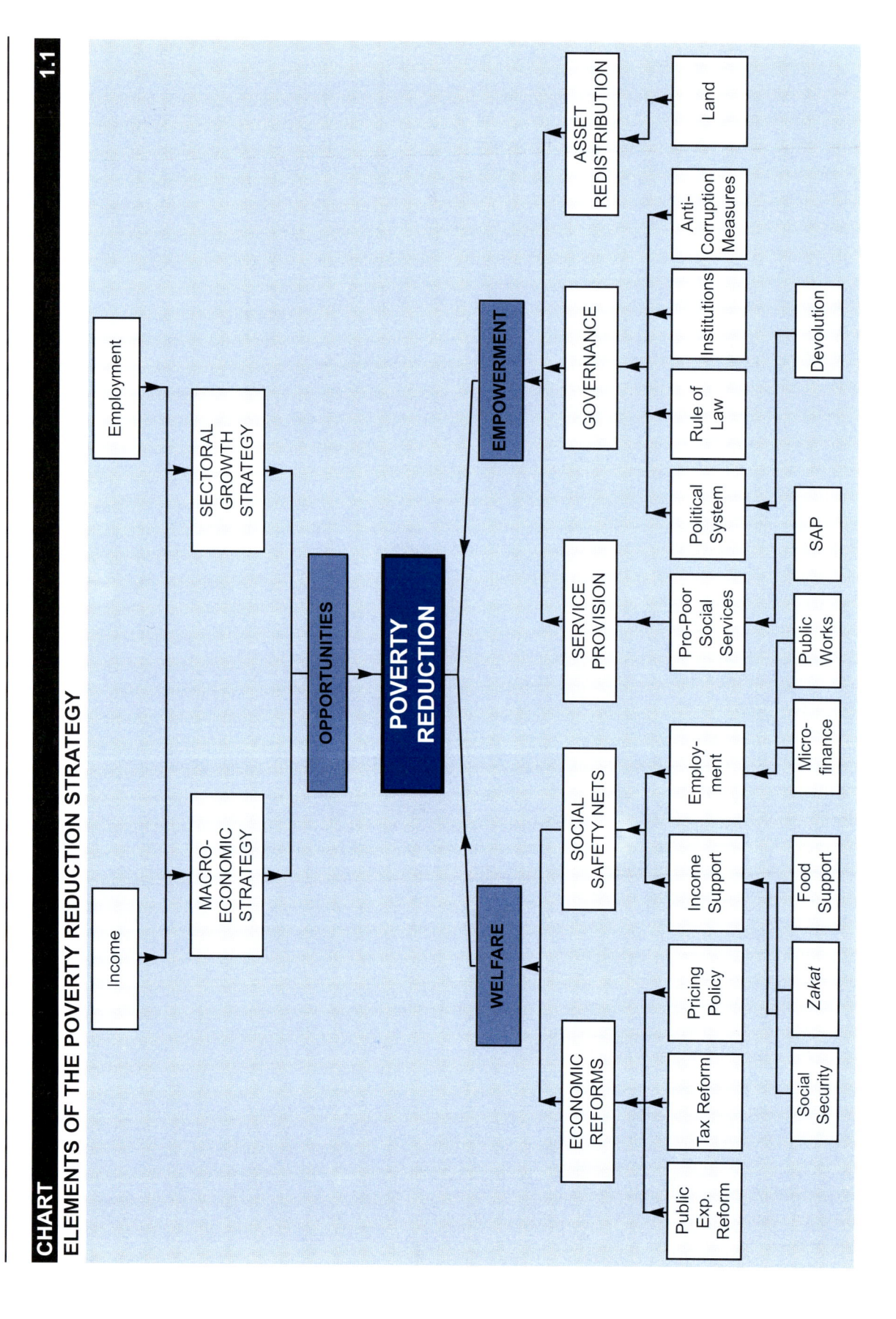

CHART 1.1
ELEMENTS OF THE POVERTY REDUCTION STRATEGY

POVERTY REDUCTION

- **OPPORTUNITIES**
  - MACRO-ECONOMIC STRATEGY → Income
  - SECTORAL GROWTH STRATEGY → Employment

- **EMPOWERMENT**
  - GOVERNANCE
    - Political System
    - Rule of Law
    - Institutions
    - Anti-Corruption Measures
    - Devolution
  - ASSET REDISTRIBUTION
    - Land
  - SERVICE PROVISION
    - Pro-Poor Social Services
      - SAP
      - Public Works

- **WELFARE**
  - ECONOMIC REFORMS
    - Public Exp. Reform
    - Tax Reform
    - Pricing Policy
  - SOCIAL SAFETY NETS
    - Income Support
      - Social Security
      - Zakat
      - Food Support
    - Employment
      - Micro-finance

These findings show that people have found ways of fighting poverty by helping each other. Their efforts have meant a significant reduction in poverty (by about one fifth). There is, in fact, a strong nexus between migration (both domestic and overseas), home remittances, and poverty reduction. But because of the loss of growth momentum in recent years, the ability of the informal economy, in particular, to absorb migrants from rural areas has diminished, while migration to the Middle East has all but ceased. Therefore, the role of migration and remittances in alleviating poverty is bound to become increasingly limited.

THE POVERTY REDUCTION STRATEGY

Given the wide and growing prevalence of poverty in Pakistan, and the increasing inability of people to organize and provide for themselves in the fight against poverty, it is clear that the government must step in and aggressively pursue, with strong commitment, the implementation of a national poverty reduction strategy. What should be the salient features of such a strategy?

Chapters 4 to 8 deal with various elements of a comprehensive poverty reduction strategy. SPDC fundamentally believes that a *three-pronged* poverty reduction strategy will have to be adopted. It should consist of (1) increased economic *opportunities* for the poor, (2) their *empowerment*, and (3) access to *welfare* and support through the development of appropriate social safety nets. **Chart 1.1** provides a schematic representation of the elements of the poverty reduction strategy recommended for Pakistan by SPDC. The 2000-01 World Development Report emphasizes similar elements for a global poverty reduction strategy.

The three major elements of the recommended poverty reduction strategy support and reinforce each other. The creation of economic opportunities alone will not sufficiently alleviate poverty unless people have the necessary human capital endowments to avail themselves of the opportunities or are adequately empowered to ensure that the benefits of growth are not largely pre-empted by the rich. Expansion of social services (as, for example, in the Social Action Programme [SAP]) will only contribute significantly to poverty reduction if employment opportunities exist that make use of higher education and skill levels.

OPPORTUNITIES

In **chapter 4**, SPDC contends that while social safety nets can begin to mitigate against the worst manifestations of poverty, the country's overall poverty outcome hinges on broader macroeconomic developments relating to such key determinants of poverty as growth in real per capita income and the employment level. In fact, the decline in poverty during the 1980s and its increase in the 1990s has a largely macroeconomic explanation. In the 1980s, per capita income increased rapidly, the rate of unemployment remained low, and the human capital endowment of the labour force improved significantly. In contrast, the 1990s witnessed slow growth in per capita income, with actual stagnation in the second half of the decade. Simultaneously, unemployment increased appreciably. By 1996-97, new entrants to the labour force, including young, educated workers, were having great difficulty finding

The creation of economic opportunities alone will not sufficiently alleviate poverty unless people have the necessary human capital endowments to avail themselves of the opportunities.

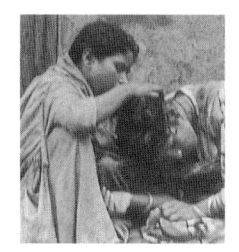

jobs; over 40 per cent remained unemployed for more than a year. Poverty was further exacerbated by the rapid increase in food prices and the steep fall in home remittances.

Macroeconomic Strategy

It is clear that if the increase in poverty is to be contained during the current decade, economic opportunities for the poor–the first key element in the poverty reduction strategy–will have to improve dramatically. The economy will need to show more dynamism with faster growth, leading to greater labour absorption and an increase in income levels. A strategy for the revival of the economy must, therefore, be central in any national programme for poverty alleviation. Constraints to economic revival include the following:

Low and falling investment and savings. The level of investment in Pakistan has fallen by almost 5 per cent of the GDP from the peak attained in the early nineties. Much of this decline is in public investment. Rising debt and interest payments, coupled with the pressure to contain fiscal deficits (as part of ongoing International Monetary Fund [IMF] programmes) have increasingly crowded out allocations for development from the budget. The decline in private investment is more recent, resulting from loss of investor confidence due to the draconian measures taken in the aftermath of the sanctions imposed on Pakistan following the country's 1998 nuclear testing. Foreign investors, in particular, have shied away because of the imposition of capital controls and lack of resolution of the Independent Power Producers (IPP) issue.

The level of national savings has fallen to only 12 per cent of the GDP. Public savings have turned negative due to the emergence of large revenue deficits, caused primarily by rising interest payments. Private savings have remained stagnant because of a lack of growth in real per capita incomes.

Lack of foreign savings. Foreign savings have traditionally been a major source of investment financing in Pakistan, especially during the 1980s. But net capital inflows diminished in the 1990s due to the worsening foreign aid environment and a rapid increase in external debt servicing liabilities. Following the freezing of foreign currency accounts (FCAs) and a major fall in Pakistan's credit rating, capital inflows dried up. In order to sustain the balance of payments position, the current account deficit (equivalent to foreign savings) will now have to be restricted, especially in light of the precariously low level of foreign exchange reserves.

Declining efficiency of capital. The problem of low and falling investment has been exacerbated by the declining efficiency of capital in the economy, with more investment now being required to achieve the same level of growth. Stagnant factor productivity, wrong investment choices, and growing problems of wastage and corruption have all contributed to a rise in the economy's capital-output ratio.

Stagnant manufacturing sector. A number of factors contributed to the sluggish performance of the manufacturing sector in the 1990s. First, unfavourable demand, both at home and from abroad, has caused the volume of manufactured exports to stagnate since 1994-95. Second, the production base has been eroded by both smuggling and the ongoing

A strategy for economic revival must be central in any national programme for poverty alleviation.

Greater access to education would dramatically improve the economic opportunities of the poor

process of trade liberalization. Third, the liquidity problems of the Water and Power Development Authority (WAPDA) and the fall in the overall level of investment have led to major declines in the output of engineering industries. Fourth, the increasing tax burden has restricted output in a number of major consumer goods industries.

Other factors that have contributed to sluggish growth in the nineties include the crisis of institutions, especially the decline in the quality of economic governance; loss of sovereignty arising from the need to implement the conditionalities embodied in IMF programmes (that have focused primarily on macroeconomic stabilization and created recessionary conditions); the inability of the economy to adjust to the process of globalization; and the presence of poor social indicators (which have implied low levels of human resource development and restricted the scope for productivity increases).

Based on the above, the macro elements of a revival strategy for Pakistan's economy should include restoring investor confidence, bringing down real interest rates, enhancing the level of development expenditure, maintaining real effective exchange rate stability, and broad-basing the tax system. Primary emphasis will have to be placed on faster growth of both the manufacturing sector and exports.

For Pakistan to return to a relatively high growth rate in the medium term, the following are essential:

- Removal of the binding constraint of a shortage of foreign exchange for external debt repayment. This could be achieved by obtaining access to significant new concessional financing from donors and a second round of debt relief.

- Restoration of investor confidence by removal of capital controls, establishment of attractive investment and privatization policies, as well as settlement of the long-standing IPP dispute, and stable and consistent economic policies.

- Reduction in current expenditure by 1.5 per cent of the GDP. This can be achieved through containment of administrative costs by right-sizing and austerity, allocations for defence expenditure beyond 2000-01 being indexed to inflation, and a fall in interest payments in relation to the GDP.

- A fall in real interest rates, brought about by fiscal deficit reduction and domestic debt retirement, facilitated by debt relief and privatization proceeds.

- Aggressive policies for resource mobilization, leading to an increase in the overall tax-to-GDP ratio of almost 3 per cent by 2002-03. This can be achieved by effective broad-basing of the tax system; greater documentation of the economy, which reduces tax evasion; major tax reforms, which lead to simplification of the tax system; and fundamental improvements in tax administration.

- An increase in development expenditure from 3 to 5 per cent of the GDP by 2002-03, including a labour-intensive public works programme that creates an additional 0.5 to 1 million jobs.

If the above reform agenda is implemented and targets are met, the economy can once again achieve a growth rate of 6 per cent by 2002-03, with the unemployment rate falling from the current 7 per cent to below 5 per cent. Simultaneously, macroeconomic stability can be enhanced if the current account deficit in the balance of payments falls to below 1 per cent of the GDP and the budget deficit is contained to 3.5 per cent. Consequently, the rate of inflation could fall from the projected rate of 7 per cent in 2000-01 to 5 per cent by 2002-03. The resulting rapid increase in real per capita income (of over 3 per cent) and the expansion in employment opportunities would mean that by 2002-03 the increase in the incidence of poverty could be arrested.

But it needs to be emphasized that if Pakistan's economy remains trapped on a low growth path, as in the second half of the nineties, there will almost certainly be an exponential increase in the number of poor. In particular, if the country is compelled to make a sharp balance of payments adjustment in the short term due to a severe shortage of foreign exchange reserves, then it is conceivable that an additional 15 million people could fall below the poverty line in the next three years.

Sectoral Growth Strategy

There is increasing recognition that stimulatory fiscal and monetary policies–to raise aggregate demand and provide more economic opportunities for employment and income generation–will need to be combined with a sectoral focus (involving supply-side measures) in order to achieve the fastest and maximum results with regard to economic revival. This will involve development of appropriate policies, improved institutional arrangements, and a regulatory framework to stimulate the chosen sectors and increase their dynamism.

As announced by Pakistan's Chief Executive, the following have been chosen as the key micro elements of the government's Economic Revival Plan:

- Revitalization of the agriculture sector;

- Promotion of small and medium enterprises;

- Encouragement of oil and gas exploration and development;

- Development of information technology and the software industry.

If Pakistan's economy remains trapped on a low growth path, there will almost certainly be an exponential increase in the number of poor.

Construction is one of the key sectors that can help lead the revival process at the micro level.

SPDC recommends various criteria for identifying sectors that can expeditiously and effectively lead the revival process. These are high labour intensity, the presence of backward and forward linkages, low import intensity, low foreign investment and technology requirements, high contributions to tax revenues, and limited requirements for policy reforms and infrastructure. In order to maximize the prospects for pro-poor economic growth, primary emphasis will have to be placed on inducing rapid growth in those sectors that, first, are labour intensive, and second, produce goods and services that figure prominently in the consumption basket of low-income groups.

Based on application of the above criteria, construction, livestock, minor crops (especially coarse foodgrains, pulses [lentils], and vegetables), and agro-processing are identified as the key additional sectors to be targeted in the revival process in order to further, at the micro level, the goal of poverty reduction as a complement to the macro strategy for economic revival.

EMPOWERMENT

The second key element of the poverty reduction strategy, and a key element of any national poverty reduction strategy, is empowerment of the poor. SPDC sees the process of empowerment as consisting of (1) increasing the poors' ownership of physical assets (e.g., land, property, livestock) in order to improve their prospects of being able to generate secure, sustainable and adequate livelihoods; (2) augmenting human capital endowments through improved access to education and health services, in order to give people the ability to get out of the poverty trap by better exploiting whatever economic opportunities are available; and (3) moving towards pro-poor governance through changes in the political system, state institutions and laws that promote decentralization and participation of the people, thereby enabling the voices of the poor to be heard in the forums of policy making.

A key element is augmenting human capital endowments through improved access to education and health services.

Land Redistribution

It is proposed in **chapter 5** that land reform must be included as a prime instrument for eliminating rural poverty in Pakistan. This proposal rests on two key facts about the nature and dimensions of rural poverty in Pakistan. First, rural poverty is high because rural income inequality is high, and rural inequality is high because of the very skewed distribution of land ownership in the country. Second, the incidence of poverty is high among the rural landless, and access to land lifts a high proportion of households out of the poverty trap.

In situations where rural markets are incomplete and interlocked, ownership of land can make a significant contribution to the food security and nutritional well-being of households, as well as to their ability to withstand shocks. For example, the obstacle of possessing collateral for access to credit is removed through entitlement to land. The political economy implications of land reform are also important. Land reform could virtually herald a revolution in the countryside and would probably constitute the single most significant act of empowerment among the poor in Pakistan. Empirical research in Pakistan also demonstrates that efficiency losses due to land reform are likely to be marginal.

The previous two land reforms, in 1959 and 1972, were both promulgated by the use of martial law regulations (MLR). Therefore, the initiative for land reform has been taken under military governments or with the help of strong provisions under martial law. Pakistan currently has a military government which at least in its initial statements seemed inclined to consider another land reform. The big challenge and true test of the commitment of the present government to the objective of poverty reduction is whether it can muster up enough will to implement deep and meaningful land reform.

Ownership of land, in situations where rural markets are incomplete and interlocked in character, can make a significant contribution to the food security and nutritional well-being of households.

Land reform is necessary for eliminating rural poverty in Pakistan.

A government building, which once housed a class room, lies in shambles.

Governance

Poverty is the outcome of interactions between economic, social, legal and political processes, mediated through a range of institutions. The extent to which state institutions are pro-poor is determined by the quality of governance and democracy, the rule of law, and the extent to which there is both political decentralization and participation of the people. The relationship between governance and poverty is examined in **chapter 6**.

Political system. The first issue, which is of contemporary relevance in the Pakistan context, relates to which system is more pro-poor–parliamentary democracy or an authoritarian military regime. Pakistan is unique in the sense that, historically, democracy has been interspersed with long periods of military intervention. Analysis of the track record of each reveals that the rate of poverty reduction has been more or less the same under both types of government. It appears that while economic growth has been slower under democratic governments, these governments have generally achieved more pro-poor growth.

What explains the apparent concern for the poor on the part of the present military government? First, SPDC believes that, in the face of rapidly rising poverty, the military regime has been compelled to focus on poverty alleviation, largely as a reflection of the enlightened self-interest of the elite in averting a social breakdown in the country. Second, in search for legitimacy, the military government has probably found in poverty reduction a viable populist slogan. Third, the regime may be catering to international donors' newly found concern for poverty alleviation, in an effort to attract more concessional assistance.

As Pakistan gears up to return to democracy by late 2002, the question is whether the momentum for state intervention in poverty alleviation will be sustained or not. The answer hinges on whether the imperfect democracy that Pakistan has experienced to date can be improved upon. True democracy will require a shift from personalized leadership to the more effective operation of institutions, particularly the legislative and judicial arms of government. An impartial and autonomous accountability mechanism will have to be put in place to prevent the worst excesses of politicians. The political environment will also have to be made more conducive to the development of NGOs and civil society at large, through the protection of civil liberties and freedom, including the preservation of press freedom.

Rule of law. The rule of law is of vital importance to the poor. The interests of the poor can be subverted either by the absence of equitable laws or the presence of inherently inequitable laws (such as those relating to property rights or the treatment of minorities and women), or by the inequitable application and enforcement of existing laws. More broadly speaking, a proper legal system should promote stable and higher economic growth while respecting property rights, guaranteeing the sanctity of contracts, and lowering transaction costs.

In Pakistan, the existing judicial system has lost the confidence of the people, especially of the disadvantaged and the underprivileged. There is a massive backlog of court cases still pending. The subordinate judiciary, which interacts the most with the poor, is seen to be corrupt, prone to political interference, inadequately trained, and underpaid. Lack of justice, a common complaint of the people, is a significant contributing factor to their state of permanent deprivation.

Judicial reform will have to focus on (1) poor governance and administration, (2) inadequate case management and long delays, (3) lack of automation and court information systems, (4) poorly developed human resources, and (5) the absence of infrastructure. Various legal aid systems for the poor will have to be established.

Institutions. In the context of improved economic governance, policies will have to be increasingly motivated by the objective of protecting the *public interest* or, more particularly, the poor, while becoming less vulnerable to the pressures of powerful special interest groups. For this to happen, the process of policy making will have to be opened up and made more transparent, information systems will have to be linked more closely to ground realities, and the bureaucracy will have to be made more responsive and accountable.

Administrative capacity and capability are important components of good governance. By affecting the quality of public service delivery, they directly raise the well-being of the poor. Merit-based recruitment and promotion–linked to performance, market-based wages, and autonomy from the political process–are perhaps the most crucial elements of improved bureaucratic performance. Civil service reforms in Pakistan will have to focus on decentralizing the organizational structure, simplifying the rules of business, modernizing management practices, changing the skills mix, enhancing in-service training, increasing accountability, promoting coordination among cadres, and improving recruitment procedures.

Anti-corruption measures. The elimination of corruption is fundamental to improved governance. Corruption is deeply entrenched in Pakistan and threatens the entire economic, political, and social fabric of the country. Petty corruption is widespread, mostly conducted by low-level personnel in the performance of some regulatory function or the provision of some service. The poor are especially vulnerable to petty corruption in the conduct of their day-to-day activities.

The rise in petty corruption is a reflection of the systemic nature of corruption. It has been reinforced by the falling real incomes of public officials, the emergence of shortages in basic services, and higher user

Lack of justice, which is a common complaint of the people, is a significant contributing factor to their state of permanent deprivation.

Poverty alleviation programmes have often neglected an important dimension-poor women.

charges. The time has come to take strong symbolic steps to reduce corruption. The government must set up an impartial and all-encompassing accountability mechanism and deliver exemplary punishments to corrupt officials of public utilities, law enforcement agencies, and the lower judiciary.

Devolution. Decentralization and devolution can be powerful ways of empowering the poor, especially if this leads to greater community involvement in the delivery of services, and to social safety nets based on local needs, local accountability, and local monitoring. The government has announced an ambitious plan for the devolution of power to local governments within the country. Implementation of the devolution plan by mid-2001 will represent a fundamental change in the system of government in Pakistan.

This plan has a number of positive features, such as greater accountability of local officials, enhanced scope for representation of the underprivileged through reserved seats, and non-party-based elections. But the plan also has major risks, including the lack of institutional capacity to handle the diverse set of functions being handed over, the reluctance of provincial governments to fully empower local governments, unclear financial arrangements, and the likelihood of control by the local elites, which could defeat the purpose of inducing greater people's participation.

Service Provision

Services can contribute to alleviating poverty in a number of ways. First, by building up the human capital endowments of the poor, services can better equip them to earn a living. Second, services can enhance income and employment opportunities by strengthening the public infrastructure for private investment and growth. Third, they can help reduce private consumption expenditure and thereby enable an improvement in the living standards of the poor.

The government in its commitment to poverty reduction must divert more resources to upgrading the coverage of pro-poor services.

Pro-poor social services. In **chapter 7**, the report quantifies the large and growing gaps in the coverage of basic pro-poor services, such as primary education, curative and preventive health care, population welfare, and water supply and sanitation. This is the consequence of a large-scale retreat by federal and provincial governments from the provision of such services, especially in the second half of the 1990s, as reflected in the sharp fall in public expenditure on social services. From a peak of 4.1 per cent of the GDP in 1995-96, expenditure on social services had fallen to 3.4 per cent by 1999-2000. Education expenditure during this period fell from 2.5 to 2.1 per cent of the GDP. Cutbacks in development expenditure have been particularly steep, and the gaps in coverage have become entrenched and are increasing. For example, the number of new schools being constructed is now down to one fifth of the peak rate attained in the first half of the nineties, and the number of hospital beds is down to one fourth.

This report observes that in an environment of resource limitations and changing priorities, expansion in the coverage of pro-poor services will have to come through higher efficiency and greater cost-effectiveness. Beyond getting more value for the money, the government will also have to demonstrate its commitment to poverty reduction by diverting more resources to upgrading and expanding the coverage of pro-poor services. The federal government must target direct spending and transfers to the provinces to ensure that at least 20 per cent of public expenditure goes to social services.

Social Action Programme. The government's Social Action Programme (SAP) appears to be in jeopardy. The large outlays under this programme have had somewhat disappointing results in terms of their impact on social indicators. In recent years, the programme has been significantly scaled down by provincial governments. Urgent reforms required within SAP include:

- Better prioritization, which would lead to the identification of core pro-poor social services that must remain protected from cutbacks.

Cutbacks in development expenditure, in particular, have been steep. The gaps in coverage have become permanent and are increasing.

- Institutional reforms that facilitate both greater decentralization and involvement of the beneficiaries.

- Changes in delivery mechanisms that enhance cost-effectiveness, sustainability, and impact.

- Greater involvement of NGOs and the private sector, through evolution of public-private partnerships and appropriate regulation.

- The use of independent and effective monitoring and evaluation systems.

WELFARE

The third key element of the poverty reduction strategy relates to welfare measures that primarily target the poor. These include economic reforms **(see chapter 5)** in the areas of public expenditure, taxation, and pricing policy, as well as the development of social safety nets **(see chapter 8)**. The latter reach out primarily to the poorest of the poor, who are unable to avail themselves of economic opportunities.

Economic Reforms

Public expenditure reform. Public expenditure reform has proven to be one of the most intractable areas of reform. As highlighted above, the key task is to increasingly orient the benefits of public expenditure towards the poor. The currently misplaced priorities of public expenditure are starkly highlighted by the following:

- Military expenditure remains at an unsustainably high level in Pakistan. At 4.5 per cent of the GDP, it is more than twice the total expenditure on public education.

- Subsidies on economic, social and community services added up to over Rs. 145 billion in 1997-98, equivalent to 5 per cent of the GDP. They had risen from about 3 per cent of the GDP in 1980-81, and 4 per cent of the GDP in 1990-91. Only about one third of these subsidies are for merit goods (i.e., primary education and health); the rest go primarily to economic services (e.g., irrigation) and higher education, which largely benefit upper income households.

- The pressure to contain fiscal deficits has led to sharp cutbacks in development expenditure, which fell from over 7 per cent of the GDP in the early 1990s to only 3 per cent of the GDP by 1999-2000. As indicated earlier, this has severely restricted the rate of expansion in the coverage of pro-poor social and economic services.

Making public expenditure more responsive to the needs of the poor will require (1) enhancing user charges for services that primarily benefit upper income households, and then using the revenues generated for cross-transfer payments to the poor; (2) placing a limit on the increase in military expenditure and exercising cost savings wherever possible; (3) rethinking the role of government and downsizing low priority areas; (4) improving the transparency and accountability of expenditures by setting up proper oversight bodies and disseminating more information on

The key task is to increasingly orient the benefits of public expenditure towards the poor.

budgets; (5) restructuring public sector institutions and service delivery; and (6) integrating planning and budgeting into a medium-term framework in order to enhance the financial sustainability of the services provided.

Tax reform. From the viewpoint of poverty alleviation, tax reform is important for two basic reasons. First, to the extent possible, such reform may play a role in the reduction of the burden of taxes on those goods and services that are consumed more by the poorer segments of society, and shift the incidence to goods and services, as well as the incomes, of relatively well-off households. Second, given the low and falling tax-to-GDP ratio, the government has found it increasingly difficult to increase the levels of public expenditure on what can be considered pro-poor services, and to expand the outreach of social safety nets. Therefore, it is imperative that the tax-to-GDP ratio be raised, but not in ways that adversely affect the poor. The additional revenues should be used, as much as possible, for financing the poverty alleviation programme.

Pakistan's current tax system manifests all the characteristics of a failed system–absence of a tax culture, high levels of tax evasion, weak and antiquated tax administration, a defective tax policy that has been exploited by special interests for wide-ranging tax concessions and exemptions, and an overreliance on indirect taxation.

This has led to the following:

- The tax-to-GDP ratio has fallen, especially in the second half of the nineties. Today, the ratio for Pakistan is below 13 per cent, whereas the average for developing countries at a comparable stage of development is 20 per cent.

- The size of Pakistan's black economy was estimated at close to Rs. 800 billion for 1998-99, equivalent to about one fourth of the economy. This represents a revenue loss due to tax evasion of almost Rs. 105 billion, equivalent to over 3 per cent of the GDP.

- Tax expenditures (representing the revenue foregone due to tax concessions and exemptions) are rampant, adding up to Rs. 120 billion or the equivalent of as much as 40 per cent of the revenues actually collected. A large proportion of these tax expenditures (especially in direct taxes) primarily benefit the rich.

- The tax burden has become more regressive with the recent increase in the share of indirect taxes and the increasing reliance on taxation of energy inputs into consumption and production.

The primary thrust of tax reforms has to be on raising the tax-to-GDP ratio while simultaneously reducing the burden on the poor and increasing it on the rich. In fact, it appears that if tax evasion and tax concessions or exemptions to the rich could be eliminated, Pakistan's tax-to-GDP ratio could approach the developing country average.

Elimination of tax evasion will have to include a series of measures for documentation of the economy, which go beyond the tax survey recently undertaken by the government, along with stronger enforcement measures. It is extremely important, however, that concurrently there be a complete restructuring of the Central Board of Revenue (CBR), including a purge of corrupt and inefficient officials, simplification of laws, re-engineering of business processes, and streamlining of the appeals process.

Tax reform must attempt to reduce the burden of taxes on goods and services that are consumed more by the poorer segments of society.

The homeless.

Beyond curbing tax evasion and eliminating tax expenditures, there are a number of areas of taxation that have hitherto been left unexplored and underdeveloped, yet have the potential to make Pakistan's tax system more progressive while at the same time raising additional revenue. These include the agricultural income tax (AIT), the urban property tax and capital gains taxes—which have the combined potential of yielding up to Rs. 25 billion.

As the above elements of tax reform are implemented, it is crucial that some of the additional revenues be passed on in the form of a reduction in the tax burden on the poor. In particular, the standard rate of the general sales tax (GST), which has become an increasingly regressive tax, should be reduced and brought down from 15 to 10 per cent. Also, the exemption limit for income tax purposes should be enhanced in order to avoid a situation whereby households with income below the poverty line are compelled to pay income tax.

Pricing policy. As far as pricing policy is concerned, the government administers the prices of a number of key commodities and services (e.g., wheat, medicine, petroleum products, urban transport, electricity, gas and water) which have a vital bearing on the cost of living of the poor. In recent months, the prices of petroleum products have risen sharply in response to rising international prices. A pro-poor pricing policy at this

An upscaled public works programme can provide the poor with what they need most: employment opportunities.

time would have been to reduce the tax content in the price of products like high speed diesel (HSD) and kerosene oil. Also, public utilities must pursue a policy of low tariffs for lifeline supplies.

Social Safety Nets

There will continue to be large pockets of the very poor who cannot benefit from more opportunities and the process of empowerment. Therefore, the development of adequate social safety nets will be a natural complement to, but not a substitute for, the other elements of the poverty reduction strategy.

An appraisal of social safety nets in Pakistan demonstrates the low priority that the government has historically assigned to direct interventions for poverty alleviation. Most schemes have weak institutional structures. Their funding is uncertain, their targeting inefficient, and their coverage very limited. The underdevelopment of social safety nets at least partly explains the growing incidence of poverty in the country.

The government has announced that it will focus on four indirect anti-poverty interventions: the Integrated Small Public Works Programme (ISPWP), establishment of a new microfinance bank (the *Khushali* Bank), the Food Support Programme (FSP), and improvements in the *Zakat* system. **Chapter 8** evaluates these initiatives in terms of their scale, design features, and implementation modalities, and evaluates their likely impact on poverty.

Employment. The ISPWP, which is allocated Rs. 21 billion for 2000-01, aims to create employment and income-generating activities through community participation and local involvement in the implementation of a large number of small projects (e.g., farm-to-market roads, water supply, electrification, and schools).

The poverty alleviating impact of a public works programme can be maximized by (1) resorting to labour-intensive construction techniques, (2) setting the wage rate below the market level to ensure self-selection, (3) targeting areas with a high concentration of poverty, (4) synchronizing

Pakistan has historically assigned low priority to direct interventions for poverty alleviation.

work with the timing of agricultural slack seasons, and (5) ensuring proper mediation by NGOs and community groups in order to protect the rights of the poor.

Based on these considerations, the ISPWP appears to have a number of problems. First, its funds have been diverted from other programmes, and therefore it is not clear whether the 0.5 million jobs created will be additional in nature. Second, the provincial governments are likely to have difficulties financing this programme due to lack of resources. Third, changes in institutional arrangements to ensure local involvement, proper targeting, minimization of leakages, and increased use of labour have not yet been specified. Fourth, the proposed wage rate (Rs. 100/day) is too high and enhances the probability of participation by already-employed workers. Fifth, the programme is biased in favour of men, given the nature of activities and existing cultural practices.

The *Khushali* Bank has been established to mobilize funds and to provide sustainable microfinance services to the poor, particularly women, in order to mitigate against poverty and promote social welfare and economic justice through community building and social mobilization. The bank will make both individual and group loans, with the loan size ranging from Rs. 3,000 to Rs. 30,000 at market-based interest rates (up to 20 per cent). Community mobilization for group loans will be undertaken by non-governmental organizations (NGOs), while special microfinance counters will be established in the branches of government-owned commercial banks.

The government's effort to implement microfinance follows many successful experiments worldwide, such as the Grameen Bank in Bangladesh. Elements of success include the reduction in both transaction costs by group-based lending and default by peer monitoring within a group. Such lending also eliminates the need for physical collateral and its substitution by social collateral. However, microfinance is not free from shortcomings. International evidence suggests that such financing is not well suited to the poor, who frequently require consumption and not production loans. Also, it rarely generates new jobs.

There are reasons, however, to be optimistic about the future of the *Khushali* Bank, because it starts with a number of distinct advantages. First, it is likely to obtain cheap (perhaps forced) equity from Pakistani commercial banks. Second, as per the ordinance promulgated for its establishment, it is not under any obligation to pay dividends to its shareholders. Third, it has been granted complete tax exemption on its income or profits. Fourth, it is not required to follow the normal reserve requirements or prudential regulations of the central bank. Fifth, it has already been promised a large and subsidized credit line by the Asian Development Bank (ADB). Sixth, it has developed a partnership with a large NGO, the National Rural Support Programme (NRSP), which already has significant experience in preparing communities for receiving microfinance. Seventh, it has free access to branches of the nationalized banks. But despite these many advantages, it is too early to say what impact the *Khushali* Bank will have on alleviating poverty in Pakistan.

Income support. The Food Support Programme (FSP) is a new initiative. The programme has been granted Rs. 2.5 billion, and is anticipated to benefit an estimated 1.2 million households earning less than Rs. 2,000 per month, with each beneficiary receiving Rs. 2,000 per year in biannual instalments. The launch of the FSP demonstrates clear recognition by the government of the need to provide basic food security to poor households following the significant increase in the price of wheat flour.

The underdevelopment of social safety nets at least partly explains the growing incidence of poverty in the country.

The access to *Zakat* is limited and some of the disabled have had to turn to begging.

The FSP has a number of potential problems. First, if the *Bait-ul-Maal's* existing lists of beneficiaries are used for identification of the recipients of the subsidy, then there is a danger of serious mistargeting since *Bait-ul-Maal* funds are notoriously prone to leakage and corruption. Second, since the subsidy is in the form of cash, there is no guarantee that the amount received will be used to enhance nutritional standards. Third, the coverage is very limited and even households which meet the eligibility criteria may be excluded. Fourth, although the programme indicates a preference for helping minorities and women, no special mechanisms are proposed for reaching them. Fifth, in the absence of an earmarked source of revenue to finance the programme, there are concerns about the fiscal sustainability of the scheme.

Zakat is the most important cash transfer scheme in Pakistan. It is mandated by religion and is officially collected from Sunni Muslims. Those eligible to receive *Zakat*, the *Mustahiqeen*, include the poor (especially widows and orphans), as well as people with handicaps and disabilities. Two main types of support are provided through the scheme: a monthly *guzara* (subsistence) allowance of Rs. 500 (recently increased from Rs. 300) and a rehabilitation grant of up to Rs. 5,000. There are currently 1.5 million *Mustahiqeen* in Pakistan.

Zakat performs fairly well as a social safety net. First, the subsistence allowance appears to be adequate. Second, administration costs are low, due primarily to voluntary inputs. Third, it is financially sustainable because of access to an earmarked source of revenue. But it also has a number of problems, including some doubts about its targeting efficiency and the fact that it may largely substitute for private transfers. There are serious delays in the disbursement of the allowance to beneficiaries and the absence of any monitoring arrangements. The government now proposes to concentrate more on rehabilitation allowances in order to reduce, to the extent possible, the state of permanent dependency among beneficiaries.

Overall, despite the greater emphasis now on anti-poverty interventions, the above social safety nets are likely to have only a small impact on the incidence of poverty in the country. The total value of public transfers is estimated at Rs. 20 billion, representing a paltry 0.6 per cent

The ineffectiveness of the present government system to respond quickly and effectively to emergencies has been amply demonstrated by the inadequate response to the recent drought.

of the GDP, and a maximum of about 3 million households are likely to be reached (out of the country's 8 million poor households). The amount of support is likely to be inadequate to lift many of these households out of poverty.

Clearly the government has to commit itself to substantially larger transfers through wider and deeper social safety nets, and to simultaneously improving the institutional arrangements for targeting and benefiting the poor. While the existing interventions need to be strengthened, other mechanisms also need to be put in place. Two sections of the population beyond those already covered need special support. The first category is that of the elderly and retired low-income workers. The existing Employees Old Age Benefits Institution (EOBI) is a potentially useful institution for providing social security and the government has recently announced an increase in pensions from Rs. 425 to Rs. 630 per month. But EOBI's coverage is extremely limited and access is difficult. It currently covers fewer than 20 per cent of workers in urban areas. The scheme could be improved by asking employers to pay a flat contribution rate per worker, and ensuring that this is matched by the government. In addition, the scheme should be opened up to the self-employed, as well as to employers in establishments with fewer than ten workers.

The other category is that of households that suffer a loss of assets or life due to natural calamities or disasters. The ineffectiveness of the present government system to respond quickly and effectively to emergencies has been amply demonstrated by the inadequate response to the recent drought in Pakistan which, in some remote parts of the country, even affected lifeline water supplies. Institutional arrangements, including the involvement of NGOs, will need to be strengthened in order to respond effectively to future calamities or disasters. In addition, the government must establish a permanent Disaster Relief Fund, to which contributions are made annually. The fund would provide support to poor families, particularly to resurrecting their economic lives in the aftermath of a disaster. Such a fund could also become the focal point for private charitable contributions.

Beyond this, the government's priority in its poverty alleviation programme should be to provide more employment opportunities by upscaling the Public Works Programme, subject to the development of adequate institutional capacity and proper implementation modalities. The present ISPWP is highly skewed towards rural areas, whereas urban poverty is also high and increasing rapidly. The additional allocations should be used for starting a *Katchi Abadis* (squatter settlements) and Slum Areas Improvement Programme, involving the provision of basic infrastructure such as roads, water supply, sewerage, and sanitation. Not only would this provide employment opportunities to construction workers in urban areas, a high proportion of whom are currently unemployed, but it would also provide significant secondary benefits to the urban poor, who generally live in *katchi abadis* and slum areas.

Finally, the government must concentrate on empowering the poor by improving access to basic services such as education and health care. Welfare initiatives of the government must not come at the expense of programmes like the Social Action Programme. This is important if the people (especially the future generation) are to be equipped to break out of the vicious cycle of poverty and not become permanently dependent on handouts from well-off households or the government.

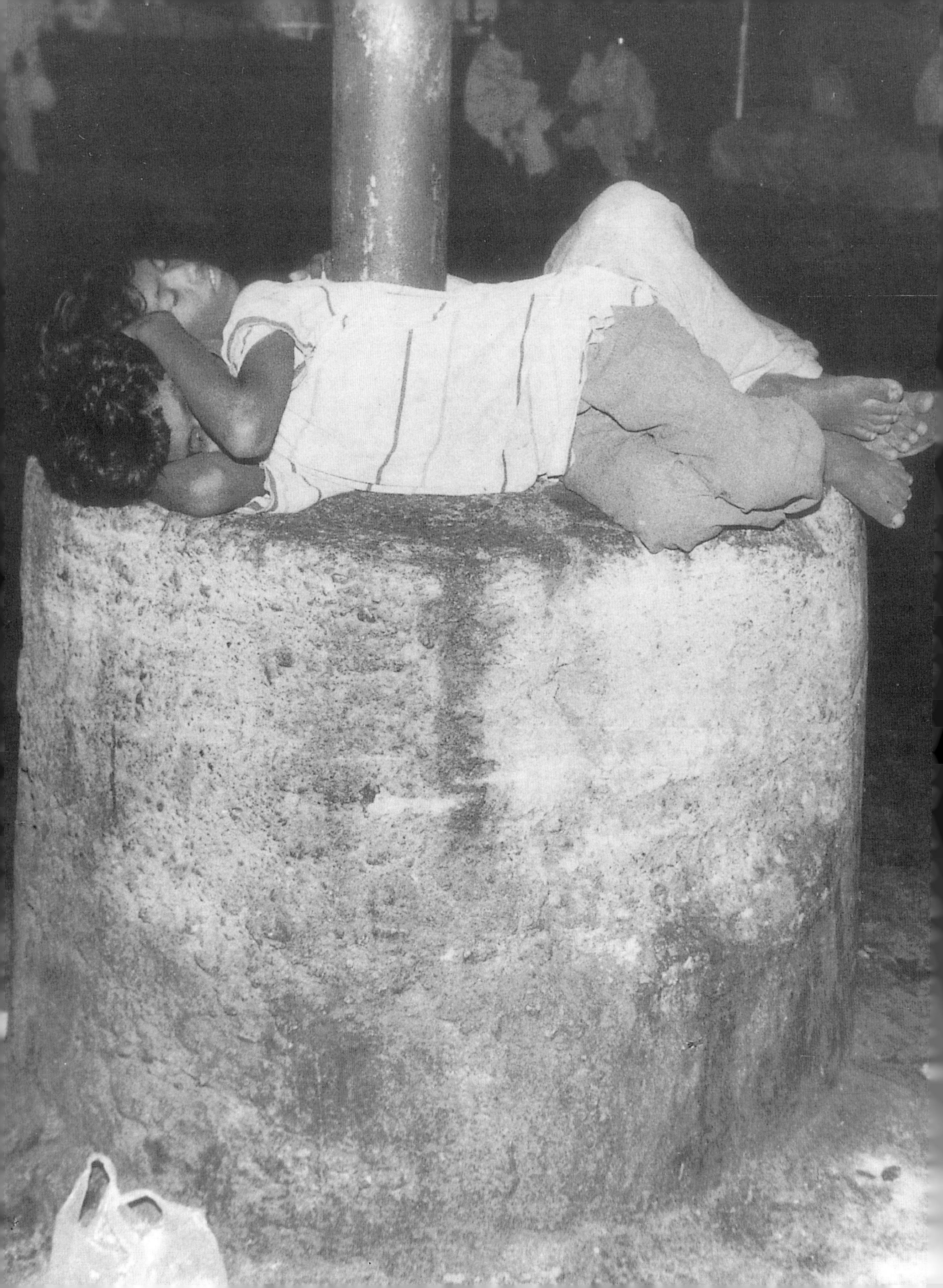

THE POOR

CHAPTER 2

"When people have some assets and job opportunities, and household members are skilled, educated and healthy, a minimum standard of living is attained and poverty is eliminated."

THE POOR

After more than a decade of preoccupation with macroeconomic stabilization, poverty alleviation is the new buzzword among policy makers in Pakistan. Recognizing poverty reduction as an important objective of economic development, the government has recently announced a poverty alleviation programme. Knowledge about the poor is essential if the government is to adopt sound development strategies and more effective policies for reducing poverty. How many poor are there? Where do they live? What are their economic circumstances? Answering these questions is a necessary first step towards understanding the impact of policies on the poor. The purpose of this chapter is to present the latest facts and figures about the extent, nature, depth and characteristics of the poor in Pakistan based on the Household Integrated Economic Survey (HIES) of 1996-97, carried out by the Federal Bureau of Statistics (FBS).

We analyse poverty not only at the national level, but also in each province of the country, for both rural and urban areas. The objective is to highlight the structural dimensions of poverty in different parts of the country and to enable proper spatial targeting of the poverty alleviation programme.

The analysis begins by identifying the differences in per capita income among the different regions of the country. Other things being equal, regions with higher incomes are likely to have a lower incidence of poverty. This is followed by an analysis of the pattern of income inequality. The more unequally income is distributed, the higher the incidence of poverty is likely to be.

Beyond this, we see poverty in two dimensions: *income poverty* and *poverty of opportunity*. Income poverty is based on the notion of a poverty line, below which households are considered to be poor. The incidence of income poverty in a given region, then, is determined by the per capita income, the extent of income inequality, and the poverty line. Higher per capita income, less income inequality and a lower poverty line are all expected to imply less poverty. Poverty of opportunity, on the other hand, is analysed primarily in relation to access to basic education and health-related services.

PER CAPITA INCOME

Income per person is the first simple indicator of whether or not people are able to attain a minimum level of well-being. **Table 2.1** presents per capita income by province for 1996-97. The average monthly income in Pakistan was about Rs. 1,000, equivalent to US$26. This figure is about Rs. 350 per month higher in urban areas (Rs. 1,270, or US$32) than in rural areas (Rs. 921, or US$24).

Significant inter- and intraprovincial differences exist in the level of income per person across the country. Interprovincially, rural Balochistan has the lowest average income at only US$17 per capita per month. The average income in rural Punjab, by contrast, is more than 50 per cent

TABLE			2.1

PER CAPITA INCOME BY PROVINCE (RURAL AND URBAN), 1996-97 (RS. PER MONTH)

	Urban	Rural	Total
Punjab	1,245	1,052	1,105
Sindh	1,352	745	1,036
NWFP	1,101	686	746
Balochistan	1,100	681	762
Pakistan	1,270	921	1,025

Source: Estimated from HIES (1996-97)

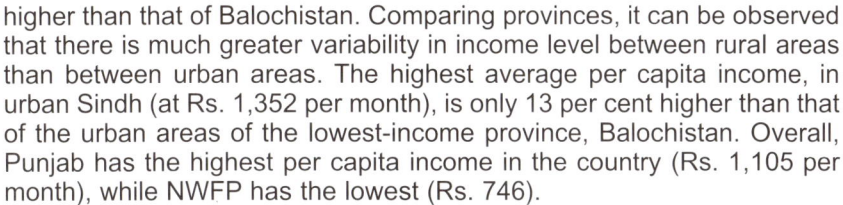

higher than that of Balochistan. Comparing provinces, it can be observed that there is much greater variability in income level between rural areas than between urban areas. The highest average per capita income, in urban Sindh (at Rs. 1,352 per month), is only 13 per cent higher than that of the urban areas of the lowest-income province, Balochistan. Overall, Punjab has the highest per capita income in the country (Rs. 1,105 per month), while NWFP has the lowest (Rs. 746).

Turning now to intraprovincial variations, Punjab has the lowest difference between urban and rural incomes (at only Rs. 193 per month), while Sindh has the highest difference (at Rs. 607 per month). The latter is an indicator of the wide gulf among the urban and rural economies in the province of Sindh.

The above figures present a general picture of regional variations in income levels across the country. Next, we turn to the crucial question of the extent of variation in income levels between households. As indicated earlier, if vast disparities exist in the levels of household income–i.e., if the distribution is highly skewed–then a greater prevalence of income poverty is more likely.

INCOME INEQUALITY

Table 2.2 highlights the differences in income across population quintiles, ranked by household per capita income. The average income of people in the highest population quintile is over seven times higher than that of the lowest. This phenomenon is the same for both urban and rural areas, and is a crude reflection of income disparities in Pakistan.

TABLE			2.2

AVERAGE PER CAPITA INCOME BY INCOME QUINTILE, 1996-97 (RS. PER MONTH)

Income Quintile[a]	Urban	Rural	Overall
First	482	334	360
Second	692	490	538
Third	912	641	713
Fourth	1,286	870	981
Fifth	2,972	2,268	2,530

[a]Ranked in ascending order according to levels of per capita income
Source: Estimates based on HIES (1996-97)

Predominant low agricultural productivity has long been a source of rural poverty.

In the following sections, various summary measures of inequality are developed in order to describe the extent and nature of inequality in Pakistan. The Gini concentration ratio is the most widely used measure of inequality. The Gini coefficient ranges from 0 (absolute equality) to 1 (absolute inequality).

Provincial and regional Gini coefficients are presented in **table 2.3**. The Gini coefficient for Pakistan is 0.40, indicating a high level of income inequality. Overall, the income inequality coefficient for rural areas (0.41) is higher than for urban areas (0.38). Provincially, Punjab has the most unequal distribution of income, followed by Sindh. Interestingly, Balochistan–the province with the lowest income level in the country–has the most equal income distribution.

The high level of income inequality in Punjab is apparently more a consequence of regional contrasts within the province than differences between households in a region. Essentially, the province can be categorized into three areas. Middle Punjab has long been regarded as the first region to have adopted agricultural innovations, and was the site of the beginnings of the 1960s green revolution in Pakistan. Much of the

TABLE 2.3

GINI COEFFICIENTS FOR PER CAPITA INCOME, 1996-97

	Urban	Rural	Overall
Punjab	0.39	0.45	0.44
Sindh	0.39	0.33	0.36
NWFP	0.39	0.30	0.33
Balochistan	0.34	0.28	0.31
Pakistan	0.38	0.41	0.40

Source: Estimated from HIES unit records (1996-97)

industrial development in Punjab, including small-scale manufacturing, has occurred in the cities and towns of middle Punjab. It is, however, also a region characterized by high population density and declining land-labour ratios. It has the lowest proportion of the workforce involved in agriculture, with relatively high landlessness; the workforce is primarily absorbed in the industrial sector (both large- and small-scale).

Upper Punjab, by contrast, is traditionally regarded as a poor region because of its predominance of low-productivity *barani* (rainfed) agriculture. It has the lowest crop yield, especially of wheat. Labour migration and employment in the armed services have been long-standing sources of income in this region.

Lower Punjab is mainly agricultural, and is relatively well-endowed with cultivable land. Unlike middle Punjab, however, there continues to be a presence of powerful landlords in parts of lower Punjab. Land distribution patterns and non-agricultural development in this region are similar to that of rural Sindh, with a high proportion of the workforce involved in agriculture.

MEASURING INCOME POVERTY

Poverty is a multidimensional concept involving not only economic but also social deprivation. The *capability concept* proposed by Sen (1982) argues that, in addition to requiring certain goods and services, an individual may also value his/her capability to be socially useful. This approach emphasizes not only access to a certain quantity of food, but also to basic services such as health care, drinking water, sanitary facilities, and education. In this section, the focus is on income poverty (to determine access to food and other basic needs). Poverty of opportunity (access to services) is discussed in a subsequent section.

The basic measure of income poverty (the absolute approach) quantifies the extent of shortfall in relation to the defined minimum standard of living. Since the focus is on the inability of poor people to attain a minimum standard of living, the questions that arise are: What do we mean by a minimum standard of living? How do we measure it?

Household incomes and expenditures per capita are generally used as a yardstick to measure people's standard of living. It is argued that the use of expenditures for this purpose is less likely to be fraught with the problem of biased reporting, as is often found when using incomes (e.g., understatement of income). However, Ercelawn (1992) maintains that similar understatement in expenditure is not only also possible but, more importantly, subsistence expenditure may well involve quasi-permanent indebtedness. Therefore, we choose to use income as a measure of the standard of living.

The Poverty Line

The poverty line is defined as the minimum income level required to achieve basic nutrition (calorie intake) and fulfilment of other basic needs. Defining the scope of basic needs and their minimum levels remains an area of debate, as shown in **box 2.1**. Following Ercelawn (1992), we use overall expenditure (economic capacity) in a calorie-expenditure relationship.

Specifically, per capita calorie consumption is regressed on per capita non-durable consumption expenditure to estimate expected

BOX 2.1

APPROACHES TO DETERMINATION OF THE POVERTY LINE

The calorie-based approach in determining the poverty line is dominant among studies of poverty throughout the developing world. Not surprisingly, most poverty analyses in Pakistan have adopted this approach.

Various variants of this approach have been applied in the Pakistani context. Havinga et al. (1989) established the poverty line as being the average food expenditure of those households who consume roughly the minimum required calorific intake.

Malik (1988) and Amjad and Kamal (1997) modified this method by adjusting for non-food expenditure. To allow for non-food expenditure in the estimation of the poverty line, the distribution of total expenditure between food and non-food categories has been calculated. More specifically, the food expenditure needed for the required amount of calories has been multiplied by the reciprocal of the food expenditure share in the total expenditure of the relevant lower-income group.

Instead of taking average expenditure, Ercelawn (1992) used what is called the calorie consumption function (CCF) to derive the expected total expenditure of those households that consume the minimum required calorie intake.

Lanjouw (1994) established the poverty line as being the sum of (1) the food expenditure that corresponds exactly to the minimum required calorie intake and (2) the expected (regression-based) non-food expenditure of that household whose total consumption is equal to the food consumption level defined in (1).

Jafri (1999) modified the approach adopted by Lanjouw by calculating the expected food expenditure (based on CCF) of the sample, along with the average non-food expenditure of those households whose food expenditure is exactly equal to the minimum requirement. It is assumed that those households whose food expenditure is exactly equal to the minimum prescribed will also satisfy their other basic needs. Jafri calls this approach the *cost of basic needs* method.

---

expenditure for the minimum calorie intake. To capture underlying differences in consumption behaviour (taste and cultural practices in obtaining calories from diverse sources), separate regressions are estimated for rural and urban areas of each province. The calorie norms are converted into per capita terms using an adult-equivalent scale (GOP 1985) in order to facilitate interpretation and comparison. Poverty lines are thus constructed separately for each province, using estimated coefficients as well as rural and urban calorie norms. The daily calorie intake norm recommended by the Working Group on Poverty Alleviation of the Planning Commission in 1997 (of 2,550 calories per capita for rural and 2,230 calories for urban areas) has been used.

Table 2.4 presents the average calorie consumption for different regions in the country. The key source of calorie intake in Pakistan is wheat. However, there do exist some interregional differences in the

TABLE 2.4

CALORIE CONSUMPTION (PER MONTH/ADULT EQUIVALENT)

	Urban	Rural
Punjab	2,954	3,322
Sindh	2,750	3,319
NWFP	2,914	3,706
Balochistan	2,726	3,380
Pakistan	2,873	3,375

Source: SPDC estimates based on HIES (1996-97)

TABLE 2.5

SOURCES OF CALORIES FOR POOR HOUSEHOLDS (%)

	PUNJAB Urban	PUNJAB Rural	SINDH Urban	SINDH Rural	NWFP Urban	NWFP Rural	BALOCHISTAN Urban	BALOCHISTAN Rural	PAKISTAN Urban	PAKISTAN Rural	PAKISTAN Total
Wheat	59	54	47	41	64	48	58	52	57	48	53
Rice	4	3	14	20	3	3	7	6	7	8	7
Maize	0	0	-	-	1	8	0	-	0	4	2
Pulses (i.e., lentils)	4	2	3	3	2	2	4	4	3	3	3
Milk and Milk Products	6	15	6	11	3	6	3	5	4	9	7
Oil and Vegetable Ghee	14	14	13	12	11	21	13	22	13	17	15
Meat, Fish, Poultry	1	1	3	1	1	1	3	2	3	1	1
Fruits and Vegetables	4	3	4	3	2	2	3	3	3	3	3
Sugar and Sugar Products	7	5	9	6	10	8	7	6	7	7	7
Others	1	3	1	3	3	1	2	1	3	1	2
Total	100	100	100	100	100	100	100	100	100	100	100

Source: SPDC estimates based on HIES (1996-97)

pattern of sources **(see table 2.5)**. For example, poor households in urban NWFP obtain 64 per cent of their calories from wheat, while the corresponding figure is 47 per cent for urban Sindh. These variations in the sources of calories across regions, as well as the underlying price differences, largely explain the difference in the poverty line across regions, as presented in **table 2.6**. The poverty line ranged from Rs. 465 to Rs. 664 per capita per month in the urban areas, and from Rs. 390 to Rs. 564 in the rural areas in 1996-97.

TABLE 2.6

POVERTY LINE ESTIMATES (RS./MONTH PER CAPITA)

Province	Urban	Rural
Punjab	639	485
Sindh	610	564
NWFP	475	390
Balochistan	664	551

Source: SPDC estimates based on HIES (1996-97)

INCIDENCE OF POVERTY

To monitor the incidence and depth of poverty, the standard measures include (1) a headcount ratio and (2) an income-gap ratio. The headcount ratio gives the proportion of individuals whose incomes are below the poverty line. However, it does not indicate the extent, or depth, to which they are poor. The income-gap ratio, or poverty gap, does illustrate this, since it quantifies the extent to which the average income of the poor is below the poverty line.

Neither nutrition nor other basic needs are adequately being met in the rural areas.

Using the poverty lines presented in table 2.6, the incidence and depth of poverty have been derived. Overall, 31 per cent of the people of Pakistan live in poverty, having income levels below the poverty line **(see table 2.7)**. This means that out of the 128 million people living in Pakistan at the time these data were collected, 40 million people were living in a state of poverty. The incidence of poverty is higher in the rural than urban areas, at 32 and 27 per cent, respectively. The depth of poverty, as revealed by the poverty gap, shows that the average income of poor households is below the poverty line by 6 per cent in urban areas, and by

TABLE 2.7

INCOME POVERTY IN PAKISTAN, 1996-97 (%)

	Urban	Rural	Overall
Punjab			
Headcount	33	29	30
Poverty Gap	7	7	7
Sindh			
Headcount	20	53	27
Poverty Gap	4	14	9
NWFP			
Headcount	18	24	23
Poverty Gap	3	5	4
Balochistan			
Headcount	35	54	49
Poverty Gap	8	14	12
Pakistan			
Headcount	27	32	31
Poverty Gap	6	8	7

Source: SPDC estimates based on HIES (1996-97)

Overall, 31 per cent of the people of Pakistan lived in poverty in 1996-97.

8 per cent in rural areas.

A comparison of the incidence of poverty across provinces and regions leads to a number of interesting and crucial insights. First, Balochistan is the most poverty stricken province in the country, with the highest incidence of both rural and urban poverty. More than half of the rural population (54 per cent) and more than one third of the urban population (35 per cent) in the province are poor. Poverty is not only extensive, but also very deep, as demonstrated by the poverty gap of 12 per cent.

Second, Sindh has the second-highest incidence of poverty in the country, at 27 per cent. The extreme dichotomy in this province's economy, as highlighted earlier, is further evidenced by the large difference in the incidence of poverty between the urban and rural areas. 20 per cent of the urban population lives under the poverty line, as opposed to more than half of the rural population. The poverty gap is also very high in the rural areas (14 per cent) in comparison with the urban areas (4 per cent). These indicators point to the acute situation of poverty in rural Sindh, the circumstances being almost as bad as in the rural areas of Balochistan.

Third, the incidence and depth of poverty is the lowest in NWFP, both in the urban and the rural areas. This conclusion, though consistent with the findings of earlier studies (Jafri 1999), has not been adequately highlighted. It appears that large inflows of remittances, both from within Pakistan as well as from the Middle East, have been instrumental in improving the lot of the people in NWFP **(see chapter 3)**.

Finally, Punjab is the only province in which poverty is more pervasive in the urban than in the rural areas. The headcount ratio in urban Punjab is 33 per cent, compared to around 29 per cent in rural Punjab. The lower incidence of poverty in the rural (versus urban) areas can perhaps be attributed to the relatively buoyant agricultural base of the provincial economy. Overall, the spatial distribution of poverty in Pakistan, as presented in **table 2.8**, shows that about 36 per cent of the poor population resides in rural Punjab, 20 per cent in rural Sindh, and 19 per cent in urban Punjab.

Why are there such significant differences in the regional incidence of poverty? **Table 2.9** summarizes the relationship between incidence of poverty, per capita income, income inequality, and the poverty line. It seems that the low incidence of poverty in NWFP, despite the relatively low per capita income, is principally the consequence of the low poverty line and the relatively uniform distribution of income (due partly to the equalizing effect of remittances).

The story for Punjab is somewhat different. Despite a high level of income inequality, the incidence of poverty in the province is relatively low. This is largely due to the combined effect of the high level of income per capita and the relatively low poverty line.

TABLE 2.8

SPATIAL DISTRIBUTION OF POVERTY IN PAKISTAN (%) [a]

	Urban Areas	Rural Areas	Total
Punjab	19	36	55
Sindh	7	20	27
NWFP	1	9	10
Balochistan	1	7	8
Pakistan	28	72	100

[a] Percentage of total population
Source: SPDC estimates based on HIES (1996-97)

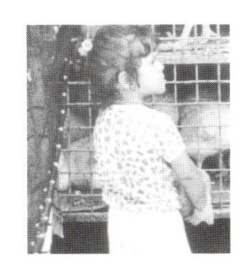

TABLE 2.9

RELATIONSHIP BETWEEN INCIDENCE OF POVERTY, PER CAPITA INCOME, INCOME INEQUALITY AND POVERTY LINE

	Per Capita Monthly Income (Rs.)	Extent of Income Inequality (Gini coefficient)	Poverty Line (Rs. per capita per month)	Incidence of Poverty (% of poor)
Urban				
Punjab	1,245	0.39	639	33
Sindh	1,352	0.39	610	20
NWFP	1,101	0.39	465	18
Balochistan	1,100	0.34	664	35
Pakistan	1,270	0.38	618	27
Rural				
Punjab	1,052	0.45	485	29
Sindh	745	0.33	564	53
NWFP	686	0.30	390	24
Balochistan	681	0.28	551	54
Pakistan	921	0.41	484	32
Total				
Punjab	1,105	0.44	527	30
Sindh	1,036	0.36	586	37
NWFP	746	0.33	401	23
Balochistan	762	0.31	573	49
Pakistan	1,025	0.40	523	31

Source: SPDC estimates based on HIES (1996-97)

Compared to NWFP and Punjab, the high incidence of poverty in Sindh is the consequence of a high poverty line, reinforced by the highly unequal distribution of income, which neutralizes the poverty reducing impact of a relatively high per capita income.

In the case of Balochistan, the high poverty line and low per capita income mitigate against the favourable implications of the prevailing low level of income inequality, and result in a high incidence of poverty.

UNDERSTANDING THE POOR

Understanding the poor requires knowledge of what types of households are unable to generate incomes above the poverty line; that is, what are the key demographic and socio-economic characteristics of the poor? And what determines the depth of poverty, as reflected by the poverty gap? The answer to these crucial questions will shed some light on the nature of poverty in Pakistan, and help policy makers judge how their economic policies are likely to affect the poor. Is poverty chronic and are households that live in poverty likely to remain poor? Or is poverty essentially transitional, whereby households live in conditions of poverty only temporarily; for example, due to unemployment between jobs or due to negative shocks of a transient nature? An understanding of

Even though employment generation has been a goal of past governments' development agendas, it remains a distant reality for some.

these attributes is an essential prerequisite for the formulation of an effective and meaningful poverty alleviation strategy, since each type of poverty has to be approached differently. For instance, if poverty is more or less of a permanent nature, a poverty alleviation strategy should emphasize a long-term, income-supplementing scheme. If, on the other hand, it is inadequate skills endowment that tends to lead to poverty, then capabilities-enhancing programmes should be the basis of the poverty alleviation strategy.

The analytical framework used to study the demographic and socio-economic attributes of the poor is described in **appendix A.2**. A two-stage Heckman model has been applied separately to the urban and rural areas of Pakistan. A number of explanatory variables relating to each household's demographic profile, asset endowment, employment status, and supplementary income sources (i.e., transfers) have been entered into the model. The demographic variables include household size, dependency ratio, age and gender of the head of the household, and number of earners. Access to asset endowments is assessed based on ownership of property and livestock, as well as the educational attainment of the head of the household. The impact of unemployment, underemployment, and self-employment on poverty has been modelled separately. To analyse the impact of informal/formal transfers on poverty, and to capture the locational dimensions, dichotomous variables have been entered into the model. The findings are discussed below.

Characteristics of Poor Households

Application of the Heckman model leads to a number of important insights into the characteristics of poor households in Pakistan. Results

TABLE 2.10

INCIDENCE AND DEPTH OF POVERTY BY TYPE OF HOUSEHOLD (%)

Characteristics	INCIDENCE Rural Areas	INCIDENCE Urban Areas	DEPTH Rural Areas	DEPTH Urban Areas
Household Size				
1 - 3	13	5	3	1
4 - 6	28	15	6	3
7 and above	37	36	10	8
Dependency Ratio				
Below 20%	11	4	2	1
20 - 50%	23	17	5	7
Above 50%	41	40	11	5
Age of Head of Household				
19 - 34	34	27	9	5
35 - 49	37	29	8	7
50 and above	27	25	6	5
Number of Earners				
One	36	29	10	6
Two	32	31	8	7
Three or more	26	23	6	4
Gender				
Male-headed Household	33	28	9	6
Female-headed Household:				
- not receiving transfers	38	29	11	6
- receiving transfers	25	17	7	4
Assets Ownership				
Owning No Property	50	29	14	6
Owning Property	31	27	8	6
Owning Livestock	21	-	5	-
Educational Attainment				
Illiterate	36	40	9	9
Primary	33	34	8	7
Higher Secondary/Matric	17	17	3	3
Graduate and Postgraduate	14	4	3	1
Employment Status				
Unemployed	33	22	8	3
Underemployed Wage Earners	42	30	11	6
Self-Employed	27	25	6	5
Transfers				
Households without Transfers	34	28	8	6
Households with Transfers	26	26	6	6
Receiving Remittances	23	22	6	4
From Outside Pakistan	12	8	2	1
From Inside Pakistan	25	31	6	6
Receiving *Zakat*	61	49	17	13
Local				
City	-	18	-	3
Town	-	39	-	9

Source: SPDC estimates

of both the incidence and depth of poverty for the rural and urban areas are presented in **table 2.10**.

Demographic characteristics. Larger households tend to be poorer because of more dependents. Therefore, the behaviour whereby poor families desire to have a large number of children, either to serve as housekeepers (to release the adults from domestic chores) or to contribute to the family income as a means for rising out of poverty, appears to be counterproductive, at least in the short to medium term. It also appears that the relationship between the age of the head of a household and poverty is of an inverted U-shape. The probability of poverty increases up to a certain age threshold, until such time as the head of the household acquires enough education/training and experience to improve his/her earnings. Thereafter, the chance of his/her being poor declines. The lower likelihood of multiple-earner families being poor is demonstrated by the findings in table 2.10.

Are women poorer than men? **Box 2.2** indicates that there are generally gender biases in terms of the impact of poverty. By and large, women in Pakistan acquire the status of head of a household in two

BOX 2.2

WHAT CAUSES THE FEMINIZATION OF POVERTY?

Income poverty analysis in developing countries has led to the conclusion that there is a *feminization of poverty*. This term implies that women are relatively poorer than men, and that the incidence of poverty amongst them is increasing in comparison with men. However, the causes of female poverty are complex, and are inextricably linked to gender inequality in human development, markets, property rights, and intra-household allocations. An overview of the position of women in developing countries establishes two facts regarding women's income-earning capacities. First, women earn less than men; one study of six developing countries shows that women's wages are about 30 to 40 per cent lower than men's wages. Second, statistics show that women in developing countries spend 31 to 42 hours in unpaid labour per week, as opposed to 5 to 15 hours for men. Generally, women's combined paid and unpaid contributions to the family exceed men's contributions to the labour market.

Women suffer disproportionately in terms of lack of access to education and health care. It is simply infeasible to view the creation of income-generating activities as a means of ending female poverty when their *capabilities* are impaired. Lower levels of nutrition for women, combined with less health care, both reflecting cultural biases, have contributed to a situation where mothers are seriously malnourished in regions like sub-Saharan Africa and South Asia. These mothers then produce low birthweight babies and increase their risks of maternal mortality. Similarly, two-thirds of the world's illiterate adults are women. In South Asia, there is a significant gender gap in primary education, especially in Pakistan and Nepal, where it is more than 20 percentage points.

Illiteracy reinforces a woman's exclusion from labour and credit markets, as well as legal systems. Taboos that restrict a woman from leaving her home and earning a living, or a situation where men appropriate their wives' earnings, are examples of the deeply-entrenched barriers faced by women in improving their financial position. Even those women who are allowed to leave the home are forced to work in low-paid, informal employment and earn less than men. Women's work outside the home is often combined with their unpaid work at home, as well as their childbearing and childcare responsibilities. At the same time, legal systems can differentiate in their treatment of men and women, and even where women do not face legal discrimination, employers treat them as casual and temporarily attached to the labour market.

Another area where women's access is limited, and thus contributes to them remaining trapped in income-inequality, is credit markets. Credit markets require collateral, which assumes that women own assets in their own right. They also assume that women are mobile, and have other transactions costs that may put off women—especially where there are cultural barriers. Even in a situation where credit is obtained by the women, as in the case of Bangladeshi microcredit, studies have found that it is unclear who ultimately controls the resources.

Land and property ownership also increase the poor's access to product and factor markets. Unfortunately, even where women have a legal right to own property, they are not always able to manage or sell it without the consent of fathers, brothers and husbands.

Furthermore, intra-household allocation of food in countries like Pakistan and parts of Africa shows that women receive lower food shares than other members of households. Thus poverty measured in terms of food consumption would reveal that females within a household could be living below the poverty line while, at the same time, the males are above it.

The feminization of poverty can only end if there is an awareness that lack of investment in women, in the form of health, education, credit facilities and employment opportunities, hinders poverty alleviation for a society as a whole and has profound implications for future generations.

"I sell chickens at a poultry stall. With my income, even one meal a day is not guaranteed."

eventualities. First, when men migrate in search of better economic prospects and women temporarily take charge of the household. Such instances are particularly common in northern areas where the phenomenon of out-migration is prevalent. Second, when the male head of a household dies or permanently abandons or departs from the household, leaving the woman to provide for her family. Our findings show that in the latter case, the probability of the household being poor is

> **BOX 2.3**
>
> ### A POULTRY VENDOR DREAMS OF SOCIAL REFORM
>
> My name is Allah Ditta and I am 45 years old. I am married with four children: two sons and two daughters. I live with my family in a *jhonpri* (shack) near Gilani Station. My mother lives with us as well. I do not have electricity in my *jhonpri*; we have to cook food by burning wood, and I have to fetch water from other people's wells and bring it to my home. I sell chickens at a poultry stall and earn about Rs. 1,800 to Rs. 2,000 per month. I am illiterate.
>
> I am originally from Bangladesh, but there life was even more difficult and I experienced many hardships. With my income, even one meal a day was not guaranteed. It was under these circumstances that I chose to come to Karachi. Since arriving, I have done a variety of jobs requiring hard work and labour, but my circumstances have not improved. I have to hand over a significant portion of my earnings to my wife so that she can manage household expenses. It is only by God's grace if I manage to buy enough food to fill myself with the leftover money.
>
> Continually rising prices are making life extremely difficult. All we wish for is that the government—any government, whether military or civilian, would reduce the prices of bare essentials and daily necessities. The government should also design the education system so that the children of the poor are eligible for free education; so that they may be literate as well. Initially my son used to attend a government school, but as times have gotten harder, I could not afford to send him anymore. With my income, if a family member is inflicted with an illness, I have to take them to the government hospitals. And when we are in great need, then either the owner of the poultry shop, or other people we know, help us financially. None of our relatives or family members helps us in troubled times. In fact, they don't even like associating with us.
>
> I realize that my children are growing up now, and I'm especially worried about my daughters. People are bad, corrupt, and we just live in a shack. My only wish is that I make enough of an effort and work hard enough to save the money to purchase even a one-room house. In times when I can't provide my children with good food, or an education, the least I can do is give them a protective roof under which they can be safe.

Women face all kinds of cultural, social, legal and economic obstacles that men, even poor men, do not.

high, more so in the rural than in the urban areas. Besides, the experience of developing countries shows that, as heads of households, women face all kinds of cultural, social, legal and economic obstacles that men, even poor men, do not (including, for example, longer work hours and lower wages).

Assets/endowments. The poor usually lack both income and assets. In economies in which wealth and status come from land/property, disadvantaged households are typically land-poor or landless. Both in the urban and rural areas of Pakistan, ownership of property is inversely correlated with poverty. Likewise, in rural areas, ownership of livestock contributes to lowering the chances of being poor.

The poor also lack human capital. They are either illiterate or have received only a low amount of formal education. Table 2.10 clearly demonstrates the decreased probability of being poor with increased educational attainment, both in urban and rural areas. The decline is particularly marked in urban areas, diminishing from 40 per cent in the case of illiterate heads of households to 4 per cent in the case of graduates.

Employment status. Besides having lower incomes and fewer assets than the non-poor, the poor are generally unemployed or underemployed, and are wage earners. The lack of employment opportunities, particularly in a period of economic recession, has dragged households into a state of acute poverty. To counter this, some opt for secondary employment (and are therefore underemployed). However, this is unlikely to fundamentally improve their status, and the probability of such households being poor is also high. Interestingly, those who manage to become small entrepreneurs (self-employed) are able to improve their standard of living and are less likely to be in a state of poverty.

In periods of low economic activity, daily wage earners are the most adversely affected. Their chances of being poor are greatest, both in the urban and the rural areas. Wage earners in the rural areas, particularly in non-farm households, are generally recognized as the most vulnerable segment of rural society. International experience and other local studies confirm this finding (Qureshi 1999; Jafri 1999).

The role of transfers. Transfers can be an important source of income for households. In most developing countries, transfers are made by relatives and friends rather than by the government. In Pakistan, remittances, both from within and outside Pakistan, are instrumental in improving the standard of living of recipient households. Table 2.10 clearly shows that the likelihood of being poor is low for households receiving remittance income. In fact, as discussed in **chapter 3**, informal transfers are successful in pulling a significant proportion of households out of poverty.

In conclusion, it appears that being poor is not a random occurrence. There are distinct demographic, social and economic factors that can force a household into a state of poverty. These insights can potentially be very useful in the design of a poverty alleviation programme.

Chart 2.1 traces the incremental steps that lead to reduced poverty in urban and rural areas, respectively. Essentially, if the head of a household is both illiterate and unemployed, and also has no access to either *unearned* income (e.g., transfers or assets) or other modes of family support (i.e., income from other employed household members), then the household is bound to be poor.

If a rural household possesses physical assets (land/livestock), the incidence of poverty tends to fall by as much as 55 per cent. As such, we

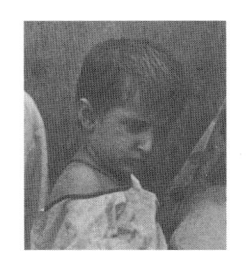

If a rural household possesses physical assets (land/livestock) then the incidence of poverty falls by as much as 55 per cent.

CHART 2.1

THE LADDER OF POVERTY REDUCTION

Probability of being Poor (%)

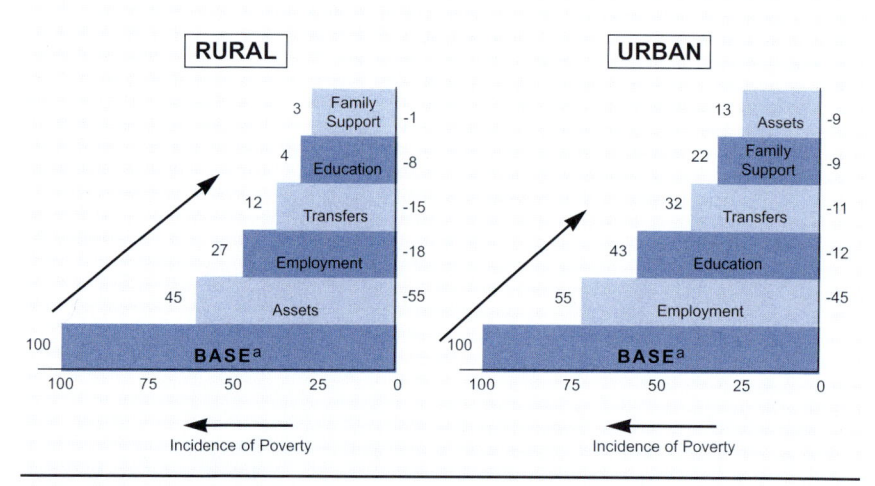

RURAL

3	Family Support	-1
4	Education	-8
12	Transfers	-15
27	Employment	-18
45	Assets	-55
100	BASE[a]	

Incidence of Poverty

URBAN

13	Assets	-9
22	Family Support	-9
32	Transfers	-11
43	Education	-12
55	Employment	-45
100	BASE[a]	

Incidence of Poverty

[a] The head of the household is illiterate and unemployed, receives neither transfers nor assets, and has no family support
[b] Primary education
Source: SPDC estimates

---

conclude that asset redistribution can be used as an effective tool for poverty reduction, particularly in rural Pakistan. Access to employment and informal transfers also tend to mitigate significantly against poverty. Finally, improvement in educational attainment reduces the likelihood of a household being poor by a further 8 per cent.

In contrast, employment tends to have a greater poverty-reducing impact in urban areas, the incidence of poverty being reduced by 45 per cent if the head of the household is gainfully employed. Transfers, followed by education, also play a significant poverty-reducing role.

We next analyse the determinants of the depth of poverty, as indicated by the poverty gap. As explained earlier, the second stage of the Heckman procedure yields these results. Interestingly, factors that determine the probability of a household being poor also, by and large, determine what the poverty gap will be (see table 2.10). As such, demographic factors like large family size and a high dependency ratio contribute to a higher poverty gap, while having multiple earners in a household lowers it. Likewise, access to assets substantially lowers the poverty gap. Heads of household with high educational attainment have the lowest poverty gap, along with those who have access to informal transfers, particularly remittance income from abroad. The highest poverty gap is evident among landless wage earners in rural areas and households receiving *Zakat*.

Finally, we turn to a quantification of the extent of chronic and transitory poverty. Within poor households, the former category essentially consists of three types of households—female-headed households (type I), male-headed households where the head of household is illiterate (type II), and male-headed households where the head of the household is

---

Employment tends to have a greater poverty reducing impact in urban areas, the incidence of poverty being reduced by 45 per cent.

TABLE 2.11

INCIDENCE OF CHRONIC POVERTY (% SHARE OF POOR HOUSEHOLDS)

Type	Rural Areas	Urban Areas	Total
Type I	5	4	4
Type II	69	53	65
Type III	1	2	1
Total	75	59	70

Source: SPDC estimates based on HIES (1996-97)

literate but old (above 60 years) (type III). The share of such households as a percentage of poor households is given in **table 2.11**.

We conclude that much of the poverty in Pakistan, especially in the rural areas, appears to be chronic in character. This would tend to justify programmes for enhancement of skills/education and for continuing income support.

POVERTY OF OPPORTUNITY

As pointed out earlier, poverty is a multidimensional concept. It refers to being denied not only adequate income, but also the opportunity to improve one's standard of living. As such, emphasis is not only on delivery of a certain quantity of food, but also on access to complementary inputs such as health care, drinking water, sanitary facilities and education. Human capital measured in terms of health status and education are considered critical measures of non-monetary dimensions of welfare, as well as important inputs into an individual's earning ability.

Various studies on human development assert that improvement in human development indicators in Pakistan has been extremely slow, and that levels remain low compared with other countries of comparable per capita income—despite the buoyant economic growth rate. During the last four decades, even though real per capita income has registered an average annual growth of about 2.5 per cent, the human development index has improved by only about 1.5 per cent. Clearly, economic growth has not translated into improvements in the level of human development in the country **(see box 2.4)**. In addition to this, social indicators are disproportionately lower for females, highlighting the existence of gender disparities. This section highlights the extent of health and education deprivation, derived from the latest Pakistan Integrated Household Survey (PIHS) of 1996-97 and Pakistan Demographic Survey (PDS) of 1996-97 in each province of Pakistan.

Education deprivation is represented by the following two indicators:

- adult illiteracy rate;
- percentage of out-of-school children.

Health deprivation is captured by the following indicators:

- divergence of actual life expectancy at birth from the norm (85 years);

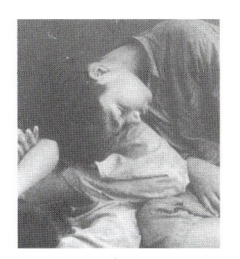

BOX 2.4

HUMAN DEVELOPMENT AND ECONOMIC GROWTH

Interest in social development policy appears to have been promoted by the observed unevenness in the economic performance of developing countries. Despite high GDP growth rates, economic development has failed to reach all segments of society. Pressed by rapid population growth and high inflation, the poorest 25 per cent of people in most developing countries receive few of the benefits of development. However, the literature on economic growth and social development has not yet adequately clarified the interaction between trickle-up and trickle-down approaches of development.

To investigate the issue in the context of Pakistan, a Human Development Index (HDI) is constructed using 9 indicators related to health (e.g., hospital beds, doctors, and infant survival rate) and education (e.g., primary, secondary, and tertiary enrolment–total and female). The Principal Component Technique is used to develop the HDI for the period from 1960 to 1999.

The comparison between the HDI and index of real GDP per capita is shown in the accompanying table. From the 1960s until the 1980s, both indices indicate that higher growth in GDP had a positive effect on HDI. The period of proclaimed trickle-up policies also supplements the argument that higher growth in income is a prerequisite for higher achievement in social and human development. Nevertheless, this result does not hold strongly in the fourth period. During the 1990s, a decrease in per capita GDP growth did not significantly affect HDI. This is indicative to some extent of the Social Action Programme's (SAP) success in improving access to basic public social services, and the dynamism demonstrated by the private sector in filling the gap in demand.

The evidence, based on the selected indicators and methodology, tends to suggest that human development, as it relates to health and education, is a product of economic growth. Nevertheless, these sectors demand special government attention in order to overcome issues such as increasing regional income inequalities.

AVERAGE ANNUAL GROWTH RATES (%)

	Real GDP per Capita	Human Development Index[a]
1960s	2.89	1.61
1970s	1.64	1.03
1980s	3.23	2.09
1990s	2.10	2.03
1960-99	2.47	1.68

[a]SPDC estimates
Source: Pakistan Statistical Yearbook (various issues)

- divergence of infant mortality from the norm (30 per 1,000 live births).

Income deprivation is measured by the headcount ratio of poverty. Magnitudes of the five indicators for each province of Pakistan in 1996-

TABLE 2.12

INDICATORS OF EDUCATION, HEALTH AND INCOME DEPRIVATION, 1996-97

Indicator	Unit	Punjab	Sindh	NWFP	Balochistan	Pakistan
Adult Illiteracy Rate	%	60	55	70	73	61
% of Out-of-School Children	%	27	36	32	42	30
Divergence of Life Expectancy from Norm	Years	25	30	28	27	28
Divergence of Infant Mortality from Norm	No.[a]	56	57	50	57	55
Headcount of Poverty	%	30	37	23	49	31

[a]Number of deaths of children under one per 1,000 live births
Sources: PIHS (1996-97)
PDS (1996-97)
SPDC estimates

TABLE 2.13

POVERTY OF OPPORTUNITY INDEX[a], 1996-97

	Punjab	Sindh	NWFP	Balochistan	Pakistan
Health Deprivation	52	56	51	54	47
Education Deprivation	53	51	60	65	54
Income Deprivation	30	37	23	49	31
POPI	47	49	50	57	49

[a] The maximum value of the index is 100. The closer the value of POPI is to 100, the greater the state of deprivation
Source: SPDC estimates

97 are given in **table 2.12**. The methodology used for constructing the composite Poverty of Opportunity Index (POPI) is given in **appendix A.3**.

The resulting magnitude of the POPI for each province is given in **table 2.13**. The results indicate that for all provinces, POPI exceeds the poverty headcount, implying that poverty of opportunity is even greater than income poverty **(see chart 2.2)**. It also appears that there are differences in provincial rankings in the two poverty measures. For example, NWFP, which has the lowest income poverty, has relatively high poverty of opportunity. Altogether, the high magnitude of POPI indicates the structural dimensions of poverty in Pakistan and the complexity of the task of alleviating poverty.

On the whole, this chapter has examined the extent, nature, and depth of poverty in the country, along with the key characteristics of the poor. It appears that when people have some assets and job opportunities, and household members are skilled, educated and healthy, a minimum standard of living is attained and poverty is eliminated. When such opportunities are lacking and access to social services is limited, living standards are likely to be unacceptably low. These characteristics of poor households help set the agenda that needs to be pursued in order to successfully tackle the problem of poverty.

CHART 2.2

COMPARISON OF INCOME POVERTY AND POVERTY OF OPPORTUNITY

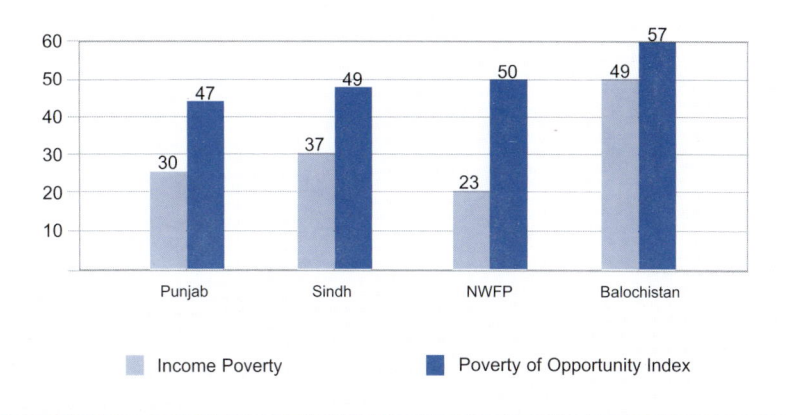

Province	Income Poverty	Poverty of Opportunity Index
Punjab	30	47
Sindh	37	49
NWFP	23	50
Balochistan	49	57

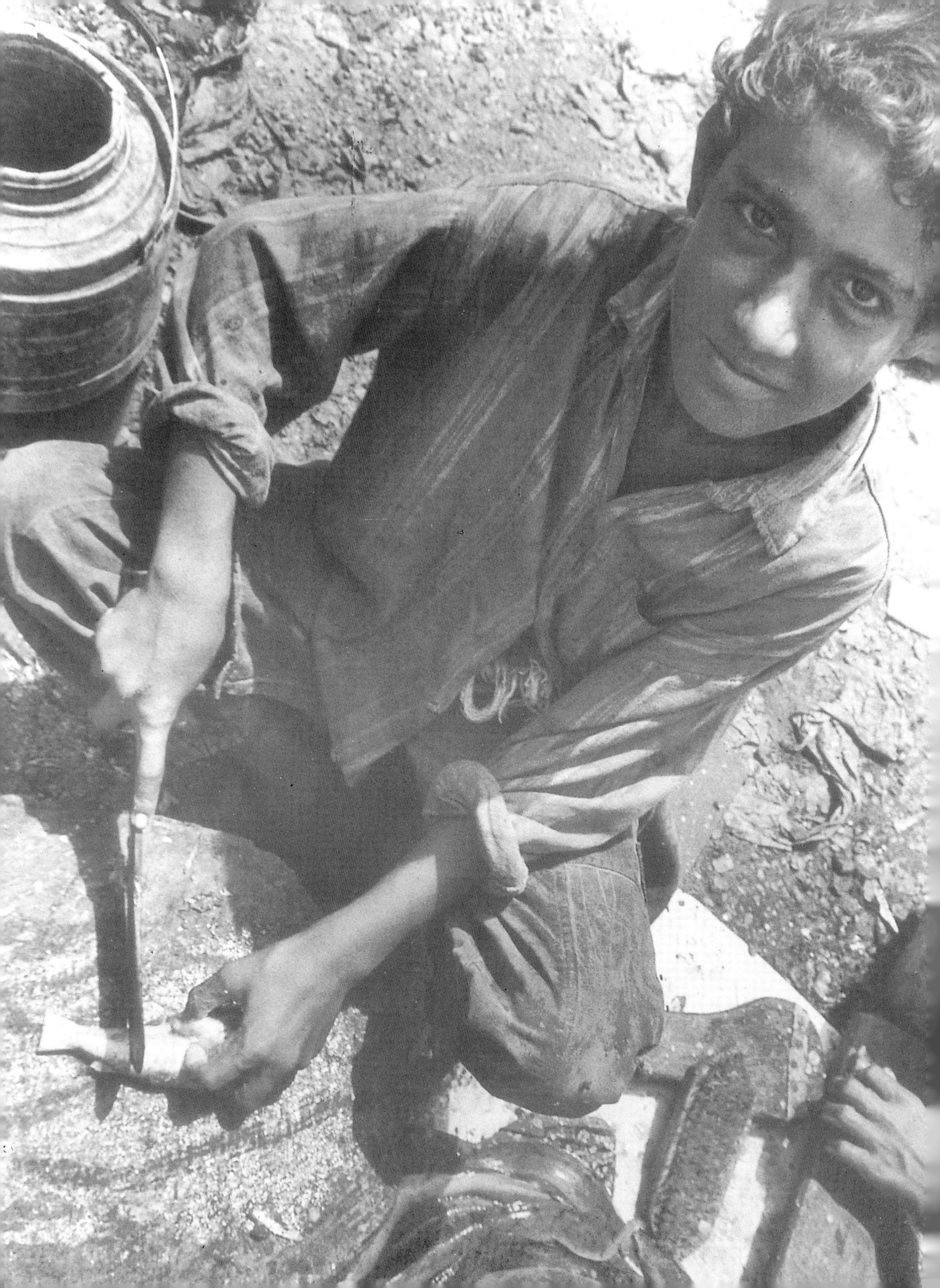

IS THE INFORMAL SECTOR A POVERTY CUSHION?

CHAPTER 3

"People have developed a way of tackling poverty by intra- and interhousehold transfers that substitute for the paltry transfer payments to the poor made through government budgets."

IS THE INFORMAL SECTOR A POVERTY CUSHION?

There is a growing view in Pakistan that the spread of poverty has fortunately been restricted by a dynamic informal sector, which, it is argued, performs two important roles in the context of poverty alleviation. First, it effectively acts as a *shock absorber*, whereby surplus labour released from the formal sector during periods of recession, or new entrants to the labour force, especially the unskilled, find employment within the informal economy and are somehow able to earn enough to stay above the poverty line. Second, through an informal and community-based welfare and support system, the people have developed a way of tackling poverty by intra- and inter household transfers that substitute for the paltry transfer payments to the poor made through government budgets.

Skeptics of this view argue, however, that it is difficult to visualize a situation where the informal economy can continue to show sustained growth on a long-term basis in the presence of a stagnant or declining formal economy. Given the linkages between the two economies, a financial crisis at the macro level is bound to eventually effect the informal economy by limiting its labour absorption and income-generating capacity. Also, as real household incomes fall or cease to grow, the informal support system comes under pressure and poor households find it increasingly difficult to rely on such transfers.

Therefore, the basic questions that arise relate to the nature, size, and role of the informal economy. Does it behave in a counter-cyclical or pro-cyclical manner with respect to the formal economy? What is its labour absorption capacity, and as it expands in employment what happens to income levels? What kinds of households engage in *giving* support and what is the nature of the recipients? How large is the informal support system and how much poverty does it alleviate? This chapter addresses these questions.

MEASURING THE INFORMAL ECONOMY

Definition

The term *informal economy* was apparently first used by anthropologist Keith Hart (1973) in the context of poor city dwellers (the urban proletariat) in Ghana. He asked the question: Do informal economic activities possess some autonomous capacity for generating growth in incomes of the urban poor?

De Soto (1989) had an essentially legalist conception of informality. According to this view, informal economic activities circumvent the costs but are excluded from the benefits and rights incorporated in the laws and administrative rules covering property relationships, commercial licensing, labour contracts, formal credit, and the social security system.

BOX 3.1

THE INFORMAL SECTOR OF PAKISTAN: SOME STYLIZED FACTS

Kemal (1998) have profiled the informal sector of Pakistan on the basis of a random survey of 1,500 urban enterprises. Their principal findings are as follows:

1. Over one third of the entrepreneurs are in the age group of 40 and above. While the majority join the informal sector when they are unable to get a job in the formal sector, a significant proportion stay on permanently.
2. Over 80 per cent of informal sector entrepreneurs are educated, but mostly with only primary or secondary education.
3. Over 90 per cent of the enterprises are individually owned. The incidence of partnerships and other legal forms is very rare.
4. Fewer than 40 per cent of the entrepreneurs own the premises of their workplace.
5. Nearly 60 per cent of the enterprises are less than ten years old.
6. Over 60 per cent of the manufacturing enterprises have a subcontracting relationship with firms in the formal sector.
7. The average number of people employed in an informal enterprise is 3.3 persons.
8. The self-employed and family helpers account for about half the labour force.
9. A major source of skill acquisition is the *ustad-shagird* (master-apprentice) system.
10. The average number of hours worked per week is 60.
11. Informal sector wages are generally relatively low, ranging between Rs. 1,500 and 1,700 per month. The self-employed earn more, averaging over Rs. 5,600 per month.
12. The average capital-labour ratio of informal enterprises is about Rs. 100,000 per worker—over twenty times less than for the economy as a whole.
13. The capital-output ratio is 0.3 as compared to over 3 for the entire country.
14. Labour productivity per worker is Rs. 85,000.
15. The rate of capacity utilization is about 70 per cent in manufacturing enterprises and 80 per cent in service enterprises.
16. Savings represent more than 50 per cent of the source of funds. The next largest source is reinvested profits. Only 8 per cent of funds are from banks.

This implies that informal activities are non-corporate in character, are mostly small-scale, and generally involve self-employment **(see box 3.1)**. It may be noted that there is a considerable overlap between the informal economy and the so-called black economy, the latter consisting of activities which evade taxes.

Measurement

Given the nature of the informal economy and the unobserved or undocumented character of economic activities within it, measuring the size of this economy is an extremely complex task. Reliance must frequently be placed only on anecdotal evidence through participant observation of the De Soto (1989) type.

The other more formal and direct, but infrequent, approach involves carrying out surveys such as establishment enquiries, and labour force and household surveys. Relevant information on labour force participation in the informal economy can also be extracted from the

Informal activities are non-corporate in character, are mostly small-scale, and generally involve self-employment.

population censuses. Given the high costs and periodic nature of such surveys, reliance has also been placed on indirect approaches applied to macroeconomic data to get annual estimates. This includes attempts at quantifying discrepancies between income and expenditure, between payments and transactions, and between tax payments and national income and product accounts (NIPA).

More recently, the currency ratio method, first proposed by Feige (1980), has become popular in the literature for sizing the informal economy. Justifications for use of this method are as follows:

1. In developing countries, currency is the predominant medium of exchange for informal transactions;
2. Informal agents typically do not have access to formal credit facilities, which employ demand deposits as the primary means of payment;
3. Even if chequeing facilities exist, currency will be the preferred medium of exchange when there are incentives to avoid detection.

A typology of different components of the economy can also be developed as follows:

<u>Agricultural Economy</u>
- limited market transactions
- transactions in cash or by barter

<u>Informal Economy</u>
- mostly market transactions
- transactions mostly in cash
- limited use of cheques

<u>Formal Economy</u>
- mostly market transactions
- transactions mostly through cheques
- limited use of cash

Therefore, most of the demand for cash originates either in the informal economy or agriculture.

Based on the characteristics of the informal economy described above, different segments of the national economy (excluding agriculture) can be categorized as follows:

<u>Informal Economy</u>
- small-scale manufacturing
- construction (private)
- road transport
- wholesale and retail trade
- ownership of dwellings
- services
- illicit activities (smuggling, drug trafficking, etc.)

<u>Formal Economy</u>
- large-scale manufacturing
- construction (public)
- mining and quarrying
- electricity and gas
- railway, air transport and telecommunications
- finance and insurance
- public administration and defence

Estimates

Based on the above classification of sectors and FBS estimates, the gross domestic product is distributed among the agricultural, informal and formal economy, as shown in **table 3.1**. In 1980-81, the informal

TABLE 3.1

SHARES OF GDP IN, AND GROWTH RATES OF, AGRICULTURE, INFORMAL AND FORMAL ECONOMIES

Years	Agriculture	Informal Economy	Formal Economy	Total
		SHARES (%)		
1980-81	31	42	27	100
1989-90	26	45	29	100
1997-98	25	47	28	100
1998-99	26	46	28	100
		GROWTH RATES (%)		
1980s	4.0	6.9	7.6	6.1
1990s	4.5	5.3	4.2	4.8

Note: Based on estimates reported in National Income Accounts by FBS
Source: Pakistan Economic Survey (1998-99)

economy represented about 42 per cent of the national economy. By 1998-99, the share had increased to 46 per cent. This demonstrates the relative buoyancy of the informal economy.

It is also significant to note that the informal economy grew faster during the 1980s, when the formal economy also showed relatively rapid growth. During the 1990s, the annual growth rate of the informal economy fell to about 5.5 per cent from 7 per cent, in line with a sharp drop in the growth rate of the formal economy from over 7.5 per cent to 3.5 per cent. This is the first evidence that growth in the informal economy is pro-cyclical in character.

However, estimates in the national income accounts of the value added in different components of the informal economy are fraught with serious measurement problems. These estimates are based either on surveys which are out of date (relating to the early 1980s) and/or on fixed

While the majority join the informal sector when they are unable to get a job in the formal sector, a significant proportion stay on permanently.

TABLE 3.2

RATIO OF CURRENCY IN CIRCULATION[a] TO DEMAND DEPOSITS[a]

1980s	Actual	Estimated[b]	1990s	Actual	Estimated[b]
1980-81	0.996	0.996	1990-91	0.975	0.991
1981-82	0.987	0.987	1991-92	0.902	0.997
1982-83	0.941	0.941	1992-93	1.081	1.003
1983-84	0.957	0.957	1993-94	1.207	1.009
1984-85	0.969	0.969	1994-95	1.144	1.013
1985-86	0.926	0.926	1995-96	1.198	1.018
1986-87	0.939	0.939	1996-97	1.392	1.022
1987-88	0.939	0.939	1997-98	1.411	1.026
1988-89	0.992	0.992	1998-99	1.027	1.002
1989-90	0.973	0.973			

[a]Annual figures are twelve-month averages
[b]Estimates made in the absence of foreign currency accounts
Sources: Pakistan Economic Survey (1998-99)
SPDC estimates

annual growth rates which remain unchanged from year to year. Therefore, not much reliance can be placed on growth patterns revealed by these estimates.

We have relied on a more refined version of the currency ratio method, as developed by Bennett (1995), to generate estimates of the size of Pakistan's informal economy from 1980-81 onwards. According to this method, a crucial determinant of the relative size of the informal economy, with respect to the formal economy, is the ratio of currency in circulation to demand deposits with the banking system. **Table 3.2** highlights the trend in this ratio. During years when this ratio is rising/falling, then the implication is that in these years the informal economy is growing relatively quickly/slowly in relation to the formal economy.

There does not appear to have been much change in the currency to demand deposits ratio during the 1980s. But first indications are that the informal economy grew relatively quickly in the 1990s, as highlighted by the rapid increase in the ratio. However, this conclusion is false because of the impact of the emergence of foreign currency deposits after 1990-91, which have displaced both currency and demand deposits. In fact, as also shown in table 3.2 that, once the effect of foreign currency accounts (FCAs) is removed, then the ratio appears to show a more gentle rising trend in the 1990s. As such, we conclude that the informal economy grew somewhat faster than the formal economy during this decade.

Application of the refined currency ratio method to the estimated currency/demand deposits ratio yields estimates of the size of the informal economy, which are presented in **table 3.3**. Comparison with the figures reported in the national income estimates reveals that the official GDP estimates generally understate the size of the informal economy. The largest error is in 1987-88, when the underestimation in the official

TABLE 3.3

REPORTED AND ESTIMATED SIZE OF THE INFORMAL ECONOMY

1980s	Reported (Rs. billion)[a]	Estimated	Ratio	1990s	Reported (Rs. billion)[a]	Estimated	Ratio
1980-81	104	104	1.00	1990-91	396	448	1.13
1981-82	121	116	0.96	1991-92	470	524	1.12
1982-83	136	135	0.99	1992-93	541	591	1.09
1983-84	156	165	1.06	1993-94	634	690	1.09
1984-85	179	182	1.02	1994-95	745	828	1.11
1985-86	196	210	1.07	1995-96	863	984	1.14
1986-87	217	247	1.14	1996-97	997	1,092	1.10
1987-88	255	291	1.14	1997-98	1,134	1,213	1.07
1988-89	292	323	1.11	1998-99	1,230	1,341	1.09
1989-90	329	370	1.13				

[a] At current prices
Sources: Pakistan Economic Survey
SPDC estimates

figures was by as much as 14 per cent—the informal economy appearing to have been almost Rs. 36 billion larger than the reported magnitude.

In terms of proportion, the informal economy now appears to represent almost 50 per cent of the national economy. As far as growth rates are concerned, both the informal and formal economies had high growth rates of close to 8 per cent and 7 per cent, respectively, during the 1980s **(see table 3.4)**. Growth rates generally fell in the 1990s, with a sharper drop to 4 per cent being registered by the formal economy, while the informal economy showed an annual growth rate of less than 5 per cent. It is of particular significance to note the loss of dynamism of the informal economy in the second half of the 1990s.

TABLE 3.4

ANNUAL GROWTH RATES OF THE INFORMAL AND FORMAL ECONOMIES (%)

1980s	Informal Economy[a]	Formal Economy	1990s	Informal Economy[a]	Formal Economy
1981-82	4.0	9.5	1990-91	6.7	5.8
1982-83	11.0	8.2	1991-92	5.0	7.8
1983-84	13.5	9.1	1992-93	3.4	4.0
1984-85	5.8	5.3	1993-94	4.8	3.0
1985-86	12.0	6.7	1994-95	7.5	4.2
1986-87	13.1	6.7	1995-96	7.9	5.1
1987-88	8.0	8.2	1996-97	-0.4	0.6
1988-89	1.5	3.3	1997-98	2.8	3.2
1989-90	6.4	5.5	1998-99	4.4	4.2
Average	8.4	6.9	Average	4.7	4.2

[a] As per SPDC estimates

The informal economy appears to represent almost 50 per cent of the national economy.

Cobbling to make ends meet.

IS THE INFORMAL ECONOMY COUNTER-CYCLICAL OR PRO-CYCLICAL?

We are now in a position to determine whether the informal economy is counter-cyclical or pro-cyclical with respect to trends in the formal economy. If it is indeed *counter-cyclical*, this would imply that during periods of rapid growth of the formal economy, the informal economy would exhibit slow growth, and vice versa. That being the case, the informal economy would, during periods of economic stagnation, provide an economic safety valve by exhibiting fast growth, and thereby contribute to poverty alleviation by preserving the rate of increase in income and employment. The counter-cyclical nature could be argued to be the consequence of increased tax evasion, which erodes production in the formal segment of the economy and diverts it to the informal sector; or it could be due to the emergence of illicit activities like smuggling and black marketing of foreign exchange, which might become more rampant during periods of economic crisis or stagnation.

The alternative hypothesis is that the pattern of growth of the informal economy is *pro-cyclical*, going up or down in line with movements in the formal economy. This could be due, for example, to the subcontracting nature of small-scale industry with respect to large-scale manufacturing. Likewise, wholesale and retail trading and transport activities in the informal economy are likely to be dependent on production levels in agriculture and large-scale industry, as well as the volume of international trade. Therefore, it is quite plausible that the informal economy bears a pro-cyclical relationship with the formal economy.

Value Added

Chart 3.1 gives the annual growth rates of value added in the informal and formal economies of Pakistan. Even visually, there appears to be a positive correlation. Years such as 1982-83 and 1983-84, when

CHART 3.1

RELATIONSHIP BETWEEN GROWTH RATES OF THE FORMAL AND INFORMAL ECONOMIES, 1981-82 TO 1998-99

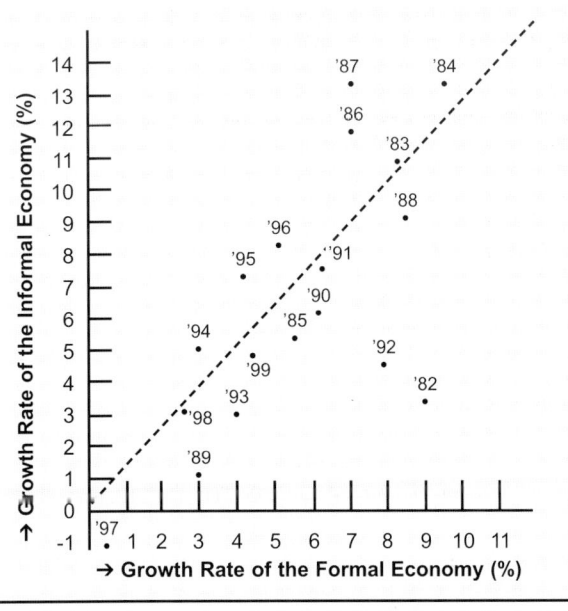

Source: As per SPDC estimates

the formal economy showed a high rate of growth, the informal economy exhibited double digit rates of growth. By the same token, in 1996-97 and 1997-98, which were relatively sluggish years for the formal economy, the informal economy also either declined or showed only modest growth.

In conclusion, contrary to the view held by some in Pakistan, growth of value added in the informal economy is pro-cyclical, and not counter-cyclical, with respect to the formal economy. Both these segments of the national economy essentially move together. The conclusion that is sometimes reached—that if the formal economy (especially large-scale manufacturing) is experiencing stagnation, then we do not need to worry too much because this is compensated for by fast growth in the informal economy—is not really valid. Therefore, there are no grounds for complacency regarding the stabilizing and growth-preserving role of the informal economy.

Employment

Estimates of the labour force in different sectors of the economy are potentially more reliable and frequent, as they are based, at least more or less, on annual Labour Force Surveys carried out by the Federal Bureau of Statistics (FBS). **Table 3.5** shows the employment shares of agriculture, the informal economy, and the formal economy. The increase in the share of the informal economy is striking, from 37 per cent in 1980-81 to over 44 per cent in 1997-98. This is almost exactly equal to the

Since value added in the informal economy is pro-cyclical with respect to the formal economy, there are no grounds for complacency regarding the growth-preserving role of the informal economy.

TABLE 3.5

SHARES OF EMPLOYMENT IN, AND GROWTH RATES OF, AGRICULTURE, INFORMAL AND FORMAL ECONOMIES

Years	Agriculture	Informal Economy	Formal Economy	Total
		SHARES (%)		
1980-81	53	37	10	100
1989-90	51	38	11	100
1997-98	45	44	11	100
		GROWTH RATES (%)		
1980s	1.8	2.4	2.7	2.1
1990s	0.2	4.2	2.0	2.0

Source: Pakistan Economic Survey (various issues)

decrease in the share of the agriculture sector. Therefore, the informal economy has contributed greatly to the increase in labour absorption in the economy, especially by employing the surplus labour released from agricultural activities. But are we essentially observing a phenomenon whereby underemployment in the rural areas is being replaced by underemployment in urban areas, in activities like trades and services?

Employment growth rates also reveal interesting trends. For the formal economy and agriculture sector, employment increased at a lower rate in the 1990s than in the 1980s. But in the informal sector, the 1990s' employment growth of over 4 per cent per annum was almost double that of the 1980s. This clearly indicates that employment growth in the informal economy is counter-cyclical with respect to the rest of the

Informal employment: Is she making enough to maintain subsistence living?

economy. It appears that when the formal economy and agriculture are unable to create additional employment, then the labour force gets increasingly diverted to the informal economy. Therefore, in terms of employment, the informal economy does appear to act as a shock absorber.

The next question that arises, then, is what happens to wages and income levels in the informal economy as it expands employment? Is there evidence of growing underemployment, as implied earlier? **Table 3.6** presents estimates of the real gross value added per worker in the informal economy from 1981-82 onwards. Labour productivity grew rapidly during the 1980s. During the 1990s, the rate of increase stagnated, and from 1995-96 onwards, there is evidence that it has actually started falling. To the extent that wages and incomes are linked to productivity, it appears that in the second half of the 1990s, while employment continued to expand rapidly, real incomes were no longer buoyant. In this respect, the labour carrying capacity of the informal economy has been exhausted. The poverty alleviating capability of this component of the national economy, therefore, has diminished.

In summary, research at SPDC reveals that the informal economy of Pakistan has the following features:

1. Growth of valued added in the informal economy is pro-cyclical with respect to growth of value added in the formal economy. Both economies exhibit similar growth trends, and the evidence points to the causality running from the formal to the informal economy. Therefore, if the formal economy falters in terms of its growth momentum then, sooner or later, this is bound to affect the dynamism of the informal economy.
2. Growth of employment in the informal economy is counter-cyclical with respect to growth of employment in the formal economy and agriculture sector. When the latter is unable to rapidly absorb more labour, then the informal economy appears to act as a residual employer and provide a *cushion* to those seeking work.
3. The contrasting behaviour of value added and employment in the informal sector has important implications for changes in real

TABLE 3.6

REAL GROSS VALUE ADDED PER WORKER IN THE INFORMAL AND FORMAL ECONOMIES (AT 1980-81 PRICES)

1980s	Informal Economy[a]	Formal Economy	1990s	Informal Economy[a]	Formal Economy
1981-82	11,502	26,304	1990-91	16,945	39,560
1982-83	11,835	28,409	1991-92	17,627	41,628
1983-84	12,227	29,463	1992-93	18,054	42,428
1984-85	12,619	31,341	1993-94	18,352	42,818
1985-86	13,467	32,081	1994-95	18,562	43,724
1986-87	14,012	33,406	1995-96	18,669	45,057
1987-88	14,684	34,685	1996-97	18,407	44,597
1988-89	15,492	36,675	1997-98	18,299	44,878
1989-90	16,377	38,218			

[a] As per SPDC estimates

The informal economy appears to act as a residual employer and provide a cushion to those seeking work.

When the formal economy fails to create enough employment, informal activity increases.

incomes and wages. During the 1980s, the formal economy grew rapidly. This implied fast growth in value added and relatively slow growth in employment in the informal economy. Consequently, labour incomes went up rapidly throughout the economy. This is one of the major factors contributing to the steep decline in the incidence of poverty during the 1980s.

In contrast, value added and employment in the formal economy expanded relatively slowly during the 1990s. The implied slow growth of value added, combined with fast growth in the labour force of the informal economy, resulted in a stagnation, and a fall in more recent years, in labour productivity and incomes. This probably explains the rise in poverty during the 1990s, especially in the urban areas of the country.

LEVEL OF INFORMAL TRANSFERS

As hypothesized above, an important reason why the prevailing high level of poverty has not yet resulted in large-scale social breakdown is because of the informal, joint household and community-based welfare and support systems which people have developed to counter rising poverty. The purpose of this section is to better understand the role of these informal transfers. Specifically, what is the level of informal transfers in the country? What form do these transfers take? Are informal transfers income-equalizing in nature; that is, do they contribute to poverty alleviation? What is their regional distribution and profile? And finally, do these transfers satisfy some of the key criteria of a *good* social safety net?

TABLE 3.7

LEVEL OF INFORMAL TRANSFERS, 1996-97

	Urban	Rural	Total
Total Annual Transfers (Rs. billion)	23.4	47.7	71.1
Share of Transfers (%)	33	67	100
Average Monthly Transfers Received per Household (Rs.)	415	360	377
Transfers Received as a Percentage of Monthly Income	6	7	7
Households Receiving Transfers (million)	0.6	2.1	2.7
Percentage of Households Receiving Transfers	13	18	17

Source: HIES (1996-97)

An initial answer to these important queries is attempted in this section. The analysis is based on household-level data from the HIES (1996-97).

In 1996-97, total informal transfers received by households in Pakistan amounted to over Rs. 71 billion, equivalent to about 3 per cent of the GDP **(see table 3.7)**. The average monthly transfer per household was Rs. 377, accounting for 6.5 per cent of household monthly income. Overall, 2.7 million households, representing 17 per cent of the total, received transfers in one form or another during the year. As such, informal transfers constitute an important source of income for households in Pakistan.

Rural areas receive about two thirds of the informal transfers. Here, the average monthly transfer received per household was Rs. 360, accounting for about 7 per cent of the household income. The significance of transfers in the urban areas was somewhat lower, at about 6 per cent. Also, a comparatively higher proportion of households in rural areas received transfers, at 18 per cent compared to 13 per cent in urban areas. On the whole, therefore, it appears that rural households rely more on informal transfers than urban households do.

What form do these transfers take? The bulk of the informal transfers (about 84 per cent) are in the form of remittances, both from within and outside Pakistan **(see table 3.8)**. Interestingly, a higher proportion, about half, are transfers from within Pakistan, while about one third of total transfers are in the form of remittances from abroad. An additional 10 per cent are made as social security transfers, which include recurrent periodical cash payments from various types of medical-related schemes (e.g., benefits for sickness, employment injury, unemployment, maternity, and convalescence). Other remittances, such as private gifts and assistance, account for about 5 per cent of total transfers. Meanwhile, *Zakat* and *Ushr* account for less than 1 percent of total transfers in the country.

Zakat payments are either made directly by households or through the government's *Zakat* scheme of transfers to *mustahqeen*. It is likely

In 1996-97, total informal transfers received by households in Pakistan amounted to over Rs. 71 billion, equivalent to about 3 per cent of the GDP.

TABLE 3.8

COMPOSITION OF INFORMAL TRANSFERS, 1996-97 (RS. BILLION)

	Urban Amount	%	Rural Amount	%	Total Amount	%
Zakat and Ushr	0.2	1	0.6	1	0.8	1
Remittances from outside Pakistan	12.2	52	11.4	24	23.5	33
Remittances from within Pakistan	7.8	33	28.3	59	36.1	51
Gifts, Assistance, etc.	1.0	4	2.3	5	3.3	5
Social Security	2.2	10	5.1	11	7.4	10
Total	**23.4**	**100**	**47.7**	**100**	**71.1**	**100**

Source: HIES (1996-97)

that *Zakat* transfers are understated because of the reluctance of households to reveal that they are beneficiaries of *Zakat*.

While remittances account for over 80 per cent of transfers in both the urban and rural areas, their origins are different. In the urban areas, remittances from abroad account for 52 per cent, whereas in rural areas, as much as 60 per cent of the rural remittances originate within Pakistan, with remittances from abroad accounting for less than one fourth of the total transfers.

The distribution of transfers is highly skewed in favour of the provinces of Punjab and NWFP **(see table 3.9)**. These two provinces respectively account for 68 per cent and 23 per cent of the total transfers, which is much higher than their share of the population. These interprovincial differences are primarily due to the pattern of outmigration observed in Pakistan. NWFP and Punjab have experienced large outmigration, which has resulted in a large flow of transfers into the provinces.

TABLE 3.9

PROVINCIAL DISTRIBUTION OF TOTAL TRANSFERS, 1996-97 (RS. BILLION)

	Urban Amount	%	Rural Amount	%	Total Amount	%
Punjab	16.1	69	32.2	68	43.3	68
Sindh	4.4	19	1.3	3	5.7	8
NWFP	2.6	11	13.6	28	16.2	23
Balochistan	0.3	1	0.6	1	0.9	1
Total	**23.4**	**100**	**47.7**	**100**	**71.1**	**100**

Source: HIES (1996-97)

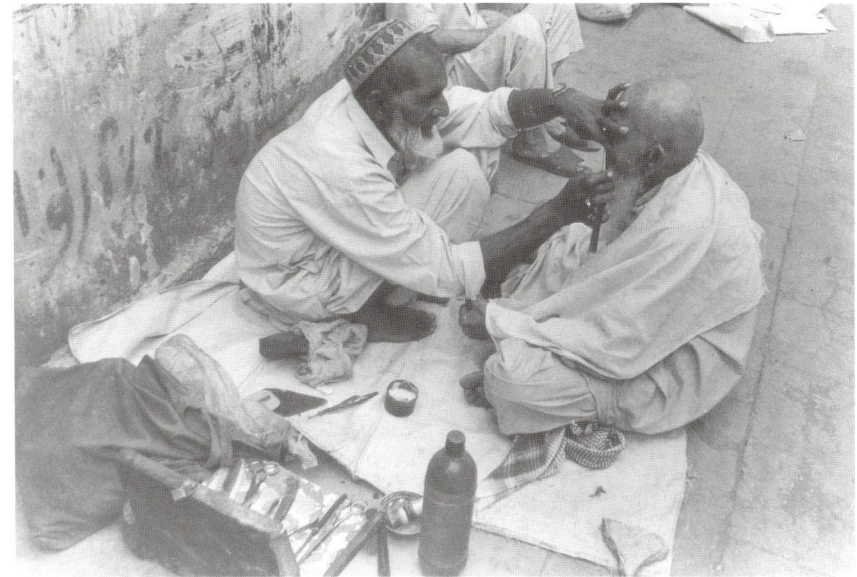

Informal transfers, coupled with long hours at low-wage jobs, help some households live above the poverty line.

IMPACT OF INFORMAL TRANSFERS

The poverty-alleviating impact of informal transfers hinges on three factors: their targeting efficiency, coverage level, and adequacy of support. *Targeting efficiency* is measured by the extent to which the transfers reach the poor, rather than the relatively well-off segments of the population. The *coverage level* indicates the proportion of poor households that benefit from transfers; if transfers accrue to only a small proportion of poor households, the ability to alleviate poverty will be very limited. Finally, *adequacy of support* measures the extent to which transfers reduce poverty among the recipients. When applied to informal transfers in Pakistan, these three evaluation criteria yield the following findings.

Targeting efficiency. On the whole, about 63 per cent of informal transfers flow to poor households **(see table 3.10)**. This indicates that informal transfers play a significant income-equalizing role in Pakistan, with as much as Rs. 45 billion reaching, and thereby supplementing the

TABLE 3.10

TARGETING EFFICIENCY OF TRANSFERS (%) [a]

	URBAN	RURAL	TOTAL
Zakat and *Ushr*	84	61	66
Remittances from within Pakistan	62	71	69
Remittances from outside Pakistan	65	67	66
Benefits / Assistance	29	44	40
Social Security	43	29	33
Total	**61**	**64**	**63**

[a] Share of transfers to poor households (pre-transfers)
Source: HIES (1996-97)

Social norms are cast aside as she makes her way on the streets to earn a living.

incomes of, poor households annually. The highest targeting efficiency is of remittances from within Pakistan (about 70 per cent), followed by remittances from abroad (at 66 per cent). As such, migration both within and outside Pakistan has very effectively countered poverty in both the rural and urban areas of the country.

Surprisingly, even though *Zakat* is exclusively meant for the poor, its targeting efficiency in rural areas is lower than that of remittances from within Pakistan. Other forms of transfers, including both private benefits/assistance and social security, are not necessarily intended for the poor, and consequently have a low targeting efficiency.

Coverage. Approximately 1.6 million of Pakistan's poor households (i.e., about 31 per cent) receive transfers in some form; 1.3 million of these are in rural areas. By far the highest coverage is of remittances from within Pakistan, benefiting over a million poor households. This implies that over 20 per cent of the poor households in Pakistan receive remittance income from within the country **(see table 3.11)**. This proportion is higher for the

TABLE 3.11

COVERAGE OF TRANSFERS (%)[a]

	URBAN	RURAL	TOTAL
Zakat and *Ushr*	2	3	3
Remittances from within Pakistan	13	22	21
Remittances from outside Pakistan	9	5	6
Benefits / Assistance	4	4	4
Social Security	n	n	n
Total	**26**	**32**	**31**

[a]Percentage of households below the poverty line (pre-transfer) receiving transfers
Notes: n = negligible
Column totals may not add up because one household may receive more than one transfer
Source: HIES (1996-97)

Many Pakistanis migrate to the urban centres in order to support their families through home remittances.

rural areas, at about 22 per cent. Remittances from abroad accrue to only about 6 per cent of the poor households, reaching a somewhat higher proportion of poor in the urban areas (9 per cent). *Zakat* and *Ushr*, the key public sector welfare intervention, benefit fewer than 3 per cent of the poor households.

The effectiveness of transfers in mitigating poverty in the urban and rural areas of NWFP is demonstrated by a high coverage level, with more than half of the poor households in the province receiving some form of transfers **(see table 3.12)**. In comparison, only about 6 per cent of poor households in Sindh and Balochistan receive transfers.

Adequacy. The final crucial evaluating criteria is the adequacy of transfers; are they large enough to bring households out of poverty? **Table 3.13** reveals that, in the case of a million households, they are. As many as 19 per cent of the poor households (20 per cent in rural areas; 16 per cent in urban) do not remain poor because of income-supplementing informal transfers. This is a very important finding, and unambiguously highlights the effectiveness of informal transfers in alleviating poverty in Pakistan.

TABLE 3.12

PROVINCIAL COVERAGE OF TRANSFERS (%)[a]

	Urban	Rural	Total
Punjab	29	38	36
Sindh	11	5	6
NWFP	49	58	57
Balochistan	11	6	6

[a]Percentage of poor households receiving transfers
Source: HIES (1996-97)

TABLE 3.13

ADEQUACY OF SUPPORT OF TRANSFERS[a] (THOUSANDS)

	Urban	Rural	Total
Households below Poverty Line without Transfers	1,241	3,940	5,181
Households below Poverty Line with Transfers	1,040	3,140	4,181
Difference	201	799	1,000
Percentage of Poor Households (pre-transfers)	**16**	**20**	**19**

[a]Households moving above poverty line because of transfers
Source: HIES (1996-97)

In the case of NWFP, the poverty mitigating role of informal transfers is truly remarkable **(see table 3.14)**. If these transfers were not available, an additional 41 per cent of households in the province would be living in poverty. The impact is also significant in Punjab, where 21 per cent more households would likewise be living in poverty were it not for transfer payments. The low impact of transfers in Sindh and Balochistan, as highlighted earlier, is borne out again in indications that only 3 to 4 per cent of these households receive sufficient transfers to get out of poverty.

In summary, the analysis in this section substantiates the significant role played by informal transfers in mitigating poverty in the country. In particular, the role of remittances from within Pakistan should be emphasized. The analysis shows that informal transfers are income-equalizing in character, as demonstrated by the high targeting efficiency, good coverage level, and adequacy of support. As many as a million additional households throughout Pakistan would be living in poverty if they did not have access to informal transfers. NWFP and Punjab are the major beneficiaries of informal transfers in the country, the bulk of these being in the form of remittances from within Pakistan. The role of informal transfers is a key factor in explaining the relatively low incidence of poverty in NWFP **(see chapter 2)**.

This analysis highlights the strong nexus between migration (and home remittances) and poverty alleviation, especially in Punjab and NWFP. Public safety nets should focus more on areas where the informal transfers are playing a relatively limited role in poverty alleviation–as in,

TABLE 3.14

PROVINCIAL ADEQUACY OF SUPPORT OF TRANSFERS (%)[a]

	Urban	Rural	Total
Punjab	18	23	21
Sindh	7	23	3
NWFP	37	41	41
Balochistan	8	4	5

[a]Percentage of poor households (pre-transfer) moving out of poverty due to transfers
Source: HIES (1996-97)

As many as a million additional households throughout Pakistan would be living in poverty if they did not have access to informal transfers.

Over two thirds of Pakistan's poor households receive no informal transfers.

for example, Sindh and Balochistan. However, since the ability of the informal economy to absorb migrants from rural areas has diminished in recent years, as highlighted in the previous section, the role of internal migration and remittances thereof in alleviating poverty is bound to become more limited.

Public safety nets should focus more on areas where the informal transfers are playing a relatively limited role in poverty alleviation.

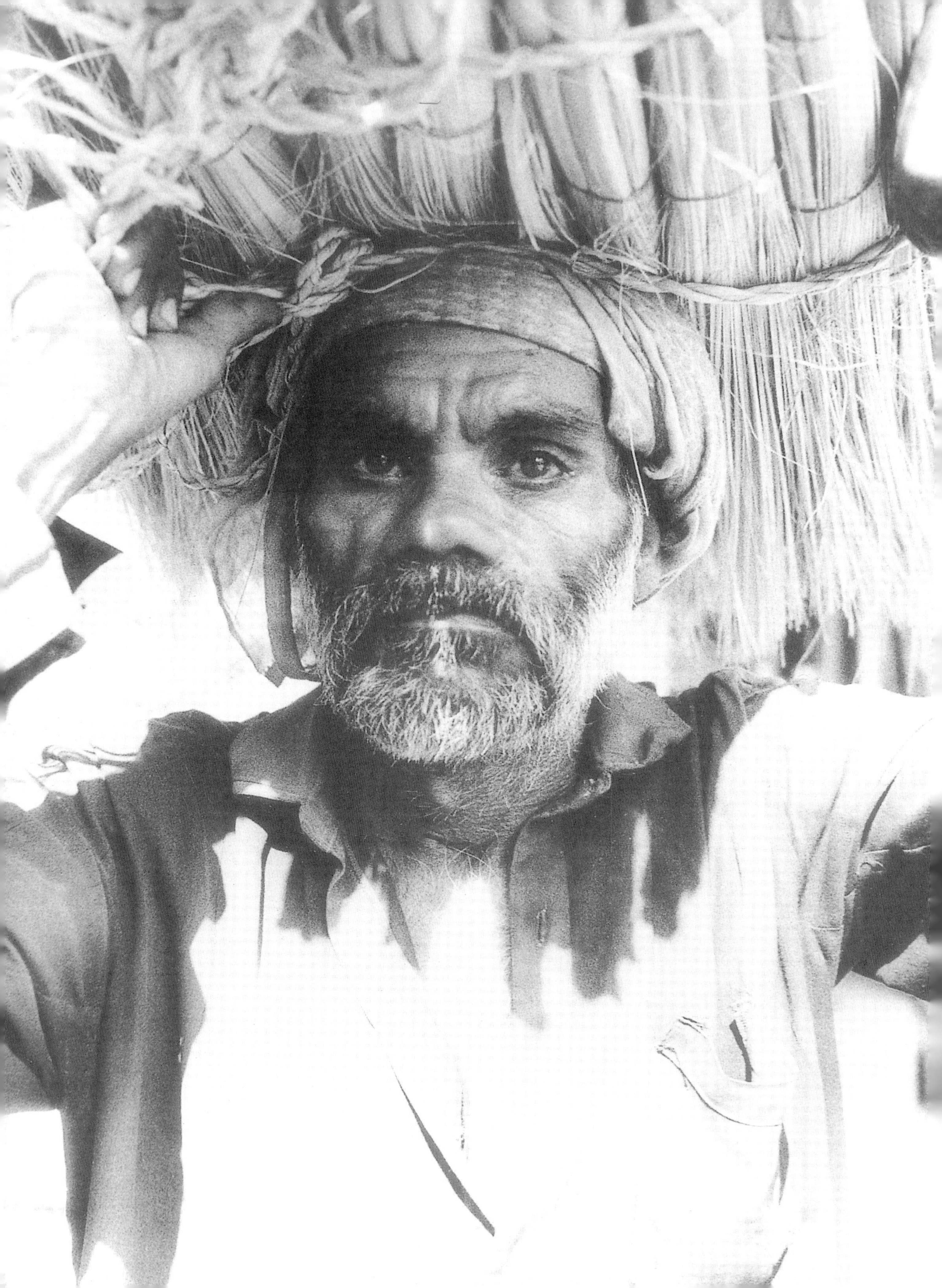

PROMOTING ECONOMIC OPPORTUNITIES FOR THE POOR

CHAPTER 4

"If macroeconomic developments remain unfavourable, then efforts directed at poverty alleviation through social safety nets are unlikely to be successful in counteracting the underlying increase in poverty."

PROMOTING ECONOMIC OPPORTUNITIES FOR THE POOR

The return of (rapidly increasing) poverty in Pakistan during the 1990s is increasingly being recognized by government, donors, and civil society at large as perhaps the principal problem requiring urgent attention if a large-scale social breakdown is to be averted, with its concomitant implications for law and order. In the early 1980s, one in every three families was poor. Poverty then diminished rapidly, having declined to one in five families by the end of the decade. Since then it has increased rapidly and it is currently estimated that we are back to the situation of twenty years ago, with one in three families being poor **(see table 4.1)**.

MACROECONOMIC EXPLANATIONS OF POVERTY

Our contention is that while social safety nets **(see chapter 8)** can begin to mitigate against the worst manifestations of poverty, the country's overall poverty outcome hinges on broader macroeconomic developments relating to such key determinants of poverty as growth in real per capita income, rate of unemployment, and level of cost of living (especially as reflected in food prices). In other words, if macroeconomic developments remain unfavourable, then efforts directed at poverty alleviation through social safety nets are unlikely to be successful in counteracting the underlying increase in poverty. As such, it is essential to focus on the relationship between macroeconomic developments and the incidence of poverty.

TABLE 4.1

TREND IN POVERTY: HEAD COUNT

Year	Total	Rural	Urban
1963-64	40.2	38.9	44.5
1966-67	44.5	45.6	41.0
1969-70	46.5	49.1	38.8
1979	30.7	32.5	25.9
1984-85	24.5	25.9	21.2
1987-88	17.3	18.3	15.0
1989-90	20.0	21.8	16.8
1990-91	22.1	23.6	18.6
1992-93	22.4	23.4	15.5
1996-97	31.0	32.0	27.0
1998-99	32.6	34.8	25.9
1999-2000	33.5	n/a	n/a

Number of Poor as Percentage of Population

Sources: Pakistan Economic Survey (1999-2000)
SPDC estimates

It needs to be emphasized at this stage that positive macroeconomic developments, as evidenced by a faster rate of economic growth, are not a sufficient condition for poverty to decline. As identified in economic literature, this depends upon whether fast growth is accompanied by significant trickle–down effects. If income inequality rises with growth, then it may even be possible for poverty to increase during periods of rapid growth (as happened during the 1960s). Alternatively, if growth causes a rapid increase in labour absorption and moderates inflationary pressures, especially on food prices, then it may play a strong poverty alleviating role. Therefore, from the viewpoint of impact on poverty, macroeconomic developments have to be analyzed not only in terms of the rate of economic growth but also in terms of factors that capture the potential magnitude of trickle–down effects. International experience demonstrates a strong relationship between economic growth and poverty reduction **(see box 4.1)**.

BOX 4.1

ECONOMIC GROWTH AND RATE OF POVERTY REDUCTION

International experience indicates that when economic growth rises, poverty falls. Conversely, where economic growth has been low or negative, poverty rates have typically been more persistent or have increased. The scatter diagram below clearly shows the relationship between poverty reduction and growth rate of GNP per capita for 40 developing countries for 1970-1992. The elasticity was close to unity, which means that income growth had a powerful impact on poverty reduction.

The People's Republic of China, Korea and Malaysia, all economies which experienced rapid growth, were able to dramatically reduce the incidence of poverty. Conversely, slower growth in Nepal and the Philippines meant that poverty reduction was more limited. It is significant to note that Pakistan lies in the middle of the scatter diagram, implying that, between 1970 and 1992, it was an average performer both in terms of growth and change in the extent of poverty.

ECONOMIC GROWTH AND POVERTY REDUCTION, 1970-1992

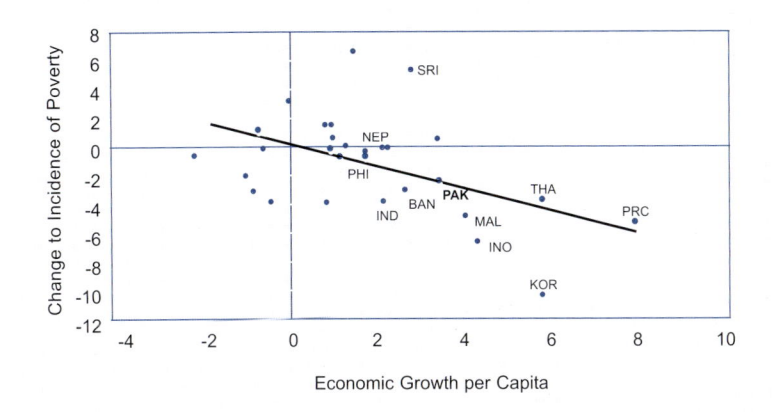

Source: *Asian Development Outlook* (ADB 2000)

Macroeconomic developments have to be analyzed not only in terms of the rate of economic growth, but also in terms of factors that capture the potential magnitude of trickle-down effects.

Surviving amidst garbage littered drains in Karachi.

Long-Term Trends in Poverty

Why did poverty rise rapidly during the 1990s? First, there was a visible decline in the growth momentum of the economy during this decade. The 1980s saw a steady growth rate of over 6 per cent, which fell to 5 per cent in the first half of the 1990s and declined further to just over 4 per cent in the second half of the decade **(see table 4.2)**. It was only 3 per cent in 1998-99, and had risen to 4.75 per cent in 1999-2000. Consequently, the

TABLE 4.2

TREND IN MACROECONOMIC INDICATORS AND INCIDENCE OF POVERTY, 1980s AND 1990s

Indicator	Unit[a]	1980s	1990-91 to 1994-95	1995-96 to 1999-2000
GDP Growth Rate	%	6.50	5.00	4.25
Growth Rate of Real Per Capita Income	%	3.00	2.00	1.00
Unemployment Rate	%	3.50	5.50	6.00
Level of Fixed Investment	% of GNP	17.00	17.75	15.25
Level of National Savings	% of GNP	14.50	14.75	12.50
Current Account Deficit	% of GNP	4.00	4.50	4.50
Budget Deficit	% of GDP	7.00	7.00	6.50
Rate of Inflation (CPI)	%	8.00	12.00	7.50
Rate of Inflation (food prices)	%	8.00	12.50	7.50
Incidence of Poverty:				
Beginning of Period	% of Pop'n	30.75	20.50	26.75
End of Period	% of Pop'n	20.50	26.75	33.50
Change during Period		-10.25	6.25	6.75

[a]Rounded off to the nearest quarter percentage point
Sources: Pakistan Economic Survey
State Bank of Pakistan, Annual Report
SPDC estimates

rise in real per capita income has tapered off. While it increased annually by almost 3 per cent during the eighties, during the last five years there has been only a 1 percent increase annually in this indicator.

The rate of inflation remained in single digits throughout the 1980s. Having risen sharply to 12 per cent during the first half of the 1990s, it moderated somewhat in the second half. Inflation in 1999-2000, at 3.5 per cent, was very low by historical standards due to less imported inflation, restricted monetary expansion (due to domestic debt retirement facilitated by the external debt relief), exchange rate stability, and staggered adjustment in administered prices of food and energy. It is significant to note that food prices have generally risen more rapidly than the overall consumer price index.

The unemployment rate increased by over 2 percentage points in the 1990s, in relation to the 1980s. This is a reflection of two factors: (1) continuing rapid growth in the labour force due to the high underlying rate of population growth and resulting concentration of the population in the younger age brackets, and (2) deceleration of labour absorption in the economy in response to the significant decrease in economic growth during the nineties **(see box 4.2)**. Given these trends, it is not surprising that while poverty fell in the eighties it started rising rapidly in the nineties.

BOX 4.2

WHAT IS HAPPENING IN THE LABOUR MARKET?

According to the Labour Force Survey of 1996-97, carried out by the FBS, the overall employment rate is 6%. What is striking, however, is the extremely high unemployment rate–at 43%—among new entrants (i.e., those who have never worked before), mostly from the younger age groups. This demonstrates a serious problem of labour absorption in the economy due to the recessionary conditions.

Within the labour force as a whole, unemployment appears to be particularly high among females (17%), young workers (10%), and those with a matric-level education (8%).

Among new entrants to the labour force, unemployment tends to be somewhat higher in the urban areas and among females. Newcomers to the labour force with relatively high levels of education appear to be having the greatest difficulty in finding suitable jobs, with unemployment rates in this category approaching 70%.

Other significant findings from the survey are as follows.
- The length of job searches is increasing, with over 42% of unemployed workers not finding a job within one year.
- Underemployment is also a serious problem, indicated by the fact that almost 43% of employed new entrants only have casual jobs.
- Only 3% of new entrants who are employed have jobs in the public sector, compared to 13% for the labour force as a whole. The government is clearly not creating many jobs, thereby adversely affecting the prospects, in particular, of educated new entrants.

All told, there is strong evidence that conditions have deteriorated severely in the labour market.

UNEMPLOYMENT RATE BY CHARACTERISTICS OF WORKERS, 1996-97 (%)

	New[a] Entrants	Total Labour Force
Location		
Rural	40	6
Urban	49	7
Sex		
Male	41	4
Female	48	17
Age (years)		
10-14	16	10
15-24	53	10
24-45	-	3
50+	-	8
Education		
Illiterate	24	6
Primary	39	5
Matric	70	8
Higher	65	6
Total	**43**	**6**

[a] Workers who have never worked before
Source: Labour Force Survey (FBS 1996-97)

Recessionary conditions have created a serious problem of unemployment.

It is legitimate to ask at this stage what the quantitative contribution of different factors is to changes in poverty during the last two decades. For this it is necessary to empirically identify which factors directly affect poverty and to what extent. Research by Kemal and Amjad (1997) and Akhtar and Ahmed (1999) indicates that the following factors are significant in explaining the variation in the incidence of poverty:

- level of real per capita income;
- extent of unemployment;
- level of food prices;
- level of real per capita home remittances;
- human capital endowment of the labour force.

Table 4.3 shows the elasticity of the level of poverty with respect to the above-mentioned factors, as estimated by Akhtar and Ahmed (1999). It is interesting to note the high elasticities of -1.58 and 0.52, respectively, with respect to real per capita income and level of food prices. Poverty alleviation efforts in Pakistan have generally focused on income supplements and employment generation. The need for basic food security for the poor, in terms of access to and stability in prices of basic food items (like *atta*, or wheat flour) has not been adequately recognized.

Table 4.4 provides estimates of the quantitative contribution of different factors to the change in the incidence of poverty during the 1980s and 1990s, respectively. It appears that poverty declined in the eighties because the adverse impact of rising food prices was overshadowed by the increase in real per capita income, along with improvement in the human capital endowment of the labour force. In contrast, there are fewer mitigating factors in the 1990s. Rising food prices, falling remittances, and increasing unemployment all contributed to greater poverty. Because of the relative stagnation of real per capita income, especially in the second half of the decade, the role of poverty-reducing factors has been more limited.

The need for basic food security for the poor has not been adequately realized.

TABLE 4.3

ELASTICITY[a] OF INCIDENCE OF POVERTY WITH RESPECT TO DIFFERENT POVERTY DETERMINANTS

Determinant	Elasticity
Level of Real per Capita Income	-1.58
Unemployment Rate	0.11
Level of Food Prices	0.52
Level of Real per Capita Remittances	-0.09
Human Capital Endowment of the Labour Force	-0.08

[a] Indicates the extent of change in poverty incidence due to a one percent increase in the determinant
Source: Akhtar and Ahmed (1999)

Short-Term Trends in Poverty

The year 1999-2000 has witnessed some favourable developments with regard to poverty alleviation. Real per capita income, which had been stagnant since 1996-97, has shown positive growth of over 1.5 per cent. Also of significance is the distribution of additional incomes in the economy. Almost one third of the increased real incomes in the economy accrued to farmers. While the income effect of the bumper crop of cotton was neutralized by the steep fall in prices, wheat growers not only enjoyed a close to 4 per cent improvement in their yields, but also received substantially higher prices due to the 25 per cent increase in procurement prices announced by the government. Altogether, over 7 per cent growth in agriculture in 1999-2000 must have contributed to some decrease in rural poverty.

The implications of macroeconomic trends in 1999-2000 are less favourable for urban poverty. The large-scale manufacturing sector registered a zero growth rate, although textiles, a relatively more labour-intensive sector, performed well. Perhaps more importantly, we have been informed that the small-scale manufacturing sector is no longer as buoyant as it once was. The sector's annual growth rate is now estimated

TABLE 4.4

CONTRIBUTION OF FACTORS TO CHANGE IN INCIDENCE OF POVERTY, 1980s-1990s (%)

	1980s	1990s
Level of Real per Capita Income	-8.00	-13.00
Unemployment Rate	-0.25	4.75
Level of Food Prices	3.25	21.75
Level of Real per Capita Remittances	0.50	2.75
Human Capital Endowment of the Labour Force	-2.50	-1.25
Unexplained	-3.25	-2.00
Change in Incidence of Poverty	**-10.25**	**13.00**

Note: Figures are rounded off to the nearest quarter percentage point
Source: Akhtar and Ahmed (1999)

to be 5.3 per cent, as opposed to 8.4 per cent in the early eighties. Since this sector is a major employer of the less-skilled category of workers, this has major implications on the process of labour absorption in the country.

Given the fact that, especially in the second half of the 1990s, the manufacturing sector has performed poorly while agriculture has shown relative buoyancy, it seems reasonable to conclude that the gap between urban and rural poverty is narrowing over time. It may be noted from **table 4.1** that there was a sudden jump in the incidence of urban poverty from about 16 per cent in 1992-93 to 27 per cent in 1997-98. It needs to be emphasized that rapid growth of poverty in the urban areas of the country has even more direct implications, potentially on the law and order situation.

As emphasized above, the unemployment situation has an important bearing on poverty. Fortunately, with the rapid increase in agricultural output in 1999-2000, labour demand has probably been relatively strong in rural areas, although the change in tenurial status and the process of mechanization that is taking place in agriculture may be having adverse implications on labour absorption in this sector.

Labour market conditions are also deteriorating very rapidly in the urban areas. The government, including the vast array of autonomous bodies, attached departments, statutory corporations and public enterprises, traditionally constituted a major source of employment, especially for the more educated. This source has more or less dried up in recent years due to the fiscal squeeze and the consequent recruitment bans that have frequently been announced. The steep fall in private investment, especially in the last two years, has limited the expansion in employment opportunities. The prospect of substantial downsizing in major government entities implies that the process of labour displacement will increase further.

Therefore, while the short-term employment situation improved somewhat in the rural areas in 1999-2000 due to buoyant agricultural output, it has clearly worsened in the urban areas. On top of all this, there is evidence that the informal economy, which has acted as the residual sector for absorption of unemployed, unskilled workers, is also running out of steam **(see chapter 3)**.

Turning to the topic of food prices, this is one area where considerable success appears to have been achieved in 1999-2000. During this period, food prices went up by only 2 per cent, according to the Federal Bureau of Statistics (FBS). This is the lowest rate of inflation in decades, and highlights the fact that the cost of living increased only modestly during the year. Food prices are of vital importance to the poor, and success achieved in restricting the increase in these prices is probably the first major achievement by government in limiting the growth in poverty. Clearly, relative food price stability will have to remain one of the major elements of the poverty reduction strategy.

A negative development from the viewpoint of poverty alleviation is the decrease of almost 10 per cent in workers' home remittances in 1999-2000. Perhaps the overall inflow has not fallen so much, and a larger part may have been diverted into unofficial channels. But the continuing decline in home remittances is an adverse long-term factor from the viewpoint of poverty reduction, and has made a significant contribution to increases in the incidence of poverty during the 1990s.

In summary, positive developments during 1999-2000 with regard to poverty alleviation are the modest rise in real per capita income, after having fallen or remaining stagnant for a number of years, and the extreme moderation in the inflation rate of food prices. Negative developments are the continued worsening of the unemployment situation, especially in the urban areas, and a steep fall in home remittances.

Rapid growth of poverty in the urban areas of the country has even more direct implications, potentially on the law and order situation.

Food price stability is essential to maintain the living standards of the poor.

Based on the changes in macro determinants of poverty during 1999-2000, SPDC's poverty forecasting model reveals that there has probably been only a relatively small deterioration in the overall incidence of poverty by less than one percentage point this past year. Consequently, the number of poor has increased by about 2 million. Although the model does not forecast urban and rural poverty separately, there is evidence that urban poverty increased more rapidly in 1999-2000. It needs to be stated that poverty measurement and forecasting remains an inexact science in Pakistan and that SPDC's estimates must only be taken as *indicators* of the orders of magnitude.

CONSTRAINTS TO ECONOMIC REVIVAL

Causes of Declining Growth

The previous section highlighted that the rapid increase in poverty during the 1990s is attributable to the relatively low rate of economic growth (implying a slow increase in per capita income), coupled with rising unemployment and a high rate of inflation in food prices (except during the last few years). It is clear that if the increase in poverty is to be contained during the current decade, then the economy will have to show greater dynamism, with faster growth leading to more labour absorption and a fall in the unemployment rate. Such growth will also have to be achieved with relative price stability, otherwise there will continue to be pressure on poverty via increases in the prices of essential commodities.

A strategy for the revival of the economy must, therefore, be central in any national programme for poverty alleviation. But before such a strategy can be found, it is essential to understand the causes of the low and falling growth of Pakistan's economy during the nineties **(see box 4.3)**. Based on such an understanding, the appropriate elements of a revival strategy can be identified. There will then be a need to determine the factors constraining the implementation of such a strategy, and how these constraints can be removed.

BOX 4.3

DETERMINANTS OF GROWTH OF PAKISTAN'S ECONOMY

Research has been undertaken at SPDC to explain the year-to-year fluctuation in the growth rate of Pakistan's economy since the early 1960s. The significant factors that explain this variation are:
- growth rate of the cotton crop
- growth rate of other major crops
- growth rate of real investment
- growth rate of dollar export prices
- home remittances as a percentage of GDP
- foreign aid as a percentage of GDP
- growth rate of real money supply.

On the basis of these variables, explanations for the decade-wise variation in growth rate are as follows:

1960s. The growth rate was 2 percentage points above average, largely due to the faster growth rate in output of other major crops (the green revolution), high levels of foreign aid, and rapid growth in investment.

1970s. The growth rate was about a half percentage point below average, caused primarily by a fall in the growth rate of cotton and other major crops and a decline in the inflow of foreign aid, compensated partly by the rise in home remittances and improvement in export prices.

1980s. The growth rate was almost 1.5 percentage points above average, a consequence of rapid growth in home remittances and increased output from cotton, dampened partly by less growth in export prices.

1990s. The growth rate was almost 1 percentage point below average. This was the result of a decline in the growth rate of investment, fall in remittances and foreign aid, and a fall in the growth rate of export prices.

Iqbal and Zahid (1998) identify the role of other factors in explaining the variation in the growth performance of Pakistan. These include the ratio of primary school enrolment (with a ten-year lag) to the labour force, the size of the budget deficit, and external debt. They show that greater openness of the economy helps boost the growth performance.

Perhaps the most popular explanation for the fall in the growth rate is the decline in the level of investment and savings in the economy. The rate of investment was high in the 1990s **(see table 4.5)**, and the economy witnessed a veritable investment boom, with private investment having attained a peak similar to the 1960s in 1991-92. This was the consequence of the policy of deregulation, liberalization and privatization, announced by the first Nawaz Sharif government. But since the mid-nineties, the investment level has been falling. By 1999-2000, it had come down to just over 13 per cent of the GDP, a fall of almost 5 per cent since the early nineties. However, much of the decline

TABLE 4.5

LEVEL OF INVESTMENT AND SAVINGS (% of GNP)

	1980s	1990-91 to 1994-95	1995-96 to 1999-2000	1999-2000
Fixed Investment	17.00	17.75	15.25	13.50
Public	9.25	8.50	6.25	5.50
Private	7.75	9.25	9.00	8.00
National Savings	14.50	14.75	12.50	13.50
Public	1.75	2.25	0.75	-0.50
Private	12.75	12.50	11.75	14.00

Note: Figures are rounded off to the nearest quarter percentage point
Source: State Bank of Pakistan, Annual Report

TABLE 4.6

EFFICIENCY OF INVESTMENT

	Level of Fixed Investment (% of GDP)[a]	GDP Growth Rate (%)[a]	Capital-Output Ratio
1980s	17.00	6.50	2.6
1990s			
First Half	17.75	5.00	3.6
Second Half	15.25	4.25	3.6

[a] figures are rounded off to the nearest quarter percentage point
Sources: Pakistan Economic Survey
State Bank of Pakistan, Annual Report

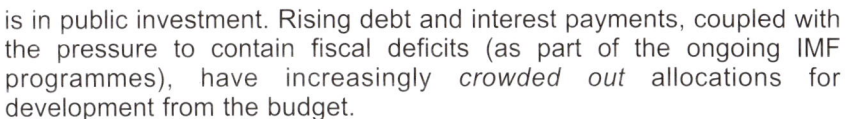

---

is in public investment. Rising debt and interest payments, coupled with the pressure to contain fiscal deficits (as part of the ongoing IMF programmes), have increasingly *crowded out* allocations for development from the budget.

The decline in private investment is more recent in character, and is fortunately not so pronounced in aggregative terms. The big shock was registered following sanctions in the aftermath of the May 1998 nuclear blasts. Foreign direct investment has fallen precipitously due to uncertainties created by the imposition of controls on the repatriation of profits and dividends in 1998, and more recently by the continued lack of resolution of the Hub Power Company (HUBCO) dispute. What is perhaps more worrying is the change in the composition of private investment. In the early 1990s, almost 30 per cent of such investment was channelled into manufacturing. By the end of the decade, this had fallen to about 20 per cent. In 1999-2000, the level of real private investment in manufacturing was 30 per cent below the peak level of 1993-94. This has restricted the ability of the manufacturing sector to create new jobs in recent years.

In addition to the falling investment rate, the negative impact on growth has been exacerbated by the declining efficiency of capital in the economy. As shown in **table 4.6**, the incremental capital–output ratio (measured as the ratio of the level of investment to GDP growth rate) has been rising in the economy. It was 2.6 during the 1980s, implying that investment of less than 3 per cent of the GDP was required to yield a 1 per cent growth in GDP. This was a low ratio, and Pakistan was increasingly being quoted as a model of efficient growth among developing countries. But this ratio rose sharply in the 1990s, to 3.6. Therefore, as a result of low investment and declining efficiency of capital, Pakistan's economic growth is now among the lowest in the South Asia region. The Indian economy, for example, performed significantly better in the 1990s **(see box 4.4)**.

Why has the economy become less efficient in converting investment into growth? The key explanation lies, of course, in stagnant productivity **(see box 4.5)**, exacerbated by wrong investment choices. On the one hand, private industrial investment was concentrated in such sectors as textiles, sugar, and cement, which, primarily due to depressed demand conditions, have experienced low rates of capacity utilization; and on the other hand, public investment has increasingly been diverted into lumpy, long-gestation projects such as motorways and air terminals, which have yielded low returns to investment. Furthermore, there is a growing perception of waste, inefficiency, and corruption in the execution

As a result of low investment and declining efficiency of capital, Pakistan's economic growth is now among the lowest in the South Asia region.

BOX 4.4

WHY IS THE INDIAN ECONOMY PERFORMING BETTER?

During the first four decades after Partition, Pakistan's economy generally performed better than India's. This pattern was reversed in the 1990s, when the Indian economy grew by about 6 per cent while the growth rate in Pakistan was 4.5 per cent.

Consequently, for the first time, in 1999, the per capita income of India in terms of purchasing power parity, at US$1,700, exceeded that of Pakistan, at US$1,560. Why has the Indian economy performed better? The reasons are as follows:
- The Indian economy has consistently invested and saved more. The savings rate in India is almost twice that of Pakistan.
- The incremental capital-output ratio of India, at 3.8, has fallen below that of Pakistan, at 4.0.
- Indian agriculture has actually performed poorly in relation to Pakistan, and there is not much difference in the growth rates of the manufacturing sectors. The difference in overall growth rate is due to the dynamism of India's service sector (including information technology) in the 1990s.
- Indian merchandise exports have grown significantly faster than those of Pakistan.
- Despite faster growth, the Indian economy is characterized by smaller macroeconomic imbalances. In particular, the current account deficit, at about 1 per cent of the GDP, is considerably lower than that of Pakistan. This has enabled India to build foreign exchange reserves in excess of US$35 billion, while those of Pakistan have fallen below US$1 billion.

MACROECONOMIC INDICATORS FOR INDIA AND PAKISTAN, 1990s

Variable	Unit	India	Pakistan	Ratio
GDP Growth Rate	%	6.00	4.50	0.75
Per Capita Growth Rate	%	3.25	1.50	0.46
Growth Rate:				
Agriculture	%	2.75	4.00	1.45
Manufacturing	%	5.50	5.25	0.95
Services	%	6.50	4.50	0.69
Gross Domestic Investment	% of GDP	23.00	18.00	0.83
Gross National Savings	% of GDP	24.00	14.00	0.58
Growth Rate of Exports	%	8.50	5.00	0.59
Current Account Deficit	% of GDP	1.00	4.50	4.50
Budget Deficit	% of GDP	4.50	6.50	1.63
Rate of Inflation	%	8.00	10.00	1.25

Source: *Asian Development Outlook*, (ADB 2000)

---

of projects by the public sector. Problems of governance, therefore, have also contributed to slowing down the growth process **(see chapter 6)**.

Throughout the history of Pakistan, foreign savings (in the form of grants, aid, and commercial credits) have contributed significantly to financing investment in Pakistan. The aid climate was particularly

BOX 4.5

WHAT IS HAPPENING TO TOTAL FACTOR PRODUCTIVITY?

A change in total factor productivity (TFP) is the change in output that cannot be attributed to a change in use of factor inputs such as land, labour and capital. Improvements in factor productivity are largely assumed to represent the gains from technical progress.

Research undertaken at SPDC reveals that the growth rate of TFP in the economy as a whole has been declining steadily, as evidenced in the enclosed table.

It appears that during the

	Annual Growth Rate of Total Factor Productivity (%)
1972-73 to 1977-78	2.0
1977-78 to 1982-83	3.7
1982-83 to 1987-88	2.8
1987-88 to 1992-93	1.0
1992-93 to 1998-99	0.4

1990s, TFP grew rapidly in agriculture and modestly in manufacturing, but declined in the services sector. Overall, only about 12 per cent of the growth in GDP during the nineties is attributable to gains in TFP. Therefore, what we now have in Pakistan is not only a crisis of investment but also a crisis of factor productivity.

The research also finds that the growth in TFP is closely linked to improvements in the human capital endowment of the labour force. Other factors that seem to affect TFP are exposure to export markets, technology transfer from abroad, increase in non-factor inputs (especially in agriculture, e.g., water and fertilizer), stage of the business cycle (reflecting the rate of capacity utilization), and vintage of capital.

Source: SPDC estimates

Problems of governance have contributed to slowing down the growth process.

hospitable in the 1980s, for geopolitical reasons in favour of Pakistan, and almost 30 per cent of investment was financed by foreign savings. But net capital inflows diminished in the 1990s due to the rapidly increasing stock of external debt and the associated increase in debt servicing liabilities. This has also affected Pakistan's credit worthiness in international capital markets. In the aftermath of the sanctions and the actions taken thereof, such as freezing of foreign currency accounts (FCAs), Pakistan's access to foreign savings has been severely impaired and it is now clear that any gap between desired levels of investment and the available national savings will no longer be filled by a corresponding inflow of foreign savings. For sustainability of the balance of payments position, the current account deficit (equivalent to foreign savings) will have to be kept low. This implies that investment will have to rely more on national savings. With such savings at only about 12 per cent of the economy, the level of investment is likely to remain low unless the savings rate (especially in the public sector) rises dramatically.

Another set of reasons given for Pakistan's poor growth performance in recent years has focused on a sectoral explanation. The loss of dynamism has been attributed to stagnation in the manufacturing sector, while agriculture, if anything, has performed visibly better (as in 1999-2000) and prevented the growth rate of the economy from plummeting even further **(see table 4.7)**.

A number of factors have contributed to the sluggish performance of the manufacturing sector, which had traditionally acted as the economy's *engine of growth*. First, unfavourable demand conditions at home or abroad have limited the growth prospects for a number of key industries, such as textiles, cement, and sugar. In fact, exports have stagnated in the range of US$7.5 billion to US$8.5 billion since 1994-95. Second, the growing phenomenon of smuggling into Pakistan has eroded production of a number of consumer goods and consumer durable industries. Third, the liquidity problems of major public sector entities such as the Water and Power Development Authority (WAPDA), and the fall in the overall level of investment, have led to major declines in output of the engineering goods industries. Fourth, the increasing tax burden has restricted growth of output in such industries as tobacco, beverages, and cement. Fifth, the ongoing process of trade liberalization, with declining customs tariffs, has meant that a number of inefficient import-substituting industries have been unable to survive. The growth rate of the manufacturing sector, for example, nearly halved between the eighties and the second half of the nineties. Small-scale industry, a major source of employment in the economy, has experienced a decline in growth from about 8.5 per cent to less than 5.5 per cent.

TABLE 4.7

SECTORAL GROWTH PATTERN (%)

	1980s	1990s First Half	1990s Second Half	1999-2000
Agriculture	5.50	4.25	5.00	7.25
Manufacturing	8.25	5.75	3.75	1.00
Services	6.75	5.00	4.15	4.75
GDP	**6.50**	**5.00**	**4.25**	**4.75**

Note: Figures are rounded off to the nearest quarter percentage point
Sources: Pakistan Economic Survey
State Bank of Pakistan, Annual Report

Other explanations offered by various writers for the outgoing "decade of sluggish growth" are as follows:

Crisis of institutions. Political governments, with an average life of less than three years, and inexperienced and corrupt leadership, have resulted in the erosion of economic management institutions, as well as wrong and inconsistent economic policies. Increased rent-seeking behaviour and loss of investor confidence are the major consequences of institutional breakdown.

Loss of economic sovereignty. Many analysts believe that the succession of IMF/World Bank programmes adopted during the 1990s has led to sacrificing the growth objective in favour of macroeconomic stabilization (which has also proven elusive). In particular, overemphasis on fiscal deficit reduction has led to severe cutbacks in development and social sector expenditures, and affected the growth potential of the economy.

Problems of globalization. Pakistan's private and public sectors have remained relatively oblivious to the implications of globalization on the domestic economy. The need to rapidly restructure the manufacturing sector and maintain the competitiveness of the export sector through well-coordinated monetary, fiscal and exchange rate policies has not been adequately realized by governments. The effects of the East Asian crisis, coupled with the sanctions imposed upon Pakistan following the nuclear blasts, have had negative effects on both exports and foreign direct investment.

Poor social indicators. Underinvestment in social development since Independence has resulted in low levels of human resource development and left Pakistan ill-equipped to raise factor productivity rapidly in the face of the onslaught of globalization in the 1990s.

The *Base* Scenario

What are the prospects for Pakistan's economy in the next few years, given this backdrop of low and falling investment due to fiscal constraints and loss of investor confidence (exacerbated more recently by the accountability and tax recovery drive); a low rate of national savings due to large public sector deficits and low household incomes; a stagnant manufacturing sector and an agricultural sector subject to growing water shortages and the usual vagaries of weather; an extremely vulnerable balance of payments position with slow-growing exports, a high import bill (due particularly to high oil prices), the drying-up of capital inflows, and extremely low foreign exchange reserves; and a labour force characterized by low human resource endowments? The obvious answer is that economic performance is unlikely to show dramatic improvement unless some of those constraints to growth are removed.

We have generated a medium-term *base* scenario for the economy for the next three years, which essentially assumes a continuation of the past trends with some modest improvement. This scenario is based on the following assumptions:

1. The gradual restoration of private sector confidence and some improvement in private investment;
2. The continued constraint on public investment by the need to bring the fiscal deficit down from the currently high level of 6.5 per cent of the GDP;

Overemphasis on fiscal deficit reduction has led to severe cutbacks in development and social sector expenditures, and affected the growth potential of the economy.

Congestion at Karachi's largest oil tanker stand due to lack of investment in infrastructure.

3. No apparent constraint to financing moderate current account deficits (of up to 2 per cent of GDP); in effect, this implies that an IMF programme with exceptional financing (including a second round of debt relief) will be put in place by the end of December 2000, when the current period of debt relief expires;
4. A modest level of fiscal effort that leads to some enhancement in the tax-to-GDP ratio, which is used primarily for budget deficit reduction;
5. Moderate growth in the world economy, leading to some increase in export prices.

In this scenario, the binding constraint is the level of investment and savings in the economy.

Based on these assumptions, macroeconomic projections have been made by using SPDC's Integrated Social Policy and Macroeconomic (ISPM) model **(described in appendix A.4)**. The resulting magnitudes are presented in **table 4.8**. The growth rate approaches 5 per cent by 2002-03, from the present rate of 4.75 per cent. Fixed investment increases by 1 per

TABLE 4.8

THE *BASE* MACROECONOMIC SCENARIO

Variable	Unit	Actual 1999-2000	Projected 2000-01	Projected 2001-02	Projected 2002-03
GDP Growth Rate	%	4.75	4.50	4.75	5.00
Unemployment Rate	%	6.75	7.25	7.50	8.00
Fixed Investment	% of GNP	13.50	14.00	14.25	14.50
Private Investment	% of GNP	8.00	8.50	8.75	9.00
Public Investment	% of GNP	5.50	5.50	5.50	5.50
National Savings	% of GNP	13.50	13.75	14.50	15.00
Current Account Deficit	% of GNP	1.75	1.75	1.25	1.00
Tax Revenue	% of GDP	12.25	12.50	13.25	13.50
Budget Deficit	% of GDP	6.50	5.25	4.50	4.00
Rate of Inflation	%	3.50	7.50	7.00	6.25
Incidence of Poverty	% of pop'n	33.50	36.25	38.50	40.25

Note: Figures are rounded off to the nearest quarter percentage point
Sources: SPDC estimates
State Bank of Pakistan, Annual Report, 1999-2000

TABLE 4.9

NUMBER OF POOR IN THE *BASE* SCENARIO (MILLION)

	Population	Incidence of Poverty (%)	Number of Poor
1999-2000	138	33.50	46
2000-01	141	36.25	51
2001-02	145	38.50	56
2002-03	148	40.25	60

Source: SPDC estimates

cent of the GDP. The unemployment rate continues to increase, while the inflation rate rises appreciably from the historically low rate of 3.5 per cent in 1999-2000. The budget deficit improves significantly, falling from 6 per cent of GDP to 4 per cent of GDP in 2002-03. Simultaneously, the current account deficit in balance of payments falls to 1 per cent of GDP in the terminal year. Altogether the *base* scenario implies modest growth, rising unemployment, and a jump in the inflation rate, combined with a degree of macroeconomic stabilization. The upsurge in the rate of inflation in 2000-01 can be attributed to the substantially higher oil prices and a faster rate of exchange depreciation.

What implication does the *base* scenario have for the future trend in poverty? It appears that poverty will continue to rise rapidly, from about 33 per cent of the population in 1999-2000 to over 40 per cent by 2002-03 **(see table 4.9)**. This implies that in the next three years, another 14 million people will be added to the poor in Pakistan, the number of poor being expected to increase from the current 46 million to 60 million by 2002-03.

MACRO ELEMENTS OF A REVIVAL STRATEGY

The *base* scenario has highlighted that in the absence of implementation of a strong and wide-ranging reform agenda, poverty will continue to increase rapidly in coming years. But if Pakistan is able to develop a comprehensive home-grown package of reforms and implement them in the context of a medium-term programme of balance of payments support by the IMF and other international donor agencies, that includes both new funds and a second round of debt relief, then the prospects for faster growth can improve significantly with the concomitant implication of a lower rate of increase in poverty. Already, there are indications that Pakistan has reached agreement with the IMF on a standby facility for 2000-01, which may be converted into a poverty reduction and growth facility after June 2001. The question then arises: What are the macro elements of a revival strategy which can promote economic opportunities for the poor?

Evaluation of Different Policy Instruments

A number of policy instruments are potentially available for promoting the process of economic revival. We highlight the pros and cons of each instrument.

Increase in the public sector Annual Development Programme (ADP). This is probably the most commonly recommended instrument for economic revival. Given the fact that much of the decline in the growth rate of the economy during the 1990s can be attributed to the declining size of the ADP, which fell from over 7 per cent of the GDP at the beginning of the decade to about 3 per cent by the end, it seems logical to argue that the prime instrument for revival of the economy should be a big jump in the level of development expenditure.

Higher development spending has a number of favourable impacts. First, directly and by a broad-based multiplier impact, it raises the aggregate level of demand and employment. Second, it promotes higher capacity utilization, especially in construction-related industries, and raises agricultural output by removing infrastructural bottlenecks. Third, there is evidence that development, particularly of economic infrastructure, *crowds in* private investment. But it also has a number of negative implications. First, if the higher expenditure is financed not by additional revenues but through larger borrowings, then it not only adds to the budget deficit but also puts pressure on interest rates, thereby *crowding out* private investment. The higher budget deficit also generally implies some net expansion in money supply, unless it is compensated for by a more or less equal contraction in private sector credit demand. The monetary expansion, in turn, exacerbates inflationary pressures Second, the increase in aggregate demand associated with higher development expenditure runs the risk of raising the level of imports into the economy and worsening the trade deficit.

Therefore, a strategy of raising development expenditure creates a clear trade-off between growth and macroeconomic stabilization **(see chart 4.1)**. While the government of Pakistan is likely, in the short term, to attach greater weight to reviving growth, the IMF is laying more emphasis on reducing the fiscal and current account deficits in the programme that it is offering to Pakistan. This will place a limit on the extent to which the level of development expenditure can be enhanced in the medium term.

Depreciation of the exchange rate. This is a popular solution, often recommended for countries like Pakistan which are experiencing serious balance of payments difficulties. Maintaining an equilibrium or somewhat undervalued exchange rate, it is argued, has a number of favourable effects. First, it stimulates exports and restricts imports, thereby improving the trade deficit. The higher level of exports encourages domestic economic activity and employment. Second, it narrows the differential between the interbank and open market exchange rates, and encourages capital inflows and remittances from abroad. It raises revenue from taxes on international trade and contributes to the reduction in the budget deficit.

Opponents of large devaluations have a number of strong arguments against the use of this instrument. First, there is *elasticity pessimism*. It is argued that given the commodity structure of Pakistan's international trade, both export and import elasticities are very low, and even big devaluations of the currency will only lead to a minor improvement in the trade balance. Second, the argument frequently used against a devaluation is that it leads to inflation in prices of tradables, and puts pressure on the cost of living of the poor, especially if food prices rise. Third, higher revenues are neutralized by the higher value (in rupees) of external debt servicing, as well as higher subsidies or lower revenues, if administered prices of food and energy inputs are not raised accordingly. Therefore, the prospect of *real* devaluation of a large

CHART 4.1

POLICY EVALUATION MATRIX OF INSTRUMENTS FOR REVIVAL

Instrument	TARGETS (increase in)			CONSTRAINTS (reduction in)		
	Output and Employment	Investment	Exports	Trade Deficit	Budget Deficit	Inflation
Increase in Public Sector ADP	favourable	ambiguous	ambiguous	unfavourable	unfavourable	unfavourable
Depreciation of the Exchange Rate	favourable	ambiguous	favourable	favourable	ambiguous	unfavourable
Decrease in Nominal Interest Rates	favourable	favourable	favourable	favourable	favourable	favourable
Broad-basing the Tax Regime	ambiguous	ambiguous	ambiguous	ambiguous	favourable	ambiguous
Privatization and Capital Market-led Revival	ambiguous	favourable	ambiguous	ambiguous	favourable	ambiguous

Public expenditures have not been utilized effectively, as the land earmarked for the *Behbood* family planning scheme hosts a football field instead.

magnitudo io not high. Most governments are likely to be averse to such an action in view of the high political costs of an immediate and visible increase in prices. However, the present government has allowed the exchange rate to float, which has already led to a depreciation in the value of the rupee by almost 10 per cent in 2000-01.

Decrease in nominal interest rates. As shown in the policy evaluation matrix, this policy does not create any trade-offs in attainment of different objectives. It generally only has favourable effects including, first, the encouragement of private investment and, second, reduction in the cost at the margin of servicing domestic debt. However, *elasticity pessimism* also exists here with respect to the sensitivity of investment to interest rates, especially in an investment climate like Pakistan's, which is characterized by a general lack of confidence. In addition, there is concern that if the profitability of the banking sector is affected, then interest rates on deposits may be brought down, thereby reducing the level of savings in the economy. It is significant to note that since January 1999, following the debt rescheduling that enabled domestic debt retirement, interest rates have come down appreciably in Pakistan, but there has been no recovery yet in private investment. More recently, presumably as a way to stop flight of capital and to encourage capital inflows, interest rates have been increased somewhat.

Broad-basing the tax regime. This policy has no direct impact on the process of economic revival. However, the government of Pakistan has shown a strong preference for this policy, having opted to broad-base the sales tax regime by extending the tax to the retail stage, and embarking on a major survey to document the economy, and to detect income tax evasion. If such a strategy leads to significant additional revenues, then indirectly it could contribute to the process of economic revival either by lowering the budget deficit (and bringing down interest rates further) or enabling higher development expenditure (without affecting the size of the budget deficit).

Privatization and capital market-led revival. Prospects for the success of this strategy have been limited by the depressed state of the capital market and the current lack of foreign investor interest in Pakistan. However, as the government embarks gradually on a programme of privatization, it is likely to encourage domestic investment and alleviate pressure on the budget of loss-making public enterprises, as well as reduce debt servicing costs through retirement of debt from the privatization proceeds.

Based on the above evaluation of the pros and cons of different revival instruments and their effectiveness in the current context, our assessment is that the macro elements of a revival strategy for Pakistan's economy will primarily include enhancing the level of development expenditure, broad-basing the tax system, resorting to exchange-rate depreciation, and reducing real interest rates. A supply-side approach to revival, involving an across-the-board reduction in tax rates, is unlikely to be adopted in view of its past failure **(see box 4.6)**. We evaluate the likely degree of success of this strategy and the emerging macroeconomic and poverty scenario in the next section.

The *Best Case* Scenario

The *best case* scenario, which incorporates the above macro elements of a revival strategy, is based on the following assumptions:

1. The presence of a new medium-term IMF programme, with significant financing and a second round of debt relief. In addition, the absence of capital controls, attractive investment and privatization policies, and settlement of the long-standing IPP dispute, all lead to restoration of investor confidence and growth in foreign private investment. Simultaneously, domestic investment also picks up.
2. An exchange rate policy that involves significant real depreciation annually of the rupee and restoration of the buoyancy in home remittances due to a policy that minimizes the differential between the official and the kerb exchange rates.
3. Aggressive policies for resource mobilization, which lead to an increase in the overall tax-to-GDP ratio of almost 3 per cent by 2002-03. This is achieved by effective broad-basing of the GST to retail trade and services; greater documentation of the economy, which leads to reduction in the level of income tax evasion; development of the agricultural income tax; more effective exploitation of the revenue potential of the urban property tax; major tax reforms, which leads to simplification of the tax system; and fundamental improvements in tax administration.
4. A 1.5 per cent reduction in the share of interest payments in GDP by 2002-03, achieved by the overall deficit reduction and domestic debt retirement (due to debt relief and from privatization proceeds), along with some reduction in real interest rates.
5. Maintenance of the overall non-tax-to-GDP ratio by greater cost recovery in major economic services like irrigation and highways, and in tertiary social services, like higher education; and restoration of the profitability of key public utilities like WAPDA, through improvement in operational efficiency and appropriate tariff reforms.
6. Containment of the costs of civil administration through recruitment bans and rightsizing; and allocations for defence expenditure beyond 2000-01 indexed only to inflation.
7. An almost 3 per cent rise in tax-to-GDP ratio by 2002-03, along with a reduction in current expenditure by 1.5 per cent of the GDP, enables a 2 per cent increase in the share of development

Macro elements for a revival strategy will primarily include enhancing the level of development expenditure, broad-basing the tax system, resorting to exchange rate depreciation, and reducing real interest rates.

BOX 4.6

A CHRONICLE OF REVIVAL STRATEGIES

Ever since Pakistan's GDP growth rate plummeted to below 2% in 1996-97 and exhibited little recovery thereafter, successive governments have kept economic revival high on their policy agenda. We present here a chronicle of the revival strategies followed since 1997.

- Soon after induction into power, the Nawaz Sharif government announced a classical supply-side package for reviving the economy, which included the following:
    - steep cuts in tax rates, with the sales tax rates brought down from 18-23% to 12.5%; the maximum import tariff down from 65% to 45%; and the maximum personal income tax rate down from close to 40% to 20%;
    - big increases in procurement prices of wheat and sugar cane, of 39% and 46% respectively, with a near doubling of agricultural credit.
- There was a significant supply response, causing the growth of the major crop sector to go up to 8% and that of large-scale manufacturing to 7%.
- But the strategy proved to be unsustainable for a number of reasons:
    - due to intercrop substitution, the output of cotton declined and exports suffered;
    - the 26% increase in sugarcane output caused actual prices to fall below the committed price, and delays in payment to farmers;
    - the 49% increase in sugar output could not be absorbed in home consumption, and exports of sugar had to be heavily subsidized;
    - the increase in the wheat procurement price resulted in a vastly increased subsidy to protect urban consumers;
    - more importantly, despite the supply response, the steep fall in tax rates led to a fall in the tax-to-GDP ratio of 0.5%, and a rise in the budget deficit. Since then, tax rates have been raised once again to 15% in the case of sales tax, and to 35% in the case of personal income tax.
- The economy went into a deep recession in 1998, following the imposition of sanctions. The Nawaz Sharif government attempted economic revival for the second time in 1999 (following the agreement with the IMF on debt relief), but with a different strategy—one focusing on incentivization of some sectors. For example:
    - the export sector was promoted by enhancing duty drawback rates (including an element of subsidy, and costing Rs. 6 billion);
    - the number of items eligible for export refinance was increased, and import tariffs were further reduced;
    - under the Prime Minister's Self-Employment Programme, a scheme of small loans at low interest rates requiring minimum collateral was launched;
    - the Small Manufacturing Enterprises Developing Authority (SMEDA) was established to facilitate the development of SMEs;
    - the Prime Minister's Housing Programme was launched, involving the construction of 500,000 housing units for low-income groups, including free provision of state land, directed subsidized credit, and numerous tax concessions;
    - urban transport was incentivized by reduced customs duties on public transport vehicles.

However, before these programmes got fully underway, the Nawaz Sharif government was removed.

Economic revival is the first item in the seven-point agenda of the military government, and an Economic Revival Plan was announced on December 15, 1999.

---

expenditure in the GDP along with a reduction in the fiscal deficit by 2.5 per cent of the GDP.

8. As part of the ADP, the launching of a labour-intensive public works programme in 2000-01, which is allocated over 1 per cent of the GDP by 2002-03 and creates an additional 0.5 to 1 million jobs.

9. A faster increase in the tax-to-GDP ratio enables larger fiscal transfers to the provincial governments, thereby leading to larger outlays on education and a faster increase in human capital endowments of the labour force.

TABLE 4.10

THE *BEST CASE* MACROECONOMIC SCENARIO

Variable	Unit	Actual 1999-2000	PROJECTED 2000-01	PROJECTED 2001-02	PROJECTED 2002-03
GDP Growth Rate	%	4.75	4.75	5.25	6.00
Unemployment Rate	%	6.75	6.00	5.75	4.75
Fixed Investment	% of GDP	13.50	14.25	15.25	16.50
Private Investment	% of GDP	8.00	8.50	9.00	9.50
Public Investment	% of GDP	5.50	5.75	6.25	7.00
National Savings	% of GDP	13.50	14.25	15.75	17.25
Current Account Deficit	% of GDP	1.75	1.50	1.00	0.75
Tax Revenue	% of GDP	12.25	13.00	14.00	15.00
Budget Deficit	% of GDP	6.50	4.75	4.00	3.50
Rate of Inflation	%	3.50	7.25	6.25	5.00
Incidence of Poverty	% of pop'n	33.50	35.00	36.25	36.00

Source: SPDC estimates

Therefore, as shown in **table 4.10**, the *best case* scenario involves an ambitious attempt at reviving the economy. It envisages an increase in the GDP growth rate from 4.5 per cent in 1999-2000 to 6 per cent by 2002-03. This requires an increase in the level of fixed investment by 3 per cent of the GDP, and a reduction in the incremental capital-output ratio to the level prevailing during the 1980s. The increase in the national savings rate by almost 5 per cent of the GDP is particularly ambitious, and is predicated on a large increase in the rate of public savings. The unemployment rate also falls sharply by 2 per cent, as a result of both growth in labour demand arising from the faster increase in national output, and the implementation of the large, labour-intensive public works programme.

The *best case* scenario also achieves considerable macroeconomic stabilization, along with faster growth. The budget deficit falls sharply to 3.5 per cent of the GDP due to the rapid increase in tax revenues and containment of current expenditure. The current account deficit is brought down to 0.75 per cent of the GDP by the generation of larger exportable surpluses, along with stronger import substitution in food and energy, and a more active exchange rate policy. The rate of inflation is expected to rise significantly in 2000-01, to 7.25 per cent, for reasons given earlier.

Overall, in comparison to the *base* scenario, the *best case* scenario implies significantly faster growth, lower unemployment, and a somewhat lower rate of inflation. Consequently, the poverty outcome is substantially better. In the *base* scenario, the incidence of poverty surpasses 40 per cent by 2002-03, whereas in the *best case* scenario, it reaches 36 per cent. In fact, in the latter scenario, the incidence of poverty declines in 2002-03, as the growth rate of the economy approaches 6 per cent. As shown in **table 4.11**, the total number of poor in the *best case* scenario is projected at 53 million, compared to 60 million in the *base* scenario: a difference of 7 million people.

TABLE 4.11

NUMBER OF POOR IN THE *BEST CASE* SCENARIO (MILLION)

	Population	Incidence of Poverty (%)	Number of Poor
1999-2000	138	33.50	46
2000-01	141	35.00	49
2001-02	145	36.25	53
2002-03	148	36.00	53

Source: SPDC estimates

The Government's Macroeconomic Strategy

In the annual plan and the federal budget for 2000-01, the government has enunciated its short-term macroeconomic targets (for 2000-01) along with a medium-term macroeconomic framework for 2002-03, including a set of targets for each. Some of these targets have been revised following discussions with the IMF. As can be seen from **table 4.12**, the government's macroeconomic targets, both in the short and medium term, are somewhat more ambitious than the *best case scenario* developed by SPDC.

During the current fiscal year, the government expects the economy to achieve a growth rate of 5 per cent. This is considered unlikely, particularly in view of the water shortage problem in agriculture, which has already affected the sugarcane crop and made the outlook for wheat and cotton crops uncertain. The year 2000-01 is also expected to witness significant macroeconomic stabilization, with the fiscal deficit expected to fall from

TABLE 4.12

COMPARISON OF MACROECONOMIC MAGNITUDES IN DIFFERENT SCENARIOS

Variable	Unit	Base Scenario	Best Case Scenario	Government Target
2000-01				
GDP Growth Rate	%	4.50	4.75	5.00
Fixed Investment	% of GDP	14.00	14.25	14.00
National Savings	% of GDP	13.75	14.25	14.00
Current Account Deficit	% of GDP	1.75	1.50	1.50
Budget Deficit	% of GDP	5.25	5.00	5.00
Rate of Inflation	%	7.50	7.25	5.00
2002-03				
GDP Growth Rate	%	5.00	6.00	6.00
Fixed Investment	% of GDP	14.50	16.50	16.50
National Savings	% of GDP	15.00	17.50	17.50
Current Account Deficit	% of GDP	1.00	0.75	0.50
Budget Deficit	% of GDP	4.00	3.50	3.50
Rate of Inflation	%	6.25	5.00	4.00

Sources: SPDC estimates
Budget Speech, Minister of Finance, GOP (2000-01)

A construction worker falls asleep while waiting for a job.

over 6 per cent to about 5 per cent of the GDP. This is predicated on exceptional growth of 26 per cent in the Central Board of Revenue (CBR) tax revenues, and an absolute reduction in interest payments on the domestic debt, which continues to grow. The target inflation rate of 5 per cent also appears low in view of the recent increases in the issue price of wheat, and in gas tariffs and transport fares. Electricity tariffs are also likely to be raised later in the year. Furthermore, the exchange rate has already depreciated significantly following the float.

For the year 2002-03, targets in the government's medium-term framework are more or less identical to the magnitudes in the *best case* scenario, with some notable exceptions. Apparently the government believes that it can minimize the trade-off between growth and inflation. As such, it proposes to achieve the same 6 per cent growth in 2002-03 as in the *best case* scenario, but with significantly lower inflation, at 4 per cent. The precise strategy for achieving these objectives of high growth with low inflation has not been indicated. Of course, if such a strategy is successfully implemented, then poverty could fall significantly in the next few years.

MICRO ELEMENTS OF A REVIVAL STRATEGY

Along with the macroeconomic framework for revival, there is a need to identify the microeconomic elements of the revival strategy, consisting primarily of sectors which are expected to lead the process of national economic recovery. This will enable development of the appropriate set of policies, institutional arrangements, and regulatory framework to incentivize these sectors and increase their dynamism. There is increasing recognition that stimulatory fiscal and monetary policies for raising aggregate demand must be combined with a sectoral focus involving supply-side measures in order to achieve the fastest and maximum results with regard to economic revival.

What should be the basis for selecting leading sectors in the process of economic revival? One obvious criterion is that such sectors must have

Stimulatory fiscal and monetary policies for raising aggregate demand must be combined with a sectoral focus involving supply-side measures to achieve economic revival.

significant excess capacity, and must be capable of being incentivized in the short term, without having to wait for the usual investment lags. Also, these sectors must be *natural* choices in terms of possessing at least *dynamic* comparative advantage, given the natural and human resource endowments of the country. Development of such sectors can then make a significant improvement in the currently adverse balance of trade position, either by import substitution or enhancement in exports, and thereby contribute to alleviating the foreign exchange constraint.

We have developed ten criteria for evaluating sectors with regard to their relative capacity for contributing to the process of revival, while recognizing the existing constraints of foreign exchange and fiscal resources. The first three criteria are:

1. *Presence of excess capacity.* As highlighted above, sectors are ranked high on this criterion if they have a significant margin of excess capacity that can be put to use quickly if the appropriate supply and demand conditions are in place.
2. *Level of foreign exchange earnings/savings.* Sectors in which output growth can contribute significantly to enhanced exports or reduction in imports clearly have priority in the revival process, since they ensure that higher growth is not accompanied by a deterioration in the balance of payments position of the country.
3. *Potential for growth.* The issue of growth potential is also important because sectors that currently have unutilized capacity may, in fact, reflect the inability to compete with international sources of supply. Therefore, a sector must inherently be in line with the comparative advantage of the country, as reflected by the resource endowments. Alternatively, it must be characterized by fast growth in world trade and in most countries (e.g., information technology), due to the rapid pace of technical innovations.

The previous criteria appear to be implicit in determining the choice of leading sectors by government. However, we have also added other criteria based on their speed of supply response, contribution to removing constraints to growth, and capacity for employment generation and thereby for poverty reduction. These remaining criteria are:

4. *Labour intensity.* Sectors which are relatively labour-intensive score high on this criterion.
5. *Presence of backward and forward linkages.* Sectors that have strong linkages with other sectors of the economy, either as a source of intermediate inputs or with regard to marketing of output, are ideal leading sector candidates because growth in such sectors has a multiplier effect on other sectors.
6. *Import intensity.* Sectors that rely more heavily on imported raw materials, intermediate goods and machinery should preferably not be targeted because their growth can significantly raise the import bill and exacerbate the balance of payments problem.
7. *Magnitude of foreign investment/technology requirements.* High-tech industries which require access to sophisticated technology, which is available only from foreign sources, along with injection of capital, are unlikely to take off quickly in the Pakistani setting because the country is not currently an attractive location for foreign investors.
8. *Level of contribution to revenues.* Given the low level of tax revenues, preference should be given to sectors that make significant tax contributions as they grow.

TABLE 4.13

EVALUATION[a] OF CANDIDATES FOR LEADING SECTOR

	AGRICULTURE			MANUFACTURING							
	Minor Crops	Livestock	Fisheries	Agro-Processing	Value Added Textiles	Engineering Goods	Oil and Gas	Construction	IT	Transport	SMEs
1. Presence of Excess Capacity	M	M	M	L	H	H	L	H	L	M	M
2. Level of Foreign Exchange Earnings/Savings	M	L	H	M	H	M	H	L	H	L	H
3. Potential for Growth	M	M	M	M	L	L	H	L	H	M	M
Cumulative Score[b]	6	5	8	5	9	7	9	6	9	5	8
4. Labour Intensity	H	H	M	M	H	M	L	H	M	M	H
5. Presence of Backward and/or Forward Linkages	M	M	L	H	H	M	H	H	L	M	H
6. Import Intensity	L	L	M	L	L	M	M	M	H	H	M
7. Magnitude of Foreign Investment/ Technology Requirements	L	L	L	L	M	M	H	L	H	L	L
8. Level of Tax Contribution	L	L	M	L	L	L	H	H	L	H	L
9. Need for Policy Reform and/or Institutional Change	M	M	M	M	M	H	H	M	M	M	H
10. Infrastructure Requirements	M	M	M	L	L	M	H	H	H	H	M
Cumulative Score[b]	25	24	23	26	30	19	23	27	18	20	29

[a] L = Low, M = Medium, H = High
[b] L = 1, M = 2, H = 4

9. *Need for policy reform and institutional change.* The speed of supply response is likely to be slow in sectors that require major policy reform relating, for example, to pricing and/or major institutional change, like corporatization or privatization.
10. *Infrastructure requirements.* Sectors in which output has been limited by infrastructure bottlenecks will require significant public investment to trigger the process of growth. This will require both time and resources and, as such, the ability of such sectors to lead the process of revival is limited.

The sectoral rankings for each criterion are presented in **table 4.13**. A sector is ranked low, medium, or high for each criterion, with three possible numerical scores also being given. Eleven sectors have been selected for evaluation as candidates for leading sectors in the process of economic revival. Of these, three are from agriculture (i.e., minor crops [primarily fruits and vegetables], livestock, and fisheries), and three from manufacturing (i.e., agro-processing, value added textiles, and engineering goods). The other five sectors considered are oil and gas, construction, information technology, transport, and small and medium enterprises (SMEs).

The resulting rankings of the sectors, on the basis of both (1) the three criteria (implicit in the government's strategy for economic revival) and (2) all ten criteria, are given in **table 4.14**. The top five sectors when three criteria are used (i.e., relating to the presence of excess capacity, level of foreign exchange earnings/savings, and potential for growth) are information technology, oil and gas, value added textiles, SMEs, and fisheries. The sectoral choice changes significantly when ten criteria are used, in which case the five sectors that emerge as prime candidates to act as the leading sectors are value added textiles, SMEs, construction, agro-processing, and minor crops. Two sectors, i.e., value added textiles and SMEs, are ranked high in both cases.

The findings for each sector in terms of its potential role as a leading sector are discussed below.

Minor crops. This sector scores high on labour intensity, and has the advantages that few imported inputs are required and no foreign investment or sophisticated technology is needed. Its principal disadvantages are that it requires proper marketing arrangements and a commitment to support prices from the government.

Livestock. This sector is also characterized by relatively high labour intensity and low import requirements. Disadvantages include the difficulty in establishing an export market for livestock products (e.g., milk) from Pakistan, and the need for more large-scale, organized production.

Fisheries. This sector has significant export potential but few backward or forward linkages with the rest of the economy. Also, deep sea fishing would require significant investment in equipment.

Oil and gas. Based on recent discoveries of gas reserves, this sector has significant growth potential and can contribute significantly to savings on foreign exchange currently being used for oil imports. It has major forward linkages with key sectors such as power and fertilizer, and can add substantially to revenues. But the sector has a number of significant handicaps. There is currently no excess capacity, labour requirements are low, the magnitude of foreign investment and technology required for development of the sector is high (but this is unlikely to be forthcoming in the short term), difficult issues related to gas pricing have yet to be

Five sectors that emerge as prime candidates to act as the leading sectors in the process of economic revival are value added textiles, SMEs, construction, agro-processing, and minor crops.

TABLE 4.14

RANKING OF LEADING SECTORS FOR THE PROCESS OF ECONOMIC REVIVAL

Rank	On the Basis of Composite Score in Three Criteria	Ten Criteria
1.	Information Technology[a]	Value Added Textiles[a]
2.	Oil and Gas[a]	SMEs[a]
3.	Value Added Textiles[a]	Construction[b]
4.	SMEs[a]	Agro-Processing
5.	Fisheries[a]	Minor Crops[a]
6.	Engineering Goods	Livestock[a]
7.	Minor Crops[a]	Oil and Gas[a]
8.	Construction[b]	Fisheries[a]
9.	Livestock[a]	Transport[b]
10.	Agro-Processing	Engineering Goods
11.	Transport[b]	Information Technology[a]

[a] Sectors chosen by the government in the Economic Revival Plan and in the export development strategy
[b] Sectors chosen by the Nawaz Sharif government as leading sectors

resolved, and key entities in the sector are undergoing the process of privatization. Also, infrastructure requirements in the form of pipelines, etc., are high.

Agro-processing. This sector has significant backward linkages and export potential in the medium term, and can significantly add value to crop production, especially of fruits and vegetables. However, there is currently little capacity in the country.

Value added textiles. Development of this sector has been much delayed and is consistent with the comparative advantage of the country. The sector has significant backward linkages, is generally quite labour intensive, and already has significant excess capacity and possibilities for exports, although there is the problem of quotas and intense competition in international markets.

Engineering goods. This sector is characterized by significant excess capacity, but it is not clear if Pakistan can compete effectively in export markets. Also, there will be the need for a major policy change in favour of import substitution in capital goods, which will imply significant enhancement in tariffs on imported machinery.

Construction. This sector was chosen as a leading sector for economic revival in the latter days of the Nawaz Sharif government, and a number of ambitious housing schemes were announced. It has large, unutilized capacity, especially of construction workers and machinery. The sector has strong backward linkages with industries such as cement, steel, and wood, and is highly labour intensive. It can also make a significant contribution to enhancing tax revenues for different levels of government. But it is a non-tradeable sector and makes no contribution to foreign exchange earnings, although it could attract significant funds from overseas Pakistanis. Perhaps the most fundamental problem is the low demand for housing in the economy at a time when purchasing power and savings are limited.

Minor crops is among the important sectors in the process of economic revival.

However, the recent decline in interest rates has improved the prospects for housing credit.

Information technology. This is the favoured sector of most governments and numerous incentives have already been granted for its development. Given rapid innovation, this sector is experiencing exponential growth worldwide. Pakistan can also enter the international markets for software development, but there is an acute shortage of trained personnel in this sector. It is unlikely to create a significant demand for unskilled labour. Other disadvantages include the considerable requirement of infrastructure, imports, and foreign investment/technology.

Transport. This sector was also targeted by the Nawaz Sharif government, because of the benefits to the urban middle class and the prospect of being able to attract significant investment in the sector through tax concessions. But growth in the sector will place a burden on foreign exchange resources and require expansion in the intra-urban road network in order to avoid congestion. A proper regulatory framework will also need to be developed, along with a policy on transport fares.

SMEs. The small and medium enterprise sector has been relatively neglected in Pakistan, although it is labour-intensive, has strong backward and forward linkages, and can generate or save foreign exchange for the country. Targeting the sector will require significant institutional reform in terms of orienting the banking system towards providing credit to the sector, emphasizing human resource development, organizing export marketing, and removing discrimination against commercial importers in the trade policy.

In the Economic Revival Plan announced by the Chief Executive of Pakistan, the following areas have been chosen as the key micro elements of the government's revival strategy:

- revitalizing the agriculture sector;
- promoting small and medium enterprises;

Incentivization of the livestock sector will provide a stimulus for agriculture and help alleviate poverty.

- encouraging oil and gas exploration and development;
- developing the informal technology and software industry.

Therefore, the government is targeting four sectors–i.e., agriculture, SMEs, oil and gas, and information technology–in its revival strategy. Our analysis of potential leading sectors reveals that, beyond these sectors, there is a strong case for the inclusion of two additional ones, i.e., construction and agro-processing, and for emphasizing within agriculture the livestock and minor crops sectors. In fact, the three sectors–minor crops, livestock, and agro-processing–form a natural cluster of sectors that can be accorded high priority in the process of economic revival. Furthermore, the construction sector, in particular, has strong linkages with other sectors of the economy, and its incentivization will also stimulate these sectors.

From the viewpoint of poverty reduction, primary emphasis will have to be placed on inducing rapid growth in those sectors that, first, are labour intensive in character and can generate significant additional employment **(see box 4.7)** and, second, produce goods or services that have a relatively high weight in the consumption basket of lower-income groups. The construction sector meets both criteria, while the livestock, minor crops, and agro-processing sectors also produce goods of importance to the poor. Therefore, the inclusion of these sectors as key sectors in the revival

From the viewpoint of poverty reduction, primary emphasis will have to be placed on inducing rapid growth in those sectors that, produce goods or services that have a relatively high weight in the consumption basket of lower-income groups.

BOX 4.7

EMPLOYMENT GENERATION CAPACITY OF DIFFERENT SECTORS

The employment generation capacity of different sectors during the process of growth can be judged by computing the sectoral employment elasticities (i.e., the percentage increase in employment due to a one per cent increase in output of a sector). These employment elasticities for the period from 1980-81 to 1997-98 are given below.

A number of key conclusions emerge from the elasticity estimates:

- Contrary to popular perceptions, the agriculture sector is no longer absorbing labour rapidly as it grows. This could be the consequence of changes in the tenurial system and the incipient process of mechanization.
- Employment in the manufacturing sector has remained virtually unchanged over the last two decades, and increases in output have translated primarily into gains in labour productivity.
- Sectors with high employment elasticities are construction, wholesale and retail trade, and transport and communications.

Therefore, an employment-oriented growth strategy would need to target the construction sector as a key leading sector in the process of economic revival. Also, dynamism of the informal economy is vital from the viewpoint of sustaining the labour absorption capacity of the economy **(see chapter 3)**.

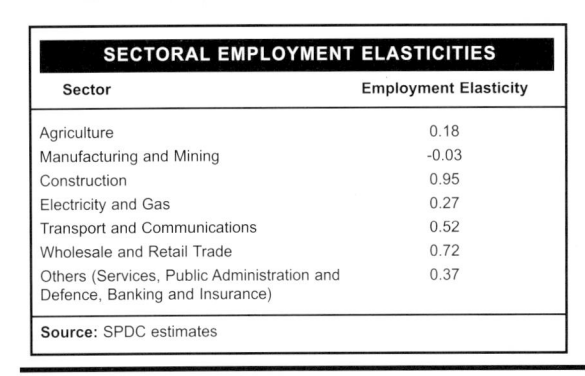

SECTORAL EMPLOYMENT ELASTICITIES

Sector	Employment Elasticity
Agriculture	0.18
Manufacturing and Mining	-0.03
Construction	0.95
Electricity and Gas	0.27
Transport and Communications	0.52
Wholesale and Retail Trade	0.72
Others (Services, Public Administration and Defence, Banking and Insurance)	0.37

Source: SPDC estimates

strategy will help significantly in furthering, at the micro level, the goal of poverty reduction as a complement to the macro strategy, which focuses on growth with employment generation and relative price stability.

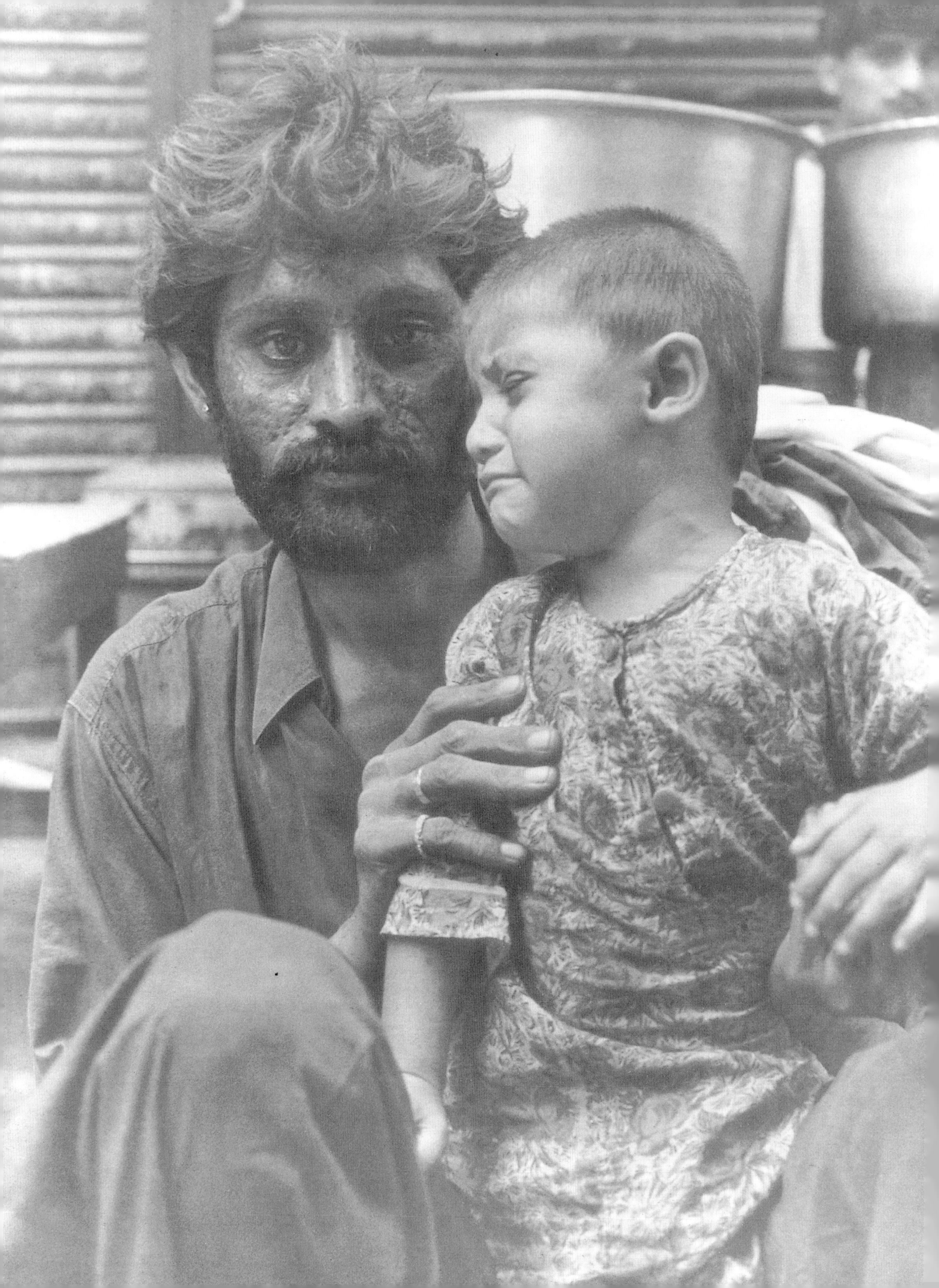

ECONOMIC REFORMS AND POVERTY

CHAPTER 5

"Economic reforms which are pro-poor in character can directly alleviate poverty."

ECONOMIC REFORMS AND POVERTY

We have emphasized in the previous chapter that the government needs to pursue a strong and comprehensive reform agenda to revive the process of growth and thereby arrest the increase in poverty. In this chapter, we discuss economic reforms which are pro-poor in character and can directly alleviate poverty. We identify three critical areas—public expenditure reform, tax reform and land reform.

PUBLIC EXPENDITURE REFORM

Public expenditure reform is vital from the viewpoint of poverty reduction. Public expenditure not only creates income and employment opportunities for the poor, but by targeting the provision of basic services towards the poor, such as education and health, it can help them break out of the vicious cycle of poverty.

Constraints

Public expenditure reform has proven to be one of the most intractable areas of reform. This is because public expenditure allocations generally reflect the roughest aspects of the political economy and problems of governance in Pakistan, whereby priorities are distorted by strong constituencies and lobbies. Politicians and senior bureaucrats frequently use the levers of concessions, subsidies, special expenditure allocations, and subventions for the purposes of patronage, and in many cases for personal gratification in the form of bribes. Rent-seeking activities flourish within the ambit of the budget-making process, whereby groups that are favoured are unwilling to give up a privilege once granted, even in times of financial stringency. Simultaneously, new groups continue jockeying for special treatment, regardless of the overall macroeconomic situation. In some respects, this is what democracy is all about. The quality of governance hinges on the ability of an administration to resist the pressures of special interest groups and to cater, instead, to the general public interest; in particular, to the poor and disadvantaged.

Rent-seeking behaviour is perhaps most acutely manifested in the granting of subsidies which erode the budgetary position of government but remain largely invisible to the public eye. Recent research by SPDC demonstrates that subsidies granted by the federal and provincial governments add up to approximately Rs. 145 billion, or 5 per cent of the GDP **(see box 5.1)**. These include subsidies on energy consumption, and social and economic services. The irony of this is that only a small component of the subsidies are targeted to the provision of *merit goods*. The political economy of Pakistan has led to the capture of the state by the most influential, vocal and organized interest groups, such as large farmers, big business (e.g., the textile lobby), public enterprises, and the military establishment. While there is considerable rhetoric on the need to protect the *common citizen* and focus on poverty reduction, in practice the actual benefits of public expenditure are skewed towards the rich and powerful.

BOX 5.1

SUBSIDIES ADD UP TO 5% OF THE GDP

Research undertaken by SPDC reveals that subsidies for economic, social and community services added up to as much as Rs. 145 billion in 1997-98; over 5 per cent of the GDP. For a particular service, the subsidy was computed as the difference between the total cost (of operations and maintenance plus depreciation) and the revenue from fees and user charges. The research also indicates that the subsidy bill has been rising steadily. It was about 3 per cent of the GDP in 1980-81 and 4 per cent in 1990-91. It is significant to note that the share of *merit goods* (i.e., primary education and health) is less than one-third; the rest goes primarily to economic services and higher education, which generally benefit the rich.

The largest subsidy is on irrigation, which is mostly pre-empted by large-scale farmers. Although small-scale, domestic consumers are charged relatively low tariffs for electricity and the tariffs increase exponentially for higher levels of consumption, the present tariff structure discriminates in favour of agricultural tubewells (operated mostly by large-scale farmers) and areas such as the Federally Administered Tribal Areas (FATA) (mostly for industrial consumption).

Gas is subsidized for all consumers, benefiting the urban middle class and the rich as well as some industries, such as fertilizer (leading to windfall profits).

Current levels of cost recovery are extremely low— even in the case of economic services, which are in the nature of private goods. For example, only 39 per cent of the annual operations and maintenance cost of the irrigation system is recovered through the *abiana* irrigation charge. With regard to higher education, the rate of cost recovery is only 4 per cent, and in the case of roads, 8 per cent.

There exists a strong case for enhancing user charges for services that primarily benefit upper income households, and then using the revenues generated for cross-subsidizing expansion of the provision of *merit goods* and for higher transfer payments to the poor.

SUBSIDIES IN PUBLIC PROVISION OF SERVICES, 1997-98
(Rs. billion)

Education	51
Primary	27
Secondary	14
Higher	10
Health	19
Curative	15
Public	3
Preventive	1
Economic Services	75
Irrigation	28
Electricity	23
Roads	14
Gas	10
Total	145

Source: SPDC estimates

Problems

The failure in public expenditure reform has meant that the public sector has become increasingly bloated and overextended. The presence of large fiscal deficits has sharply highlighted this feature of the economy. Overall, the public sector of Pakistan misallocates resources, is poorly managed, inefficiently spends scarce public resources, and does not effectively target the poor. The long list of problems includes the following:

Misplaced priorities. The fundamental problem is that high-priority social and physical infrastructure investments that could benefit the poor, and transfer payments for poverty reduction, have increasingly been *crowded out* by growing interest payments (due to the persistently large fiscal deficits) and military expenditure. An indication of misplaced priorities is the fact that, in Pakistan, military expenditure is more than twice the total expenditure on public education.

Improper utilization of scarce funds. This is the consequence of faulty institutional structures for service delivery, poor financial management practices, and defective planning. Service delivery is mostly by line departments and parastatal organizations, which are characterized by overcentralization of management and a supply-driven approach, rather than by responsiveness to effective demand. There is overemphasis on salary payments (given the employment fixation) in relation to non-salary

An indication of misplaced priorities is the fact that, in Pakistan, military expenditure is more than twice the total expenditure on public education.

inputs, which reduces the effectiveness of spending. Lumpy capital expenditures are generally preferred over operations and maintenance because of the greater scope for *commissions.*

Financial management practices have led to loss of control and leakages because of the absence of proper accounting systems, appropriate reconciliation procedures, and audit. Reliance only on cash flow accounting means that there is inadequate knowledge of public assets and of contingent liabilities. The planning process has been rendered ineffective by too much *politicization* of project selection and execution. This has also contributed to the development programme being *spread too thin* in order to accommodate competing claims. The consequence is delays, cost overruns, and the stretching of limited implementation capacity. Overall, the improper utilization of funds has implied scaled–down and wasteful delivery of services. Programme initiatives pursued by governments with populist agendas, supposedly aimed at benefiting the poor, have the greatest potential for eroding the normal budgeting process and distorting priorities. Programmes such as subsidized urban housing and transportation have been demonstrated to be notoriously prone to leakages and defective implementation, with much of the benefit being pre-empted by the more powerful segments of society. Such programmes are often eventually abandoned because of lack of financial sustainability, without any significant gain, meanwhile, to the poor.

More recently, the launching of poverty reduction strategies has led to somewhat increased outlays for social safety nets, including generalized food subsidies, targeted food support programmes, cash transfer payments, enhanced social security, and labour-intensive public works programmes. But the institutional arrangements for such anti-poverty interventions are generally fragile and underdeveloped. Consequently, overhead costs are high, targeting is poor, coverage is limited, leakages are common, and negative incentive effects are frequently the result. A lot more needs to be done to effectively implement poverty reduction strategies **(see chapter 8).**

Absence of transparency and accountability. Large components of public expenditure remain outside the realm of public scrutiny. For example, the military budget, which consumes almost 25 per cent of Pakistan's federal resources, is presented as merely a one-line item in the budget documents. There is also a lack of explicit accounting of subsidies and tax expenditures. The problem of inadequate information dissemination is especially acute in the case of statutory corporations and utilities, which account for the major part of the *quasi-fiscal* deficit. There is a virtual absence of effective oversight mechanisms of the legislature, consumers, and civil society at large.

The consequence of misplaced priorities, lack of responsiveness to needs and preferences, and ineffective and wasteful delivery, is growing disillusionment among the people, especially the poor, with the provision of goods and services by government. There is a search for alternatives, and greater reliance on the private sector and non-profit organizations. This is most evident in the areas of education and health where, especially in the urban areas, much of the demand has moved away from the government, and most public service facilities lie underutilized. However, this has meant that while the rich have found ways of accessing high quality, privately-provided services, the poor have been relegated to consuming public services of poor quality.

A stage has also been reached where, in the absence of reforms,

Quality of education has been adversely affected by teacher absenteeism.

public sector entities have begun to collapse in Pakistan. Closure has been temporarily forestalled by the building-up of large overdrafts with the banking system, and by deferring payments of liabilities to the likes of suppliers and contractors. In the case of many of the large public utilities, such as WAPDA and the Karachi Electric Supply Corporation (KESC), which provide vital services (e.g., power and water), the government recently had to step in and bail them out by effectively writing off their debts through debt-equity swaps. Inefficiency and corruption have translated into high tariffs, which have adversely affected the living standards of the poor.

Physical indicators of the public sector crisis include lack of improvement in the coverage, and deterioration in the level of services; for example, the high incidence of power outages, interruptions to the supply of drinking water (especially in low-income neighbourhoods), and breakdowns in telecommunication services. Also, there is visible depletion of physical infrastructure in the absence of adequate repairs and maintenance.

A particularly worrying consequence of the growing public perception of waste, corruption and inequity in public expenditure is the resulting breakdown of taxpayer compliance in Pakistan. Given the absence of any visible link between tax payments and benefits received, citizens are inclined to withhold their tax contributions and defy tax laws through higher levels of tax evasion. This has been most acutely manifested in the recent traders' strikes against the levying of GST at the retail stage. This phenomenon reinforces the need for greater accountability of public expenditure, greater exercise of economy, and in some cases, earmarking of revenues, if the process of developing a tax culture is to be promoted. Otherwise, the tax-to-GDP ratio is likely to remain low and limit the financial capacity of the government, in particular, to expand its poverty alleviation programme.

Altogether, a stage has been reached where, unless there is radical reform of the public sector, the process of growth and development in Pakistan will be retarded by the lack of social and physical infrastructure, which has already begun to hinder the process of production and

In the absence of reforms, public sector entities have begun to collapse in Pakistan.

Given scarce drinking water, growing inequity in distribution of this resource will lead to acute distress among poor communities.

investment by the private sector. More importantly, it has rendered the task of poverty alleviation even more difficult.

Directions of Reform

What are the key reforms required to realize this new vision of the public sector as an efficient entity oriented towards serving the interests of the general public, and in particular the poor?

Rethinking the role of government. Based on the new vision, there will have to be a fundamental rethinking of the role of government. Each function (and the entity discharging it) will have to be carefully studied from the viewpoint of the following: Is the public entity producing a public good or a purely private good? Is the entity performing a significant poverty alleviating function? Is the entity facing competition from the private sector? Is the entity surviving only because of some special protection or preferential treatment? Is the entity so overextended that all it can do is to cover the cost of its own establishment? Has the mission of the entity disappeared? Is there a duplication of activities with other agencies? Does the entity represent encroachment upon functions of a lower level of government? If it is a public commercial venture, is the entity showing losses?

Based on the above assessment, a decision will have to be taken as to whether the entity should be retained in its present form, or closed, downsized, privatized, or devolved to a lower level of government. Such an audit will not only have to be undertaken of government ministries and departments, but also of statutory corporations, public enterprises, autonomous bodies and attached departments. This is clearly a mammoth task and may have to be undertaken in phases, starting first with the more peripheral activities. The body charged with the responsibility of conducting this review will have to be seen as independent and impartial, and made immune from the inevitable

A worrying consequence of the growing public perception of waste, corruption and inequity in public expenditure is the resulting breakdown of taxpayer compliance in Pakistan.

lobbying pressures. Fortunately, in Pakistan, commissions or high-powered committees have already looked at the role of different entities. The problem is not so much one of identifying the nature of the restructuring programme, but of implementation—for which the requisite political will is required. The human dimension of downsizing would, of course, have to be carefully managed through the maintenance of a surplus pool, severance payments, and labour-training facilities. On the balance, if user charges or tariffs could be brought down by way of cost savings, and funds diverted to more pro-poor expenditures, then the poor would be the net beneficiaries.

Improving transparency and accountability. This will require developing proper budgetary classification systems; instituting information-disclosure requirements, especially for parastatals, corporations and security agencies; setting up proper oversight mechanisms with requisite powers and representation from the legislature (following the restoration of democracy), consumer bodies and civil society at large; implementing mechanisms to ensure that spending is only for authorized purposes; and establishing a strong and independent legal and institutional framework for accountability of corruption and inefficiency. The military government has recently established public accounts committees at the federal and provincial levels, consisting of retired civil servants, professional accountants and members of civil society and academia.

Prioritizing effectively among broad expenditures and programmes. This will require focusing, first, on an increase in non-wage operations and maintenance-spending in key sectors; second, on the rehabilitation of infrastructure and the consolidation of existing investments through better utilization of available capacity, rather than expenditure on new investments in expansion of capacity; and third, an increase of public expenditure in high priority areas like social development and poverty reduction. Emphasis will have to be placed in ensuring that military expenditure is diverted to these high priority needs. As part of the Economic Revival Plan announced by the Chief Executive, it was proposed that Rs. 7 billion be saved from the defence budget and diverted to the poverty alleviation programme. Unfortunately, the revised expenditure estimates for 1999-2000 indicate that not only did this saving not materialize, but that defence expenditure actually exceeded the original budget allocation.

Restructuring public sector institutions and service delivery. Wherever possible, the approach should be one of commercializing and corporatizing public service delivery agencies. Greater autonomy will need to be granted to the management boards of such entities, and representation on these boards broadened to allow for greater civil society and consumer representation. There will also have to be more emphasis on cost recovery, especially on services that are largely consumed by upper-income households, in order to create financial sustainability and some degree of market-based accountability. Simultaneously, independent regulatory entities will have to be set up for prescribing minimum service standards and tariff-setting rules. Wherever possible, cross-subsidies will need to be put in place to protect the poor from unaffordably high tariffs. As such, tariffs for a basic *lifeline* level of service should be kept relatively low.

Too close for comfort—public drinking water in close proximity to sewage water.

Integrating planning and budgeting in a medium-term framework. Annual budgets and programme allocations should be consistent with a medium-term planning framework and projections of fiscal resource availability. This will ensure that sustainable levels of recurrent expenditure drive sectoral investment programmes, rather than vice versa. This is especially true in the context of basic social services such as primary education and health, which involve high operations and maintenance costs, largely financed from tax revenues. In Pakistan, the rapid construction of primary schools and rural health facilities in the first phase of the ambitious Social Action Programme, supported liberally by donors, has now run into serious problems of staffing, along with recurrent funding problems, especially for non-salary inputs. Since it is primarily the poor who benefit from such services, it is important to ensure at least a minimum level of quality and sustainability in the provision of such services by making adequate funds available for the balanced provision of inputs. A balance will, of course, be required in the implementation of the medium-term planning framework. On the one hand, there will need to be sufficient flexibility to adapt to changed circumstances while, on the other hand, there will have to be enough commitment and discipline in adherance to targets and allocations to preserve the credibility of the process.

In summary, as identified above, key areas of public expenditure reform should include rethinking the role of government, improving transparency and accountability, effectively prioritizing among broad expenditures and programmes, restructuring public sector institutions and service delivery, and integrating planning and budgeting in a medium-term framework. Success in public expenditure reform will go a long way towards strengthening efforts for poverty reduction.

TAX REFORM

From the viewpoint of poverty alleviation, tax reform is important for two basic reasons. First, to the extent possible, such reform must attempt to reduce the burden of taxes on those goods and services that are consumed more by the poorer segments of society, and shift the incidence to the incomes and consumption of relatively well-off households. Second, given the low and falling tax-to-GDP ratio of Pakistan, the government has found it increasingly difficult to increase the levels of public expenditure on what can be considered pro-poor services, and to expand the outreach of social safety nets. Therefore, it is imperative that the tax-to-GDP ratio be raised, but not in ways that adversely affect the poor. The additional revenues should be used to the extent possible for financing the poverty alleviation programme.

The Existing Situation

Pakistan's current tax system manifests all the characteristics of a failed system—absence of a tax culture, high levels of tax evasion, weak and antiquated tax administration, a defective tax policy that has been exploited by special interests and thereby distorted the allocation of resources, wide-ranging tax concessions and exemptions, and an overreliance on indirect taxation.

Given all these weaknesses, it is not surprising that the tax-to-GDP ratio fell steadily in the second half of the 1990s, as shown in **table 5.1**. From a peak of 14 per cent of the GDP, attained in 1995-96, it had fallen to below 13 per cent by 1999-2000. The temporary upsurge of revenues in 1998-99 was largely due to the windfall of revenues from the petroleum development surcharge, arising from that year's steep fall in oil prices and a lack of corresponding downward adjustment in retail prices. Pakistan's relatively low fiscal effort is demonstrated by the fact that the average tax-to-GDP ratio for countries at a comparable stage of development is close

TABLE 5.1

TAX[a]-TO-GDP RATIO AND SHARE OF INDIRECT TAXES (%) [b]

Year	Tax-to-GDP Ratio	Share of Indirect Taxes
1990-91	12.75	84.75
1991-92	13.50	82.50
1992-93	13.25	79.25
1993-94	13.25	79.00
1994-95	13.75	76.00
1995-96	14.00	74.25
1996-97	13.50	73.75
1997-98	13.25	71.25
1998-99	14.00	72.75
1999-2000	12.75	73.00

[a]Inclusive of surcharges and provincial taxes
[b]Rounded off to the nearest quarter percentage point
Sources: CBR Yearbooks
Pakistan Economic Survey
State Bank of Pakistan, Annual Report

It is imperative that the tax-to-GDP ratio be raised, but not in ways that adversely affect the poor.

BOX 5.2

COMPARATIVE FISCAL EFFORT OF PAKISTAN

Burgess and Stern (1993) have estimated the level and composition of tax revenues for a sample of developing countries with per capita incomes ranging from US$360 to US$750. Their estimates are compared with those for Pakistan (whose per capita income is US$450), in the enclosed table.

In relative terms, the fiscal effort of Pakistan appears to be particularly weak in direct taxes, where the difference is 3 per cent of the GDP. The other tax with a relatively low tax-to-GDP ratio is import duties. This is the consequence of trade liberalization in the nineties, which has led to a steep reduction in import tariffs.

LEVEL AND COMPOSITION OF TAX REVENUES (% OF GDP[a])

	Developing Countries	Pakistan (1998-99)	Difference
Direct Taxes	6.75	3.75	-3.00
Income Tax	5.50	3.50	-2.00
Wealth and Property Tax	0.25	0.25	0.00
Social Security Taxes	0.75	-	-0.75
Others	0.25	-	-0.25
Indirect Taxes (domestic)	4.75	5.00	0.25
Sales, Turnover, Value Added Tax	2.25	2.50	0.25
Excises	2.00	2.00	0.00
Others	0.50	0.50	0.00
Indirect Taxes (foreign)	7.50	5.00	-2.50
Import Duties	6.75	2.25	-4.25
Export Duties	0.50	-	-0.50
Others	0.25	2.75	2.50
Others	0.50	0.00	-0.50
Total Taxes	19.50	13.75	-5.75

[a]Rounded off to the nearest quarter percentage point

---

to 20 per cent **(see box 5.2)**. It appears that if Pakistan could improve its revenue performance and approach this average, then an additional fiscal space of over 7 per cent of the GDP (equivalent to over Rs. 200 billion) would become available for deficit reduction, higher development expenditure, and larger allocations for the poverty alleviation programme.

Why did the tax-to-GDP ratio fall in the second half of the 1990s? Alternative explanations have been offered, including first, a growing failure of the tax administration to curb tax evasion and to resist the pressures of vested interests for tax concessions; second, the relative lack of buoyancy of the key tax bases in recent years, such as large-scale manufacturing and imports; and third, falling tax rates as a result of both supply-side initiatives to revive the economy and the ongoing process of trade liberalization. We analyze the impact of different factors by dividing the change in the tax-to-GDP ratio into two separate effects: the rate effect and the base effect. The rate effect quantifies the extent of decline in the tax-to-GDP ratio—due to either a fall in statutory tax rates, or an increase in the erosion of given tax bases (due to exemptions or evasion). The base effect derives the impact of the relative growth of the various tax bases on the ratio, in relation to the economy as a whole. Results of this analysis are summarized in **table 5.2**.

TABLE 5.2

FACTORS CONTRIBUTING TO CHANGE IN TAX-TO-GDP RATIO, 1995-96 TO 1999-2000 (%)

Tax	Change in Tax-to-GDP Ratio	Rate Effect	Base Effect
Direct Taxes	-0.25	-0.25	0.00
Customs Duty	-2.00	-1.50	-0.50
Sales Tax	1.50	1.00	0.50
Excise Duty	-0.75	-0.75	0.00
Surcharges	0.00	-1.50	1.50
Provincial Taxes	0.25	0.25	0.00
Total	**-1.25**	**-2.75**	**1.50**

[a]Rounded off to the nearest quarter percentage point
Source: SPDC estimates

BOX 5.3

THE SIZE OF PAKISTAN'S BLACK ECONOMY

The standard Vito Tanzi currency ratio method has been used to size the black economy of Pakistan. The assumptions underlying this method are that currency is the predominant means of exchange in illegal economic activities, and that the underground, or black economy is primarily the consequence of high taxes. Estimates of the black economy and the implied revenue loss are given in the accompanying table.

It appears that the share of the black economy in the GDP declined during the 1990s, primarily because of falling tax rates. But even recently, it was the equivalent to over one-fourth of the economy, the revenue loss due to tax evasion having been estimated at Rs. 105 billion for 1998-99.

SIZE OF THE BLACK ECONOMY AND REVENUE LOSS

Years	Size of Black Economy (Rs. billion)	% of GDP	Revenue Loss (Rs. billion)
1990-91	394	39	50
1991-92	462	38	63
1992-93	466	35	62
1993-94	559	35	74
1994-95	635	34	84
1995-96	743	35	105
1996-97	744	30	97
1997-98	815	30	108
1998-99	784	26	105

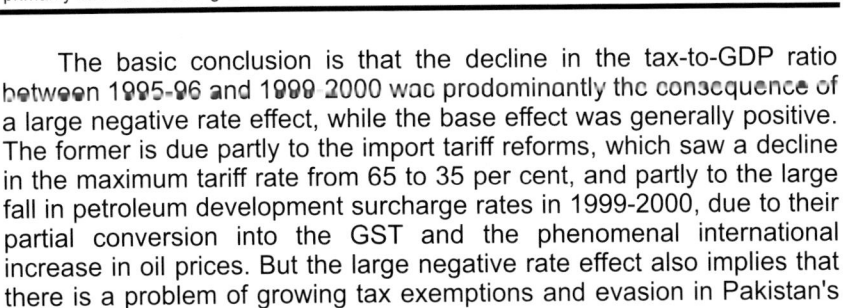

Source: SPDC estimates

The basic conclusion is that the decline in the tax-to-GDP ratio between 1995-96 and 1999-2000 was predominantly the consequence of a large negative rate effect, while the base effect was generally positive. The former is due partly to the import tariff reforms, which saw a decline in the maximum tariff rate from 65 to 35 per cent, and partly to the large fall in petroleum development surcharge rates in 1999-2000, due to their partial conversion into the GST and the phenomenal international increase in oil prices. But the large negative rate effect also implies that there is a problem of growing tax exemptions and evasion in Pakistan's economy.

One approach to quantifying Pakistan's revenue potential is to estimate, to the extent possible, the size of the black economy. This has been attempted in **box 5.3.** The conclusions are striking. Currently, the black economy is estimated at over one fourth of the GDP. This implies that the revenue loss due to tax evasion is almost Rs. 105 billion, equivalent to 3.5 per cent of the GDP. The research indicates that there has been some success in controlling the growth of the black economy during the 1990s, achieved primarily by following a policy of reducing tax rates, especially in the second half of the decade. However, levels of tax evasion still remain unacceptably high.

We next turn to the cost to the exchequer of revenues forfeited due to tax concessions and exemptions. These are sometimes also referred to as tax expenditures, but are seldom highlighted in the budget documents. As shown in **table 5.3**, these are estimated in 1998-99 at Rs. 120 billion—equivalent to as much as 40 per cent of the revenues actually collected, and amounting to 4 per cent of the GDP. Rs. 40 billion of the tax expenditure is in direct taxes, including the undertaxation of agricultural incomes (Rs. 13.5 billion), exemption to independent power projects (Rs. 6 billion), interest income on non-resident deposits (Rs. 4 billion), rupee accounts converted out of foreign currency accounts (Rs. 4 billion), area-specific, time-bound exemptions in the form of tax holidays (Rs. 2 billion), exemption to statutory corporations (Rs. 1.5 billion), and concessionary tax rate on exports (Rs. 1.5 billion). Wealth tax exemption on FCAs, foreign exchange bearer certificates (FEBCs) and dollar bonds has cost the exchequer Rs. 4 billion, while the exemption on agricultural land implies an additional revenue loss of Rs. 1.5 billion.

TABLE 5.3

TAX EXPENDITURE IN PAKISTAN, 1998-99 (RS. BILLION)

Tax	Revenue	Tax Expenditure	%
Direct Taxes	110	40	36
Customs Duty	65	33	50
Excise Duty	61	-	-
General Sales Tax	72	47	65
Total	**308**	**120**	**39**

Source: Central Board of Revenue

The recent abolition of the wealth tax, at a time of growing income inequality in Pakistan, is yet another demonstration of the ability of the rich and powerful to influence the process of policy making in Pakistan. This move has been justified on the grounds that the tax retarded the process of investment in the economy and was of marginal importance, anyway, because of its low revenue yield (of less than Rs. 5 billion). However, it should be emphasized that revenues from taxation had been seriously eroded because of exemptions on a number of assets, as highlighted above. Nevertheless, the wealth tax had provided a handle on detecting tax evasion in the economy in view of the greater visibility of physical assets, in particular, in relation to the flow of income. It is indeed ironic that at a time when the government has launched a major, nationwide tax survey to unearth undeclared assets, especially property, the wealth tax has been abolished, abandoning thereby one of the major potential sources of additional revenue from the survey.

The prevalence of Statutory Rules and Orders (SROs) in customs duties is responsible for a tax expenditure of Rs. 33 billion, equal to half the revenues collected. This includes the cost of SROs for protection of local industry (Rs. 10 billion), exemptions under the investment policy (Rs. 7 billion), SROs for public health provisions (Rs. 6 billion), goods imported under grants-in-aid (Rs. 5.5 billion), exemption of customs duty on imports of machinery by Independent Power Producers (IPPs) (Rs. 2 billion), and so on.

Tax expenditure in sales tax is estimated at Rs. 47 billion for 1998-99. This includes the exemption of GST at the retail level (Rs. 20 billion), from services (Rs. 6 billion), defence stores (Rs. 5 billion), cement (Rs. 4 billion), domestic production of edible oils and ghee (Rs. 3 billion), and fertilizer, insecticides and pesticides (Rs. 4 billion), as well as area-specific exemptions (Rs. 2 billion). A GST on services has been levied through the provincial finance acts of 2000-01, largely by replacement of excise duties. However, the revenue loss of Rs. 6 billion is due to the exemption of services, which are currently not subject to excise duty.

Altogether, revenues could be enhanced by almost 40 per cent if tax expenditure could be eliminated. While it can be argued that some of the tax expenditure in general sales tax and customs duty protects the interests of the poor, the bulk of tax expenditure in income and wealth taxes clearly benefits the rich. Powerful lobbies jealously guard against withdrawal of these concessions and exemptions.

The overall conclusion is that if tax evasion and tax concessions or exemptions to the rich could be eliminated, then Pakistan's tax-to-GDP ratio could come close to the low-to-medium income developing country average of 20 per cent of the GDP.

The recent abolition of the wealth tax is yet another demonstration of the ability of the rich and powerful to influence the process of policy making in Pakistan.

Growing disparity: An area for immediate public action.

Incidence of Taxes

The next question is: Who bears the burden of taxes in Pakistan? In particular, we are interested in determining how much of the burden falls on the poor. Earlier research, by Malik and Saqib (1989), Alauddin and Raza (1981) and Jeetun (1978), has demonstrated that the overall tax incidence by income group is initially regressive up to the middle-income brackets, and then becomes progressive in the upper income groups, primarily because of the payment of direct taxes. In effect, however, a relatively large tax burden falls on the poorest households because the dominant share of indirect taxes either directly or indirectly affects the prices of essential commodities and services. Table 5.1 quantifies the share of indirect taxes as a percentage of total tax revenues. It indicates that over 70 per cent of tax revenue in the nineties accrued from indirect taxes. The worrying thing, in recent years, is a trend of an increase in this share.

Within indirect taxes, it has also been shown that the most regressive incidence is in the case of surcharges (on petroleum products and gas), followed by import duties, excise duties, and sales tax, respectively. The recent conversion of the petroleum development surcharge partially into GST is bound to increase the regressivity of the sales tax. In fact, a recent study by SPDC on the incidence of the sales tax, which is now the largest indirect tax, reveals that a disproportionate burden of this tax falls on the lowest income groups. As shown in **table 5.4,** the incidence of the tax is about 5 per cent of the income of households in the lowest quartile, falling sharply for households in the uppermost quartile. The recent extension of the GST to electricity and gas has accentuated this problem of adverse incidence by increasing the effective tax burden on sectors that had hitherto been exempt from the GST, through an increase in tax payments on energy inputs. Most of these exempt sectors produce basic commodities, such as food products and fertilizer, and the rise in the effective tax burden means that the cost of living in general, and in particular for the poor, has increased.

TABLE 5.4

BURDEN OF GENERAL SALES TAX AS A PERCENTAGE OF INCOME, 1999-2000

Income Quartile	Rural Areas	Urban Areas
First (lowest)	5.00	5.00
Second	4.25	4.50
Third	3.75	4.25
Fourth (highest)	2.00	3.75
Overall	**3.00**	**4.00**

Source: SPDC estimates

Altogether, the tax burden in Pakistan is regressive in character, having an adverse impact on the poor. This has been exacerbated in recent years by the rising share of indirect taxes, especially those levied on energy inputs into consumption and production.

Directions of Reform

The above section has identified the areas of tax reform from the viewpoint of raising the tax-to-GDP ratio, while simultaneously raising the burden on the rich and reducing it on the poor. The precise nature of these reforms is described below.

Documentation of the economy. We have demonstrated that there are substantial revenue gains from a reduction in tax evasion. This will require steps towards documentation of the economy which will enable better knowledge of economic transactions and help in detecting both nondeclaration and underdeclaration of income. Both a *carrot* and *stick* approach will need to be adopted, whereby documentation is rewarded and lack of documentation is penalized. Suggested steps include:

- maintenance and filing of basic accounts (trading account, profit and loss account) to qualify for the universal self-assessment scheme;
- a higher tax rate (of 10 percentage points) on the income of taxpayers not maintaining basic accounts;
- subjecting all returns filed under the universal self-assessment scheme to the probability of an audit, with selection of audit cases by computer ballot;
- granting no immunity from audit, irrespective of the increase in declared income or tax paid;
- enforcement of a law requiring prescribed sets of accounts to be maintained by self-employed professionals, such as medical practitioners, lawyers, accountants, auditors, architects, engineers, etc.;
- requiring all transactions of Rs. 25,000 and above to be made only by cheque, bank draft, pay order, demand draft, or telegraphic transfers, in order to be eligible for tax deductibility;
- assignment of a common taxpayer identifier (CTI) to major taxpayers (mostly companies), and compulsory disclosure of the CTI on all tax-related documents of transactions in accordance with the relevant provisions of the Income Tax Ordinance (ITO);

Will more revenues from the rich be used to provide relief to low-income taxpayers?

- requiring industries still on fixed-GST to move to normal VAT-mode, based on filing of monthly returns with tax-invoicing of inputs and outputs;
- the development of an integrated and computerized database to monitor withholding of tax payments.

The government recently launched a major tax survey for documentation of the economy, beginning in 13 major cities of the country. All businesses and properties (owners and tenants) are being required to fill out a questionnaire asking for information on income (total and by source), assets, and major expenditures. The tax survey is proceeding at a reasonable pace, although there has been resistance, especially from the trading community. Initial analysis of returned forms reveals that there is a significant component of underdeclaration. The government expects to collect as much as an additional Rs. 100 billion on the basis of information obtained from the survey. This estimate appears to be optimistic since the 0.7 million self-employed taxpayers (including traders) currently contribute a total of less than Rs. 4 billion. Clearly, the focus will have to be on better documentation of the corporate sector, for which implementation of the above-mentioned package will be essential.

Anti-tax evasion measures. In addition to the process of documentation, explicit anti-tax evasion measures will need to be taken, as follows:

- effective enforcement of existing legal provisions relating to raids against notorious tax dodgers;
- the power to ascribe value to undeclared or unexplained assets, and allow provisional assessment;
- the publication of a tax directory on actual income tax payments made by individual taxpayers;
- the power to confiscate plants, machinery and goods of registered persons deliberately not filing four consecutive returns of GST.

Inequality amongst the classes is an impediment to reducing poverty.

There is a danger, however, that these strong provisions can lead to coercion, harassment and corruption by officials of the Central Board of Revenue (CBR). Therefore, it is extremely important that concurrently there be a complete restructuring of the CBR, including a purge of corrupt and inefficient officials, simplification of laws, re-engineering of business processes, streamlining of appeals, and large-scale automation and use of IT. The government has already put together a high-powered committee to facilitate the reorganization of CBR, which is expected to submit its report by December 2000.

Elimination of tax expenditures. We have highlighted above that tax concessions and exemptions currently cost the country as much as Rs. 120 billion annually, with a large portion benefiting relatively well-off taxpayers. Such tax expenditures need to be eliminated to the extent possible, and the revenues used to provide relief to small taxpayers. The government has taken the first step in this regard by announcing that in future there will be no whitener schemes such as the Foreign Exchange Bearer Certificates (FEBCs). However, much more needs to be done in this area. As part of the redrafting of the income tax law, it is important that the committee appointed for this purpose achieve the following:

- simplify income tax laws, which have become too cumbersome and complicated for the ordinary taxpayer;
- ensure that all forms of income are treated alike for tax purposes, and that the second schedule of the ITO (containing a list of exemptions) is considerably rationalized;
- prepare a scheme for the transition of presumptive income taxes to normal income taxation, as the former have essentially operated as indirect taxes and placed a burden on the poor.

In addition, as import tariffs continue to fall, concessionary rates embodied in the SROs should be merged into the statutory tariff schedule. This will reduce the discretion of customs officials and lead to a simpler, more transparent system that is less prone to corruption.

It is extremely important that there be a complete restructuring of the CBR.

Taxing the rich. Beyond curbing tax evasion and eliminating tax expenditures, there are a number of areas of taxation that have hitherto been left unexplored and underdeveloped, but which have the potential not only to make Pakistan's tax system more progressive, but also to raise additional revenue.

The first is the agricultural income tax (AIT). The extremely low collection (of only about Rs. 1.5 billion) under this head has become the prime symbol of the lack of vertical equity in Pakistan's tax system. Even with conservative estimates, it is expected that the agricultural income tax can yield upto 0.5 per cent of the GDP (equivalent to over Rs. 15 billion). However, effective imposition of this tax has been strongly resisted by the powerful feudal lobby. More recently, an impetus has been provided to reform the AIT, under pressure from international agencies. Being a provincial subject, such reforms would have to be enacted and implemented by the provincial governments. For the 2000-01 budget, these governments have made a significant move in this regard, with the introduction of a dual-system AIT. First, there will essentially be a small, graduated land tax on farms that are above the exemption limit of 12.5 acres. Second, for farms earning a net income of more than Rs. 80,000 per annum, an income tax has been introduced which will require filing returns. The tax rate will range from 5 to 15 per cent. It remains to be seen how much additional revenue will be generated by the new AIT in Punjab. Meanwhile, the other provinces will have to be motivated to introduce similar reforms.

The second promising area for resource mobilization, which will essentially tax the relatively well-off households, is the urban property tax. This tax is expected to get a major boost following its transfer to local governments as part of the devolution plan **(see chapter 6)**. Current collection for the entire country is only Rs. 1 billion, which is less than 2 per cent of the estimated rental values of urban properties, compared to the statutory rate of 20 to 25 per cent on assessed rental values (ARVs). Reasons for the extremely low exploitation of this potential revenue include wide-ranging exemptions, lack of periodic reassessments of ARVs, extremely low taxation of owner-occupied properties, and a lack of incentive on the part of provincial governments to develop this tax (with only 15 per cent being retained by them and the rest transferred to local bodies).

Tax relief to the poor. As the above elements of tax reforms get implemented, and the tax burden on the relatively well-off increases due to declining levels of tax evasion, rationalization of tax expenditures, and the development of progressive taxes, it is crucial that some of the additional revenues be passed on in the form of a reduction in the tax burden on the poor.

The first such initiative should be in the area of GST. It has been shown that this tax is becoming increasingly regressive, with its broad-basing to petroleum products, electricity and gas. The recent extension of the tax to the retail level will further exacerbate the burden on the poor. Therefore, if the government is able to substantially augment revenues through a tax survey and documentation of the economy, then the standard GST rate should be brought down from 15 to 12.5 per cent, initially, and eventually to 10 per cent. In addition, the government is apparently contemplating extending the GST to agricultural inputs (e.g., fertilizer, pesticides, tractors and agricultural machinery) under pressure from the IMF. This step must be avoided both on efficiency and equity grounds. A tax on agricultural inputs is likely to impose a major excess burden and have deleterious consequences on agricultural production. It

TABLE 5.5

INDEX OF PRICES[a] OF PETROLEUM PRODUCTS (1995-96 = 100)

	1996-97	1997-98	1998-99	1999-2000
Retail Prices				
Gasoline	117	121	166	187
Kerosene Oil	130	130	145	155
High-Speed Diesel Oil	129	129	143	172
Light Diesel Oil	136	136	149	183
Furnace Oil	139	122	134	246
Import Price (Rs.)	130	101	94	173
Consumer Price Index	112	121	127	132

[a] As of the last day of the fiscal year (i.e., June 30)
Source: Ministry of Petroleum and Natural Resources, GOP

will tend to raise the prices of basic food items produced by the agricultural sector, and disproportionately affect the household budgets of the poor.

Beyond this, it is important that the government exercise extreme caution in enhancing the prices of petroleum products from the viewpoint of sustaining or enhancing revenues from the petroleum development surcharge. As shown in **table 5.5,** these prices have risen very rapidly during the last few years, especially during 1999-2000 and more recently. For example, the prices of kerosene oil and high-speed diesel (HSD) oil, which either have a direct or indirect impact on the common person, have shown cumulative increases since 1995-96 of 55 and 72 per cent, respectively, whereas the overall consumer price index has gone up by 32 per cent during this period. The prices of light diesel oil (input into agricultural tubewells) and furnace oil (input into power generation and various industries) have gone up even more, by 83 and 146 per cent, respectively. The tax content in prices is given in **table 5.6.** It is as high as 60 per cent in the case of gasoline, 28 per cent for HSD, and 26 per cent for kerosene oil.

Research has been undertaken at SPDC, with the help of an Input-Output Table for Pakistan, to derive the implications of an across-the-board rise in the prices of petroleum products on the final prices of consumer goods and services, especially those which are important to the poor.

TABLE 5.6

OVERALL TAX CONTENT IN PRICES OF PETROLEUM PRODUCTS (% OF RETAIL PRICE)

	1995-96	1996-97	1997-98	1998-99	1999-2000
Gasoline	59	58	66	56	59
Kerosene Oil	25	11	44	19	26
High-Speed Diesel Oil	23	18	45	42	28
Light Diesel Oil	31	7	36	9	18
Furnace Oil	15	23	27	10	0

Source: Ministry of Petroleum and Natural Resources, GOP

TABLE 5.7

IMPACT ON COST OF LIVING OF HOUSEHOLDS DUE TO A DOUBLING OF PETROLEUM PRICES (%)

Quartile of Households	Rural Areas	Urban Areas
First (lowest)	7.00	7.00
Second	5.50	6.00
Third	5.00	6.50[a]
Fourth (highest)	3.75	7.50[a]
Total	**5.00**	**7.50**

[a] A bigger increase due to the rise in price of gasoline used in private transport
Source: SPDC estimates

Based on the sectoral price increases and household consumption patterns, we have derived the impact on households **(see table 5.7)**. A doubling of the retail prices of petroleum products for example, raises the cost of living significantly among lower-income households (in the first quartile and partially in the second quartile), by over 7 per cent. Therefore, future changes in petroleum prices will have to be minimized as part of the policy of poverty alleviation. In fact, if CBR revenues from other sources begin to show rapid growth, then the rates of petroleum development surcharges should be scaled down, especially on products such as HSD, light diesel oil, and kerosene oil.

LAND REFORM

Most economic reforms aimed at poverty reduction are oriented either towards augmenting income and employment opportunities for the poor, moderating their cost of living, improving their human capital by access to basic services, or mitigating against the worst manifestations of poverty. These are all important elements of a comprehensive and integrated poverty reduction strategy. But the impact of many of these reforms takes time. Furthermore, there is no guarantee that improvements made will endure over the long term. One approach that is seldom emphasized, but that has the potential of achieving both results, is a change in the underlying distribution of assets, especially agricultural land, brought about either through reform or sequestration of such assets and their subsequent redistribution.

We therefore propose that land reform must be included as a prime instrument for eliminating rural poverty in Pakistan. This proposal rests on two key stylized facts about the nature and dimensions of rural poverty in Pakistan. First, rural poverty is high because rural income inequality is high, and rural inequality is high because of the highly skewed distribution of land ownership in the country. Second, as is demonstrated earlier **(see chapter 2)**, the incidence of poverty is high among the rural landless, and access to land takes a high proportion of households out of the poverty trap.

What is the empirical evidence on the extent and change of income inequality among rural households in Pakistan? **Table 5.8** shows that inequality of income has been increasing in Pakistan's rural areas since

Land reform must be included as a prime instrument for eliminating rural poverty in Pakistan.

TABLE 5.8

LEVEL OF, AND TREND IN, RURAL INCOME INEQUALITY IN PAKISTAN

Year	SHARE OF INCOME OF Highest 20% of Households	Lowest 20% of Households	Approximate Ratio	Gini Coefficient
1979	41	8	5:1	0.32
1985	43	8	5½:1	0.34
1991	47	6	8:1	0.41
1994	43	7	6:1	0.40
1997	49	7	7:1	0.41

Source: Pakistan Economic Survey (1999-2000)

the late 1970s. According to the most recent estimates, almost one half of the income is pre-empted by the top 20 per cent of households, in comparison with only 7 per cent by the lowest quintile. The Gini coefficient, which, as has been explained, is the standard measure of inequality, has risen rapidly from a moderate magnitude of 0.32 in the late seventies to the relatively high level of 0.41 in the late nineties.

Opponents of land reform have argued that, at least in intergenerational terms, agricultural land cannot remain unevenly distributed because of the inevitable fragmentation of ownership due to the Islamic inheritance laws. But evidence points to extreme slowness of this process. **Table 5.9** gives the farm-size distribution by ownership, as observed in the last two agricultural censuses. The proportion of area occupied by farms of over 50 acres has shown little change in the intercensal period. If there is any evidence of land holdings becoming smaller, it is at the lower end of the distribution. The persistence of large farms can be attributed to factors such as the process of mechanization, the rising indebtedness of small farms, and eviction.

For those who have either never owned land or been evicted from their holding, what is the likely poverty outcome? We have constructed a poverty ladder **(see chapter 2)** which shows that for households where the head is illiterate, ownership of assets (either land or livestock) takes close to one half of the households out of their state of poverty. This demonstrates that acquisition of assets, following the process of land redistribution in the aftermath of a land reform, could lead to a major once-and-for-all reduction in the incidence of poverty. Particularly in

TABLE 5.9

FARM SIZE DISTRIBUTION IN PAKISTAN

Farm Size (acres)	PERCENTAGE OF Farms 1981	1990	Area 1981	1990
< 5	47	53	9	12
5 to 25	43	39	38	39
26 to 50	6	5	17	15
Over 50	4	3	36	34
Total	**100**	**100**	**100**	**100**

Source: Mahmood (1999)

Squalid conditions in urban slums.

situations where rural markets are incomplete and interlocked in character, as is the case of Pakistan, access to land can make a significant contribution to the food security and nutritional well-being of households, as well as to their ability to withstand shocks. For example, the obstacle of collateral for access to formal credit is removed through entitlement of land.

The political economy implications of land reform are also important. Traditionally, the feudal elite has enjoyed enormous political power because of their monopoly over the votes of their tenants in elections. The nexus of relationships between the feudal class, the bureaucracy, and agencies of law and order has also ensured that the rural rich enjoy privileged access to such inputs as irrigation and credit, while smaller farmers are marginalized in the process. Implementation of land reform will fundamentally alter the power structure in many rural parts of the country, giving the poor a greater voice in institutions of governance and enabling them to increasingly easily access publicly provided services. Land reform could virtually herald a revolution in the countryside and would probably constitute the single most significant act of empowerment of the poor in Pakistan.

The timing for embarking on major land reform in the near future is also right. The present military government has announced an ambitious plan for the devolution of power to the grass-roots level through the establishment of district and lower level governments with wide-ranging functions and considerable autonomy. Embarking on land reform at this time would greatly facilitate genuine people's participation, and prevent the capture of these newly-established governmental structures by strong feudal interests.

Unfortunately, the experience with land reform in Pakistan has largely been one of failure and weak implementation. A strong coalition of vested interests has successfully thwarted attempts at any meaningful reform. Since Independence, three land reforms have been introduced, in 1959, 1972 and 1977, respectively. The first two reforms are considered more significant since the reform of 1977 remained largely unimplemented because of the fall of the Zulfiqar Ali Bhutto government.

Implementation of land reform will fundamentally alter the power structure in many rural areas, giving the poor a greater voice.

Multi-purpose use of water.

The 1959 and 1972 reforms were essentially ceiling-based redistributive reforms. The former prescribed a ceiling of 500 irrigated acres, or 1,000 *barani* (non-irrigated) acres. Only 5,000 landowners ended up declaring land in excess of 500 acres. Approximately one million hectares of land was resumed and distributed among 85,000 beneficiaries.

The 1972 land reform was more far-reaching. It involved a reduction in the ceiling to 150 irrigated acres (300 non-irrigated acres) or 15,000 produce index units, whichever was greater. It was also proposed that no compensation be provided for the expropriated land. About 0.5 million hectares were appropriated in this reform and handed over to 71,000 beneficiaries. Cumulatively, the land reforms undertaken to date have led to the redistribution of 1.8 million hectares of land, equivalent to 8 per cent of the cultivated area in Pakistan.

Khan (1998) has highlighted that a substantial portion of the land redistributed was of poor quality. Numerous exemptions were allowed during the implementation process. Not all the beneficiaries were existing sharecroppers. There was no follow-up support system to provide protection and facilities to the new landowners. Altogether, the general perception is that the land reforms carried out have made no contribution to changing the process of differentiation observed in the agrarian structure of Pakistan.

There is also the view that implementation of land reforms could impose significant costs in terms of foregone agricultural output. In other words, there is a positive relationship between farm size and productivity, and truncation of large farms will lead to a loss of output. The empirical evidence for this relationship is, at best, ambiguous. It has frequently been argued that there might even be an inverse relationship, because small farms use more labour (largely family labour) per unit of land and, therefore, achieve higher yields. Cropping and land intensities also tend to be higher in small farms. Nabi (1991), Waqar (1998), and Qureshi (2000) find empirical evidence of this inverse relationship in the Pakistani context.

Land reforms: A powerful mechanism for ensuring their empowerment.

On the other hand, large farms may enjoy economies of scale in transaction costs for credit, input purchases, and output marketing, and also in transport and post-harvest operations. In the presence of imperfections and information asymmetries, especially in the credit market, large farms may have the advantage of differential access to inputs and cheap credit. These differentials in access at least partially explain why the diffusion of new technology was faster to large farms during the green revolution.

We believe that efficiency arguments in favour of not implementing land reforms fail to override the equity concerns, especially in view of the absence of any conclusive evidence on the higher efficiency levels of large farms. Meaningful land reform will contribute directly to the reduction of poverty in the rural areas, through the redistribution of land away from the rich, to the landless. It will also constitute an extremely powerful mechanism for empowering the poor and enable greater participation by them in the process of governance.

It is significant to note that the two land reforms, in 1959 and 1972, were both promulgated by use of martial law regulations (MLR 64 in 1959 and MLR 115 in 1972). Therefore, the initiative for land reforms has been taken under military governments or with the help of strong provisions under martial law. Pakistan today has a military government, which at least in its initial statements seemed inclined to consider another land reform. However, strong and entrenched interests will continue to frustrate any attempts at such reform. The big challenge, and a true test of the commitment of the present government to the objective of poverty reduction, lies in whether it can muster up enough will and courage to bring about fundamental structural economic and political change by implementing deep and meaningful land reforms.

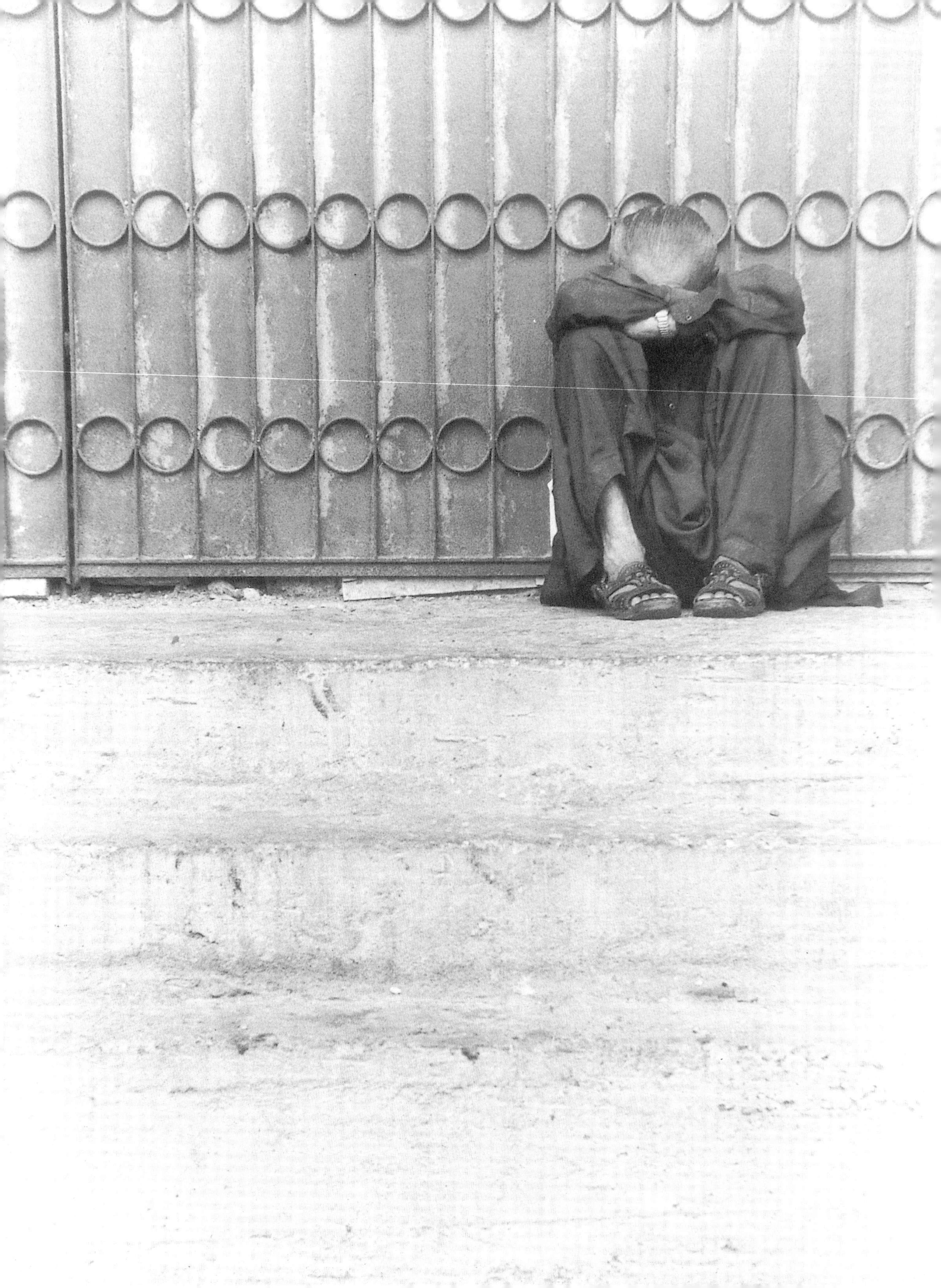

GOVERNANCE AND POVERTY

CHAPTER 6

"The inherent rights to freedom of expression and to form civil society groups greatly enhance the likelihood that the voices of the poor are heard in the forums of policy making."

GOVERNANCE AND POVERTY

Governance is generally conceived of as being the exercise of political and administrative authority in the management of state affairs. It can legitimately be argued that the ultimate goal of good governance must be improvement in the quality of people's lives, including the elimination of the worst forms of deprivation and poverty. Governance has three dimensions: one, the political regime; two, the systems and procedures for exercising authority; and three, the capacity of governments.

Poverty is the outcome of interactions between economic, social, legal and political processes, mediated through a range of institutions. The extent to which state institutions can be considered to be pro-poor is determined by the quality of governance and democracy, the rule of law, and the extent to which there is both political decentralization and participation of the people.

This chapter focuses on how good governance contributes to poverty reduction, including discussions on the role of an effectively functioning democracy, the rule of law, corruption, institutional capacity, and decentralization and devolution.

DEMOCRACY

The issue of which system of government is more pro-poor–parliamentary democracy or an authoritarian military regime–has acquired contemporary relevance in the Pakistani context, following the military takeover on October 12, 1999. Pakistan is, in fact, unique in the sense that, historically, democracy has been interspersed with long periods of military intervention. This enables an empirical analysis of the track record of each of the two types of government with regard to poverty reduction.

It can be argued that effectively functioning democracies are inherently more likely to have built-in institutional arrangements for addressing the concerns of the poor. Because democracies are more likely to promote inclusive participation, without excluding any groups or classes of society, people have greater civil and political liberties. The inherent rights to freedom of expression and to form civil society groups greatly enhance the likelihood that the voices of the poor are heard in the forums of policy making. Likewise, the emergence of a free press and a strong independent judiciary encourage greater transparency and accountability, thus diminishing the likelihood of corruption and making the state more responsive to the needs of the people.

But in countries such as Pakistan, which lack the strong and long-established tradition of a parliamentary system, democracies are far from perfect. The poor are excluded from the process of governance for a number of reasons, including their lack of education, knowledge, opportunity and economic power. The state is controlled by the feudal and industrial classes of the elite. Such domination by vested interests, coupled with weak institutions, leads to subversion of the law, lack of

Poverty is the outcome of interactions between economic, social, legal and political processes, mediated through a range of institutions.

The ramshackle state of the lower judiciary.

accountability, high levels of corruption, and a process of decision making that remains largely outside the formal institutional framework. In effect, sovereignty has become equated with powerful governments, not with free citizens. This helps explain people's widespread disillusionment with how democracy functions within Pakistan, and also provides a rationale for the frequency of military takeovers.

In contrast, military governments in Pakistan are actually considered to be more effective with regard to both governance and their ability to deliver basic services to the citizens. The strong and centralized command structure that characterizes a military regime enables timely and coordinated decision making, as well as the ability to surmount lobbying pressure from vested interests. Although military governments have no formal mechanism for hearing the concerns of the poor, improved governance does have significant indirect advantages that are of benefit to the poor. Some analysts have even argued that authoritarian governments are better for economic growth, and in keeping with the theory of the *trickle-down* effect, that the consequences are also more favourable for the poor.

The period since Pakistan's independence can be divided into five periods of democratic and authoritarian rule, with a total of 31 years under democracy, and the remainder under military governments. During the initial period of nation building, from 1947 to 1958, Pakistan witnessed a succession of rapidly changing civilian governments. The resulting constitutional crisis led to an army takeover in 1958. From 1958 to 1971, there was a long, uninterrupted period of military rule, mostly under Field Marshal Ayub Khan, which ended following the loss of East Pakistan in December 1971. The next six years witnessed a return to democracy under the Pakistan People's Party (PPP), with Mr. Zulfiqar Ali Bhutto as the leader. In 1977, General Zia ul Haq staged a coup, and martial law continued until 1985 when non-party elections led to the induction of Mr. Junejo's government. Thereafter, Pakistan was ruled by democratic governments, the PPP and the Pakistan Muslim League (PML) each serving two terms. Democracy was terminated once again by the military coup of October 1999. All in all, Pakistan has experienced three periods of democratic government–1947 to 1958, 1971 to 1977, and 1985 to 1999–alternating with two periods of military rule–1958 to 1971 and 1977 to 1985.

Table 6.1 quantifies the overall performance of Pakistan's democratically-elected and military governments since Partition, using indicators to assess economic growth, social development, and poverty reduction. The broad conclusion is that while military governments have generally been better with regard to Pakistan's economic growth, both types of government have fared comparably with regard to poverty reduction.

On the whole, while economic growth has been slower under democratic governments, these governments have achieved greater pro-poor growth. Social development also appears to have fared better under democratic governments, with all indicators, such as school enrolment, literacy, and health, having performed better. The one exception is life expectancy.

The first military government of Field Marshal Ayub Khan followed a strategy of industrialization that artificially raised the profitability of manufacturing enterprises, thereby promoting the emergence of an indigenous entrepreneurial class. This was achieved by twisting the terms of trade between agriculture and manufacturing in favour of the latter, keeping real wages low, providing subsidized credit, maintaining an overvalued exchange rate for the cheap importation of capital goods and industrial raw materials, and providing high tariff protection and tax holidays. The consequence was double-digit industrial growth, and overall economic growth well in excess of 6 per cent per annum. But poverty actually increased despite the rapid growth.

Mr. Bhutto's government, on the other hand, came to power in 1971 on an essentially socialist agenda, and then proceeded to implement a

TABLE 6.1

PERFORMANCE BY MILITARY AND DEMOCRATIC GOVERNMENTS IN PAKISTAN, 1947 TO 1999

Indicator	Unit	Performance by Military Governments[a]	Performance by Democratic Governments[b]
Change in:			
Real per Capita Income[c]	% growth per annum	3.1	1.5
Employment	% growth per annum	2.2	2.5
Incidence of Poverty[d]	% point per annum	-0.4	-0.4
Literacy Rate	% point per annum	0.5	0.8
Primary School Enrolment	% growth per annum	5.0	7.8
Female Primary School Enrolment	% growth per annum	7.7	9.8
Life Expectancy - Male	number of years per annum	0.8	0.4
- Female	number of years per annum	0.9	0.4
Mortality Rate	number per 1,000 per annum	-0.2	-2.1
Hospital Beds	% growth per annum	3.4	4.0

Notes: [a]Military-led governments existed from 1958 to 1971 and from 1977 to 1985
[b]Democratic governments existed from 1947 to 1958, from 1971 to 1977, and from 1985 to 1999
[c]From 1949-50
[d]From 1963-64
Source: Pakistan Economic Survey (various issues)

While economic growth has been slower under democratic governments, these governments have achieved greater pro-poor growth.

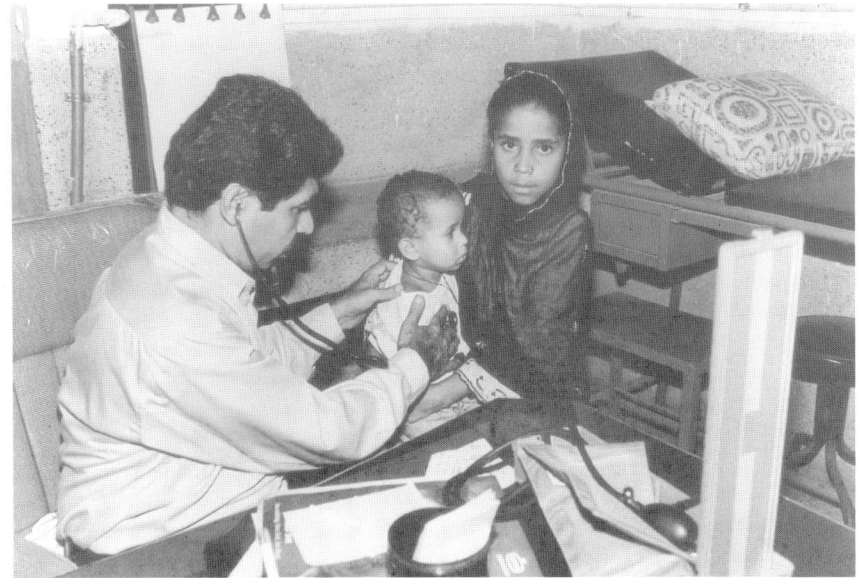

Democratic governments have historically focussed more on pro-poor growth.

large-scale programme to nationalize industries and banking. Trade union activities were encouraged, and a conscious attempt was made to politically emancipate the masses. But the growth rate plummeted significantly (for reasons **see chapter 4**), and the inflation rate rose appreciably on the back of internationally rising oil prices. But despite the fall in growth and high inflation, there was a perceptible decline in poverty.

What were the pro-poor characteristics of this growth? First, there was an upsurge in employment, primarily because of the rapid expansion of the public sector. Second, a large-scale migration to the Middle East, which was actively promoted by the government, led not only to a quantum leap in home remittances, but it also bid-up real wages in the domestic labour market. Third, given the populist agenda, and in the face of high inflation, a conscious effort was made to stabilize the prices of essential commodities by subsidizing the consumption of such basic items as wheat, sugar, edible oil, kerosene oil, and fertilizer. At its peak, the subsidy bill approached 4 per cent of the GDP. While it may be argued that the pro-poor growth strategy was fiscally unsustainable, it was nevertheless successful in decreasing the incidence of poverty at a time of relatively low economic growth.

The Zia ul Haq period of martial law, between 1977 and 1985, enjoyed the bonanza of continued large inflows of home remittances and concessional aid, which fuelled both the process of growth and poverty reduction. In addition, the inflation rate was kept down by avoiding monetization of the large fiscal deficit, through the development of government savings schemes. As part of the process of Islamization, the *Zakat* and *Ushr* Ordinance was promulgated. This, for the first time, provided a redistributive system involving taxation of the rich and transfer payments to the poor. At its peak, annual subventions from the *Zakat* fund approached 0.3 per cent of the GDP. This period was unique in that, unlike the Ayub Khan era, it achieved both rapid growth and poverty reduction. But public debt mushroomed during this period, and was primarily responsible for the fiscal problems in subsequent years.

The Junejo government, which came into power in 1985 on the basis of non-party elections after eight years of military rule, must be given credit for being the first government to explicitly give high priority to poverty alleviation in this policy agenda by launching the Five Point Programme. This programme was designed to accelerate socio-economic development by way of eradicating unemployment and poverty and ensuring social justice. With a total financial allocation of over Rs. 117 billion spread over four years, the focus was on the provision of basic social and economic infrastructure to help uplift the rural areas. The largest share of allocations was proposed for village electrification, rural education, rural water supply and sanitation, and the establishment of a national employment fund. The Five Point Programme eventually floundered due to inadequate funds and a lack of implementation capacity within the line departments.

The 1990s witnessed, for the first time, a combination of the worst outcomes—low growth and rising poverty. Democratic governments during this period were not only unable to achieve high growth, but also to ensure that growth was pro-poor in character. What explains this failure? First, the accumulation of debt reduced the fiscal capacity for development expenditure and pre-empted expansion of the public sector, thereby restricting the growth of employment. Second, home remittances plunged sharply due to the significant return of Pakistani migrants. Third, labour absorption into the agriculture sector diminished as a consequence of both the ongoing process of mechanization and changes in tenurial status. This forced an increasing number of workers into the urban informal economy, where incomes are relatively low **(see chapter 5)**. In addition to all this, the general quality of governance declined, and corruption and misuse of public funds increased.

However, democratic governments during the 1990s were not entirely insensitive to poverty concerns. Under the first Nawaz Sharif government, the ambitious Social Action Programme (SAP) was inaugurated as a natural follow-up to the Five Point Programme, but with greater emphasis on the provision of basic social services in rural areas. The subsequent Benazir Bhutto government increased allocations to SAP by over 20 per cent per annum. To date, over Rs. 323 billion has been spent on SAP, however this expenditure does not appear to have led to a significant reduction in the incidence of poverty. This can be explained by a lack of cost-effectiveness, combined with a failure to implement the corresponding institutional reforms required for its success **(see chapter 7)**. Meanwhile, gains from investments in education and health have not been fully realized due to the lack of employment absorption capacity in the economy.

We have now a military government, which appears to be pursuing a relatively pro-poor growth agenda and has already announced a poverty reduction strategy involving the widening and deepening of a number of social safety nets **(see chapter 8)**. What explains this apparent concern about poverty on the part of the military government? First, the military regime has taken over after a decade of rising poverty and there are visible manifestations of acute distress in the country. With the incidence of poverty approaching one in every three families, the military government has been compelled to focus on poverty alleviation, largely as a reflection of the enlightened self-interest of the elite in averting a social breakdown in the country. Second, in search of legitimacy, the military government has probably found poverty reduction to be a viable populist slogan. Third, the regime may be adopting the expedient strategy of catering to international donors' new-found concern for poverty alleviation, in an effort to attract more concessional assistance.

In search for legitimacy, the military government has probably found poverty reduction to be a viable populist slogan.

Ensuring the protection of a fundamental human right.

As Pakistan gears up to return to democracy by the end of 2002, the question is whether this momentum for state intervention in poverty alleviation will be sustained or not. The answer hinges on whether the *imperfect* democracy that Pakistan has experienced to date can be improved upon. True democracy will require a shift from personalized leadership to the more effective operation of institutions, particularly the legislative and judicial arms of the government. An impartial and autonomous accountability mechanism will have to be put in place in order to prevent the worst excesses by politicians. The political environment will also have to be made more conducive to the development of NGOs and civil society at large, through the protection of civil liberties and fundamental rights, including the preservation of press freedom. All of these transformations are required if genuine participation of the people is to be promoted, and the voice of the poor is to be increasingly heard in the corridors of power.

RULE OF LAW

The rule of law is of vital importance to the poor. The interests of the poor can be subverted either by the presence of inherently inequitable laws (such as those relating to property rights or the treatment of minorities and women) or by the inequitable application and enforcement of existing laws. More broadly speaking, a proper legal system should promote stable and higher economic growth while respecting property rights, guaranteeing the sanctity of contracts, and lowering transaction costs.

In Pakistan, the existing judicial system has lost the confidence of the people, especially of the disadvantaged and the underprivileged. There is a massive backlog of court cases still pending, and the subordinate judiciary, in particular, is seen to be corrupt, prone to political interference, inadequately trained, and underpaid. The lack of justice, which is a common complaint of the people, is a significant contributing factor to their state of permanent deprivation.

The existing judicial system has lost the confidence of the people, especially of the disadvantaged and the underprivileged.

Which interest group is the government catering to?

Beyond this, the higher judiciary has been unable to deal with large loan defaults in the banking system (with court decrees not being enforced), large-scale financial embezzlements and misappropriation, and high-profile corruption. The consequence is a weakened financial system and a significant loss to small savers. The judiciary has also failed to adequately deal with the violation of building laws and zoning regulations by large construction companies in the megacities, and to properly redress grievances against police brutality to in-trial prisoners, women, and minorities. These examples of the absence of protection from blatant violations of the law have all contributed to the people's deep sense of injustice.

In some critical areas regarding the protection of people's rights, laws have yet to be even promulgated. For instance, land registration laws require that only deeds be registered, not actual ownership. Monopolies abound, encouraged by existing legislation–particularly in the utilities sector. There are no consumer protection laws or laws to make state transactions (e.g., privatization) more transparent. Laws against environmental pollution are insufficiently developed, and the freedom of information ordinance promulgated by the interim government in 1996 was allowed to lapse. All of these laws, however, are necessary for a more pro-poor environment.

An Asian Development Bank project on judicial reform has identified the following problems with judicial administration in Pakistan: (1) poor governance and administration, (2) inadequate case management and long delays, (3) lack of automation and court information systems, (4) poorly developed human resources, and (5) an absence of infrastructure. The proposed areas of reform are:

Judicial administration. Alleviate problems in the judicial system related to organization and administration, procedures and policies, human resources, financing, and infrastructure.

Access to justice. Reduce financial, institutional, procedural, physical, and information barriers to justice; and improve key economic laws, as well as the administration of civil and commercial litigation.

Legal profession and education. Improve the human resource capacity of the legal profession and the judiciary.

Legal information systems. Address the information management needs of the judicial and legal systems in order to improve feedback to society, which is so necessary for building trust and respect.

Government legal services. Improve government legal services using modern public sector management methods.

On a priority basis, the project proposes establishing a national judicial policy-making body and a council for legal education, and appointing a legal ombudsman. It also recommends the equalization of pay and allowances for the subordinate judiciary across the provinces, as well as a reduction in the disparity between the highest and the lowest echelons.

The breakdown of the judicial system and its failure, in particular, to address the common problems of the poor, has led to the emergence of Pakistani civil society organizations to help the poor through class action. Two notable entities that have attempted to redress the balance in favour of the poor are Lawyers for Human Rights and Legal Aid (LHRLA) and the Citizens-Police Liaison Committee (CPLC) **(see boxes 6.1 and 6.2)**

Replication of such support mechanisms at the national level, along with legal and judicial reforms of the types identified, are necessary prerequisites for removing the sense of injustice and despair that is felt among the poor and underprivileged people of Pakistan.

BOX 6.1

LEGAL AID FOR THE POOR

Lawyers for Human Rights and Legal Aid (LHRLA) was established in 1989 by a group of 50 zealous lawyers willing to provide free legal services to the disenfranchised, principally to fight against human right abuses in Karachi. It was initially supported by the Edhi Foundation, but is today funded by donors and community contributions, in equal proportions. LHRLA provides preventive, remedial, and direct legal aid, as well as free counselling, to aggrieved parties who would not otherwise be able to afford it. It also provides an arbitration mechanism to help resolve disputes outside the courts. LHRLA has helped release prisoners, mainly women and children, who were being held under discriminatory laws such as the *Hadood* Ordinance (which technically applies to adulterers, but is sometimes applied to rape victims). Often these people are the victims of trafficking. It has successfully campaigned, for example, against the trafficking of children for the camel races in Dubai. LHRLA has also been at the forefront of the fight for jail reform and the introduction of juvenile courts and penitentiaries, and is actively helping the government draft legislation for a juvenile justice system. The organization operates a Working Women's Support Centre, which actively fights against the discrimination, harassment and abuse of women in the workplace. It has also set up an awareness campaign that informs prisoners of their rights and privileges, as well as the procedure for such processes as filing applications for bail and filing petitions. In the realm of child labour, LHRLA participates with other agencies in the field and provides a 24-hour hotline service and crisis centre for children in need.

BOX 6.2

FIGHTING CRIME

The Citizens-Police Liaison Committee (CPLC) was established in 1989 by a group of Karachi business people, initially to support police efforts to stop the spread of kidnapping. To gain police acceptance, volunteers formed neighbourhood watch committees and began working in harmony with police patrols. Working on the premise that corruption in the police was due to an antiquated pay and benefits structure, the CPLC gave area police stations money to improve their equipment and work environment, as well as the living conditions of the personnel and their families.

Expenditure management was introduced through computerizing the systems. The CPLC's work has now progressed beyond the narrow confines of the more affluent segments of society. The United Nations Development Programme (UNDP) has helped prepare a system that now records all crimes committed and thefts reported, along with the follow-up action taken. In the past, first information reports (FIRs) were not readily accepted by police stations. However, since CPLC has been authorized, a letter from CPLC will ensure that FIRs are registered so that a timely investigation of the crime can

be initiated. The fact that these letters can also serve as court documents has been a deterrent to police high-handedness, and has diminished citizens' apprehensions (particularly among the poor and the disenfranchised) about reporting to police stations. CPLC helps improve law enforcement and assists citizens in human rights issues on a daily basis. The centre has also hired female staff so that women can benefit from its services. In terms of finances, the CPLC functions mostly through community contributions, with some supplemental government funding and assistance.

ECONOMIC GOVERNANCE

The basic goal of economic governance must be to fully harness the productive potential of both human and physical resources, for broad-based, sustainable, and pro-poor growth.

One of the key problems hindering efficient and focused economic management in Pakistan is that the government is too capacious in unproductive areas and too small in essential areas. The government's over-involvement in manufacturing, trading, and regulatory activities can be attributed to the presence of greater opportunities for patronage, rent seeking and corruption in these areas. In contrast, the government's performance is weak in areas that are deemed essential from the viewpoint of poverty alleviation, such as providing basic social services, redistributing resources through the taxation system, and developing adequate social safety nets.

It is clear that the state's primary agenda must be limited to providing collective goods and services that have large positive externalities (e.g., primary education and health care), as well as to equity considerations such as the prevention and amelioration of poverty, and the development of backward areas. If this agenda is strictly followed, then the state's energy can be focused on achieving better results with regard to growth and poverty reduction. The resulting savings in expenditure can then be diverted to higher priority uses, thus feeding back into the system.

Another set of serious problems with regard to economic governance includes the overcentralization of decision making, a lack of openness and transparency, the non-involvement of stakeholders (including civil society institutions, which are in a position to articulate the concerns of the poor), and the absence of a serious technical analysis of different policy options. The consequence of these shortcomings is that a number of serious mistakes have been and continue to be made in the design, sequencing, and implementation of major economic reforms. These have a negative impact on the country's prospects for growth, macroeconomic stability, and incidence of poverty. Some of these mistakes have also occurred either because of adherence to a faulty

The basic goal of economic governance must be to fully harness the productive potential of both human and physical resources, for broad-based, sustainable, and pro-poor growth.

Squalid conditions outside Karachi's *reputable* Chamber of Commerce.

paradigm or in response to advice from international agencies. Such mistakes include:
- the liberalization of the financial sector and a switch to market-based interest rates, without prior fiscal reforms to reduce the budget deficit. As a result, excessive government borrowing has caused debt-servicing liabilities to mushroom, thus crowding out pro-poor expenditures on basic social and economic services.
- too-rapid trade liberalization, which has involved steep import tariff reductions and a removal of quota restrictions, but without either accompanying institutional improvements in the export sector or the diversion of resources towards labour-intensive exports. This has led, on the one hand, to the increased displacement of labour and unemployment; on the other, to a loss of revenues which, in turn, has led to restricted public expenditure on human resource development and pro-poor services.
- a reduction in the growth of intergovernmental transfers, as a result of a new NFC award, without enhancing provincial fiscal powers or better exploiting subnational resources. This has implied major cutbacks in provincial outlays on social services **(see chapter 7)**.

An important test of the quality of economic governance is whether policies are oriented towards powerful special interest groups, or are motivated by the objective of protecting the *public interest* or, more particularly, the poor. This can be seen within the political economy of the policy-making process in terms of winners and losers. If it becomes clear that the government is catering to particular interest groups, then the quality of economic governance becomes suspect. Some recent examples illustrate this point:
- Special concessions are widespread in the cotton and textile sector of Pakistan. The All Pakistan Textile Manufacturers' Association (APTMA), one of the strongest lobbies in Pakistan, obtained permission to import over one million bales of cotton just prior to the bumper crop of 1999. In addition, the government effectively abandoned its cotton support pricing policy. Consequently, cotton prices crashed, and the windfall profits were conferred on the big textile manufacturers to the detriment of cotton growers, many of whom are small-scale farmers.

If it becomes clear that the government is catering to particular interest groups, then the quality of economic governance becomes suspect.

- Sugar production has fallen precipitously this year, by over 24 per cent, yet the government has maintained a high, 35 per cent regulatory duty on sugar import in order to protect domestic sugar manufacturers. Despite a huge deficit of over 0.5 million tons of sugar, the government continued to restrict public sector imports and delayed the decision to reduce the duty. The consequence is that the retail price of sugar has increased by over 50 per cent, partly due to hoarding and speculation. This has adversely affected the living cost of all households, especially among the poor.
- In early 2000, the government announced a 25 per cent increase in the wheat procurement price, in order to induce a domestic supply response. This has led to a bumper crop, and for the first time, Pakistan has a surplus of wheat. As a result, the price of wheat flour should have stabilized; instead, it has gone up by 10 to 15 per cent, depending on the location. The government delayed its decision to allow the interprovincial movement of surplus wheat, and simultaneously withdrew the wheat subsidy by enhancing the issue price. This increase in the price of a staple food in the diet of the poor will have major implications on the incidence of poverty.
- Pakistan has been under pressure from international agencies to introduce an agricultural income tax. In an effort to mobilize greater revenues, the government of Punjab made the rather strange decision to reduce the exemption limit to 5 acres rather than raise additional revenues, primarily from large farmers. Given that a subsistence landholding is about 12.5 acres, the reduction in the exemption limit implied a tax burden on very small farmers. Fortunately, this decision was recently reversed by the Chief Executive.

These and other examples demonstrate the callousness and lack of concern on the government's part, with regard to the impact of economic decisions on the living conditions of the poor.

A litmus test for economic governance is how crises are anticipated and managed, and how the burden of adjustment is distributed among different levels of society. A good example of pro-poor policy in the event of crisis is how the government managed the exchange rate following the imposition of sanctions on Pakistan in the aftermath of the 1998 nuclear tests. A dual exchange rate was introduced, whereby the import of essential items like wheat, pulses (lentils), pharmaceuticals, and edible oil and petroleum products was kept at the lower exchange rate of Rs. 46 per dollar, while the higher, interbank rate (of over Rs. 51 per dollar) applied to all other transactions. This policy effectively insulated the poor from the negative impact of a deep depreciation in the value of the currency, and the inflation rate in 1998-99 remained low at about 6 per cent.

More recently, international oil prices have attained a ten-year peak, while during the last few months, Pakistan's currency has depreciated by over 10 per cent. These factors, combined, imply a major increase in the landed cost of petroleum prices. This time, the government has decided to pass along the full cost to the consumer through a corresponding increase in the retail prices of petroleum products. Consequently, during the last year, the price of high speed diesel oil has increased by 44 per cent, leading to a rise in both the general price level and urban transport fares. This, in turn, has disproportionately affected the poor **(see chapter 4)**. A pro-poor policy option at this point would be to at least partially insulate the poor by reducing the tax on essential products such as high speed diesel oil and kerosene oil.

A litmus test for economic governance is how crises are anticipated and managed, and how the burden of adjustment is distributed among different levels of society.

Governance should become more responsive to the needs of the poor.

Overall, the quality of economic governance, both at the macro and micro levels, has significant implications on the incidence of poverty. For economic management to become more responsive to the concerns and needs of the poor, the process of policy making will have to be opened up, information systems will have to be linked more closely to ground realities, the bureaucracy will have to be made more responsive and accountable, and governments will have to insulate themselves more effectively from the pressures of special interest groups.

CORRUPTION

We come now to an important element of governance: the level of corruption in the fulfilment of government functions. The 1999 Human Development Centre (HDC) report has rightly referred to corruption as a "menace", and emphasized that it is one of the most damaging features of poor governance. When corruption becomes deeply entrenched, it can devastate the entire economic, political and social fabric of a country. There is, in fact, a vicious mutually-reinforcing cycle between corruption and human development. Corruption hinders human development directly by limiting access to basic social services, and indirectly by reducing economic growth due to loss of investment. Low levels of human development contribute to an environment that breeds corruption and reduces governance still further. The end results, both directly and indirectly, are unfavourable to poverty reduction.

Corruption in developing countries, including Pakistan, has a number of distinctive features. First, it occurs upstream at the highest levels of government, thereby distorting fundamental decisions about development priorities, policies and projects. Second, corruption money is usually smuggled out to safe havens abroad and so, in this sense, there is no local multiplier effect. Third, there are no effective accountability mechanisms against corruption. Fourth, corruption generally occurs in an environment of deprivation and poverty. These features make corruption all the more damaging.

There is, in fact, a vicious mutually-reinforcing cycle between corruption and human development.

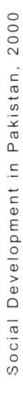

Petty corruption in particular adds to the harassment of the poor.

There are essentially three types of corruption. The first is petty corruption, mostly carried out by low-level personnel during the performance of some regulatory function (e.g., traffic police) or the provision of some service (e.g., black marketing of drinking water through tankers). The poor are especially vulnerable to petty corruption, and constantly face this problem in the conduct of their day-to-day activities **(see box 6.3)**. Middle-level corruption is normally conducted by bureaucrats at the enterprise level, in areas such as industrial licensing, awarding of contracts, allocation of quotas, and tax collection. Grand corruption occurs at the highest levels of the state and frequently involves foreign money (e.g., in defence contracts).

BOX 6.3

HOW CORRUPTION HITS THE POOR

The impact of corruption on the poor, particularly in their daily lives, is manifested in a number of ways. Some examples of this in Pakistan are:

- A hawker peddling his/her goods from the footpaths of any city or town must pay *bhatta* (protection money) to the local police officer on the beat. S/he is exposed to harassment when streets are being cleared of encroachments, and must contribute *in kind* at festivals to the officials.
- A squatter first has to pay the *land mafia* (largely composed of officials of the land departments and the police) to gain access to a piece of land; next, his application for regularization must be accompanied with a *bakhshish* (commission), his registration of the title deed being levied as an *informal* fee.
- The poor living in remote villages face difficulties accessing justice. They must pay to travel and stay overnight, pay *speed* money to ensure hearings are held, and bribe the judge to ensure justice for themselves.
- Standard police procedure is to pick up a substantial number of itinerants and squatters for *interrogation* without cause, particularly close to festivals and in *law and order* drives. These hostages are then ransomed-off for the maximum amount the *market* can bear. Non-payment leads to illegal incarceration, torture (at times until death), or death by shooting "in police action".
- A poor patient is not attended to in a government hospital, but is *recommended* to visit the private clinic of the doctor or specialist where s/he pays several times the cost of the government facility.

Corruption can be said to be premised on discretionary and monopolistic powers, a lack of accountability, and low government salaries. Exclusive provision of a service enhances discretionary power with regard to the discharge of a function, thereby leading to more corruption. Trade restrictions, government subsidies, and price controls, to name a few, are well-known sources of corruption. Accountability has traditionally been low in Pakistan at all levels–state, judicial and civil society. Because of public officials being poorly paid, Pakistan is also more susceptible to corruption.

The extent of corruption is particularly difficult to quantify because by definition it is unobserved. The HDC report makes a preliminary estimate of corruption in Pakistan of Rs. 100 billion, with the caveat that this is a conservative estimate. The biggest areas of corruption in Pakistan include tax evasion in connivance with the tax collector; illicit trade across borders with the tacit approval of security forces; theft and underpayment of public utility bills in collaboration with meter readers; bribes on the award of engineering contracts for development or maintenance works in the public sector; corruption in the granting of bank loans; and judicial and police corruption.

There are indications, however, that the level of corruption has been decreasing in Pakistan. The Corruption Perceptions Index of Transparency International had ranked Pakistan as being second among its 1996 sample of countries. Since then, Pakistan's ranking has fallen. It was ranked fifth in 1997 and fourteenth in 1998. In 1999, the ranking deteriorated slightly to twelfth place in light of the perception that towards the end the Nawaz Sharif government, the country had become vulnerable to higher levels of corruption.

It must be remembered that the Corruption Perceptions Index is based primarily on the views of foreign and local business people regarding the amount of corruption involved in conducting their activities in a particular country. As such, this index is probably geared more towards measuring the level of middle-level and grand corruption rather than petty corruption. In 1996, the perception of grand corruption in Pakistan was at its peak, which explains why Pakistan was ranked second that year.

Despite Pakistan's improved performance in Transparency International's index, corruption continues to be perceived by the people as a major problem, and there is a growing clamour for establishing strong, independent and even-handed mechanisms of anti-corruption and accountability in the country. This process has commenced under the new government, although there is a feeling that the process is being selectively applied and is proceeding more slowly than anticipated. We believe that while grand- and middle-level corruption may have declined in recent months, there continues to be a high and possibly rising level of petty corruption in the country. Petty corruption affects the lives of the largest number of people, thus explaining the growing public frustration.

The rise in petty corruption is a reflection of the systemic nature of corruption. It has been further reinforced by falling real incomes of the low-level public officials, in the absence of regular upward adjustments in salaries. In addition, as shortages have emerged in key public services due to the lack of investment (e.g., in the provision of drinking water in water-scarce metropolitan areas, a large and entrenched tanker mafia has come into existence). With regard to other services, a sharp increase in tariffs (e.g., electricity tariffs) has increased the potential gains from theft or underpayment.

In summary, integrity in the formulation and conduct of economic policy, and in the discharging of government functions, or regulation and

Multitude of structural shortcomings at the rail ticket office.

provision of services, remains a vital element of governance. A wide-ranging programme for the elimination of corruption in Pakistan has become absolutely essential. Given the systemic nature that corruption has acquired, it is necessary that strong symbolic actions be taken to reduce corruption. The government must identify and give exemplary punishment to major tax evaders, a few dishonest judges, and corrupt officials of public utilities and law-enforcing agencies. This will raise morale, especially among the poor, who undergo frequent harassment by corrupt officials. Ultimately, decreased corruption will increase people's chances of escaping from the poverty trap.

INSTITUTIONAL CAPACITY

Administrative capacity and capability are important components of good governance. By affecting the quality of public service delivery, they directly raise the well-being of the poor. Merit-based recruitment and promotion, linked to performance, market-based wages, and autonomy from the political process, are perhaps the most crucial elements for improved bureaucratic performance. Combined, they will help reduce corruption, as well as bureaucratic inefficiencies and delays. Most bureaucrats today have forgotten that they are civil servants, and that their primary function is to serve the people.

Public institutions in Pakistan are plagued with a multitude of shortcomings. There is a skills shortage for identifying and enunciating coherent policies; the prevailing work ethos discourages officials from hard work and dedicated service; systems and procedures are cumbersome and outdated; mechanisms to ensure coordination exist, but have ceased to function; there is continuous interference in day-to-day management by influential vested interests; staff members are inadequately trained, both at the outset and on-the-job, because of the short duration of job postings; staff selection, posting and promotion are not merit related; and the incentive structure does not reward improved performance.

Given the systemic nature that corruption has acquired, it is necessary that strong symbolic actions be taken to reduce corruption.

The passport office: An example of cumbersome, and outdated systems and procedures.

The quality of civil servants has eroded, largely because of quota-based employment and the politicization of the public services. In Pakistan, only 10 per cent of entrance into the public service is based on merit, compared to 40 per cent in Bangladesh. Furthermore, the decline in real wages and the widening gap between public and private sector wages have led to a consequential increase in corruption, at times in collusion with politicians. In Pakistan, the most highly remunerated public sector jobs pay only 30 to 40 per cent of the salary of comparable positions in the private sector. Thus talent is not attracted.

HDC (1999) concludes that, in Pakistan, "the bureaucracy has had to face intense political interference in the form of both coercion and patronage." Those who are loyal receive better (more "lucrative") postings and more rapid promotions. Demotion, political appointment, lateral entry, ad hoc transfers, and bureaucratic reshuffles are only a few of the mechanisms used to ensure loyalty. Large-scale arbitrary termination and transfers have resulted in a further lowering of morale and commitment.

Institutional reform of the civil service is a necessary component of structural reforms. The objective should be to make the service more professional and accountable. While these reforms could be painful in the short term, their benefits will be substantial in the long term. Benefits will include, but not be limited to, a smaller civil bureaucracy, a lower per unit cost for service and infrastructure, and greater efficiency in governance. The current status of permanent, non-terminable employment will have to be replaced by a system whereby the inefficient or the corrupt can be weeded out, and staff skills will need to be developed to use modern management techniques.

A framework for civil service reform in Pakistan was proposed by the World Bank in 1998. The study says that the problems faced by, and the shortcomings of, the civil service in Pakistan include an overcentralized organizational structure; rigid, often irrelevant, and unevenly enforced rules; inappropriate management practices; the wrong skills mix; the absence of compulsory continuing education, particularly for the higher echelons; lack of accountability, both internally as well as to the public;

The bureaucracy has had to face intense political interference in the form of both coercion and patronage.

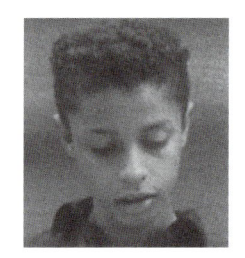

the politicization of civil service decision making; highly compartmentalized cadres; tensions, and a lack of cooperation and coordination, across cadres; and overemployment.

Civil service reforms will necessarily be a complex process and take time. Entry points into this process will need to be identified, and proceeded with on a strategic basis. It is clear, however, that improvements in bureaucratic performance will make the government more people-friendly.

DECENTRALIZATION AND DEVOLUTION

Decentralization represents the ceding of power from the central government to a local government or agency, with the former retaining a measure of oversight. Devolution is a more complete and permanent form of decentralization, in which the subnational unit is granted greater autonomy. Effective decentralization is considered to be pro-poor if the process of the delivery of basic services and social safety nets effectively draws on community involvement, based on local needs, local accountability and local monitoring.

Yet there are important caveats to decentralization and devolution. In settings where the local power structure is unequal, such as in feudal or tribal societies, or where there is a skewed distribution of economic power, local institutions are liable to be captured by the elite, who pre-empt funds for the benefit of special interests rather than for the people at large. Also, in the absence of adequate fiscal equalization, through targeted transfers from higher levels of government, reliance on local sources of revenue can intensify regional inequality and exacerbate problems of poverty in the backward areas. Furthermore, unless local institutional capacity is augmented, there is even the danger of impairing the quality of the delivery of services.

Therefore, decentralization and/or devolution cannot by themselves make state institutions pro-poor. There is a need for adequate institutional safeguards, as well as the establishment of proper mechanisms to facilitate people's participation in the process of governance. The relationship between local agencies and communities will have to be carefully designed and nurtured to ensure that the poor and otherwise disenfranchised segments of the population begin to be given a voice in the allocation and management of public resources. As such, devolution will have to be approached with caution and care. But if implemented effectively, it has the potential to improve development outcomes and to act as a catalyst for the broader process of empowering the poor.

On August 14, 2000, the Chief Executive announced an ambitious plan for the devolution of power to local governments within the country. The basic principles of the devolution plan, which was prepared by the National Reconstruction Bureau, are that it is people- and service-centred, and aims to carry government down to the grass-roots level. The plan recognizes three basic rights of the people: the rights to development, participation, and information. The plan's operational mechanisms include a bottom-up methodology, consensus building, ownership promotion, and issue-based politics. The plan aims to bridge the urban-rural divide, promote human resource development, and achieve corporate governance with an entrepreneurial approach. The empowerment targets of the plan include the devolution of political power, the decentralization of authority and functions, the diffusion of the power-authority nexus, and the distribution of resources **(see box 6.4)**.

Devolution, if implemented effectively, has the potential to improve development outcomes and to act as a catalyst for the broader process of empowering the poor.

BOX 6.4

SALIENT FEATURES OF LOCAL GOVERNMENT IN THE DEVOLUTION PLAN

District Government

The *Zila* (district) government will include the *Nazim* (administrator) and *Naib Nazim* (deputy administrator), the *Zila* council, and the district administration. The *Zila Nazim*, assisted by the *Naib Zila Nazim*, will be the executive head of the district, and the administration and police will be responsible to him. They will both be indirectly elected as joint candidates. All heads of the union councils in the district will automatically become members of the district council. The *Zila Nazim* and *Naib Zila Nazim* will be elected by the union council members of the district.

The number of general seats in the *Zila* council will vary depending on the number of unions in the district. In addition to the general seats, the *Zila* council will have thirty-three per cent of its seats reserved for women, five percent for workers/peasants, and five per cent for minorities.

The district administration will be coordinated by a District Coordination Officer (DCO). There will be twelve departments in the district government: district coordination; finance and planning; works and services; agriculture; health; education; community development; information technology; revenue; law; and magistracy.

Tehsil Council

The *Tehsil* (sub-district) government will include the *Tehsil Nazim*, the *Naib Tehsil Nazim*, the *Tehsil* council and the *Tehsil* administration. The *Tehsil* council will comprise *Naib Union Nazims* of all the unions of the *Tehsil*. Under the *Nazim*, there will be a *Tehsil* Municipal Officer (TMO) who will coordinate the Tehsil administration. There will be four *Tehsil* Officers (TOs) reporting to the TMO, each responsible for finance; budget and accounts; municipal standards and coordination; land use control; and rural-urban planning. Functions of the *Tehsil* council will include provision of municipal services, regulation of fees and charges, approval of the *Tehsil* budget, and land use control and master planning.

Union Council

The union government will comprise the *Union Nazim*, the *Naib Union Nazim*, the union council, and the union administration. The union council will have 21 members, 18 of whom will be elected: 12 men and 6 women. Six seats will be reserved for representatives of peasants/workers. The council will be headed by a *Union Nazim* and assisted by a *Naib Union Nazim*. They will be directly elected as joint candidates. Every union will have three secretaries under the control of the Union *Nazim*. The union councils will carry out their functions through the union government and the monitoring committees. At a minimum, there will be monitoring committees for municipal services; finance; public safety; health; education; literacy; works and services; and justice. The monitoring committees, or the citizens themselves, may facilitate the creation of Citizens' Community Boards (CCBs) in both rural and urban areas.

Village Council

The *Zila* council will determine the strength of each village council. *Tehsil Nazims* will arrange to hold elections for each village council, through secret ballots. The candidate who secures the highest number of votes will become the chairperson. The village council will be responsible for assessing finances required for projects and mobilizing contributions of the people; promoting civic education and community learning; organizing recreational and youth activities; and promoting gender issues. It will also facilitate the creation and functioning of CCBs.

Source: National Reconstruction Bureau, Chief Executive's Secretariat, Government of Pakistan; Local Government (Final Plan 2000), August 2000, Islamabad.

Local government finances will consist of federal and provincial transfers and grants, as well as self-generated funds, including revenue from taxes, fees and rates, and community contributions. Federal and provincial transfers will be formula-based, considering fiscal needs, fiscal equalization on the basis of backwardness, fiscal effort, and the maintenance of minimum standards of provision of services. Transfers will be determined by a Provincial Finance Commission.

Each district will have a district government as well as councils at *tehsil* (sub-district), union and village levels. The councils, or the citizens

The current transport system will need to be developed in order to effectively bridge distances.

themselves, will form voluntary citizens' community boards at all levels. The elected bodies will have general seats, plus one third reserved for women and five per cent each for peasants/workers and minorities.

Implementation of the devolution plan by mid-2001 will represent a fundamental change in the system of government in Pakistan. This plan has many positive features that could promote increased people's participation and local accountability in the provision of services. First, the civil administration and district-level functionaries of line departments are being placed, for the first time, directly under the control of elected local representatives. This could make the bureaucracy more responsive and accountable. Second, seats have been reserved for otherwise disenfranchised groups, such as minorities, peasants, workers and women. This should ensure that the poor are better represented in the local councils. Third, citizens' community boards are being constituted to monitor the process of the delivery of services. This will ensure greater transparency and accountability in the system. Finally, local elections are to be held on a non-party basis. Although this runs the risk of intensifying divisions within the community along ethnic and *baradiri* (clan) lines, it could provide greater opportunity for local community workers to contest elections, whereas under a party-based system, tickets are generally awarded to the rich and influential.

There are also some major risks. First, the plan is being implemented with a *big bang*, with a large number of diverse functions being handed over all at once to the local governments. It is not clear

Giving a voice to the poor is an essential element of good governance.

whether there will be adequate institutional capacity to handle these functions. Second, the common perception is that the devolution plan will undermine the authority of provincial governments, who may resist this change and not hand over sufficient financial resources for effective performance of the devolved functions. The sustainability of this change remains doubtful after the return to democracy. Third, local resources are likely to be inadequate to finance the provision of services, and financial arrangements remain unspecified. Finally, as highlighted above, there remains the ever-present danger of control by the local elites, which would defeat the purpose of inducing greater people's participation.

At this stage, the impact of the process of devolution, especially in terms of giving a voice to the poor, remains unclear. Following implementation, this process will need to be carefully monitored to determine if the stated objectives are being achieved or not.

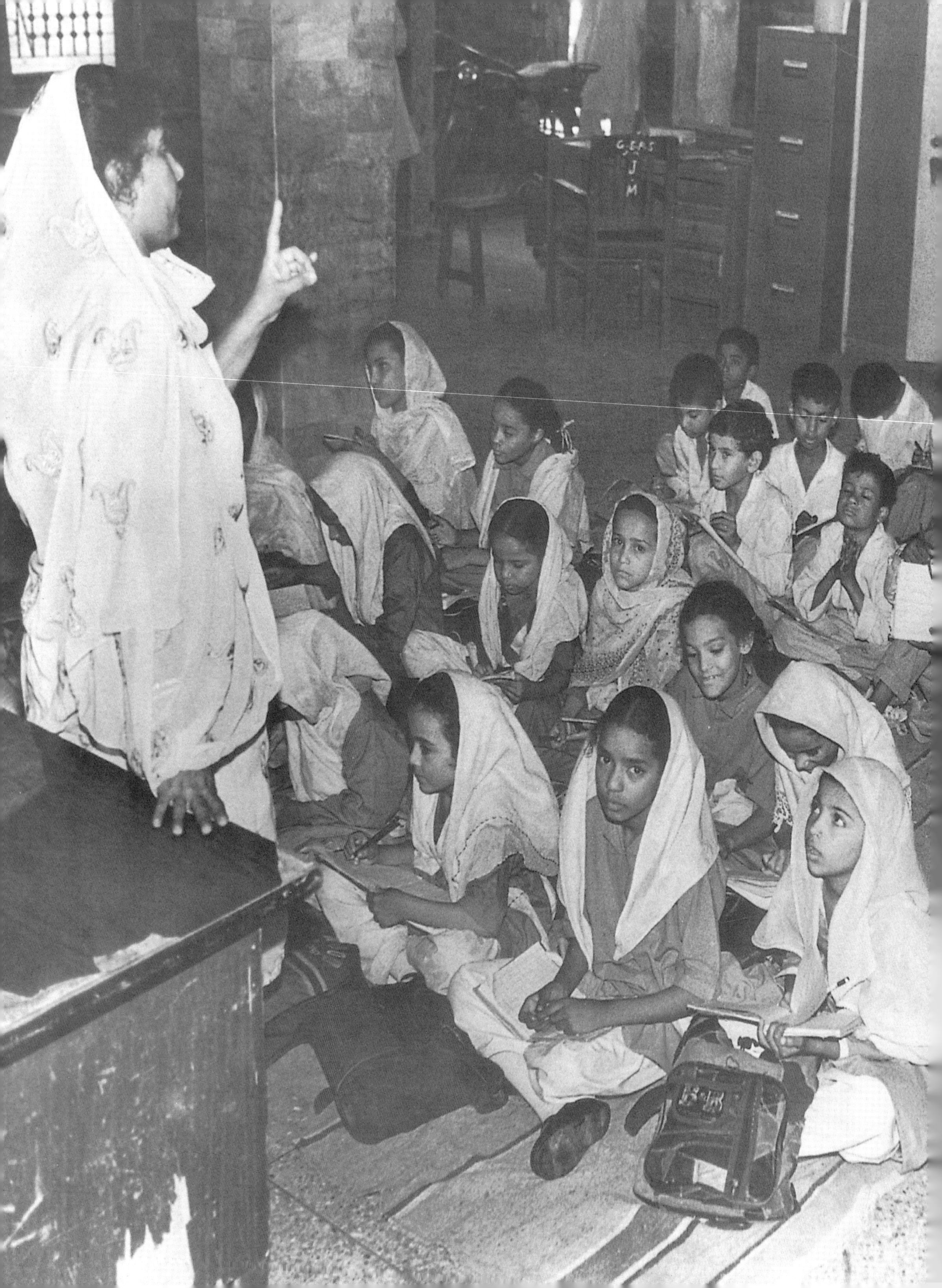

PROVIDING SERVICES TO THE POOR

CHAPTER 7

"Government must aim to improve the human capital endowments of the poor, thereby empowering them in their struggle against poverty."

PROVIDING SERVICES TO THE POOR

As part of a strategy for improving the prospects of the poor and enhancing their chances of surmounting poverty, it is essential that their access to services be increased. Services can contribute to alleviating poverty in a number of ways. First, by building up the human capital endowments of the poor, services can better equip them to earn a living. Second, services can enhance income and employment opportunities by strengthening the public infrastructure for private investment and growth. Third, they can help reduce private consumption expenditure and thereby enable an improvement in the living standards of the poor.

This chapter focuses, in particular, on identifying trends in the provision of pro-poor social and economic services, noting that one of the reasons for the rapid increase in poverty during recent years is a retreat by government from the provision of basic pro-poor services. This is a disturbing trend, and has fundamental implications on the long-term prospects for the successful implementation of a poverty reduction strategy. In this context, we discuss the performance of the Social Action Programme, which for some time was considered to be the flagship among government and donor efforts to improve the human capital endowments of Pakistan's poor, and to empower them in their struggle against poverty.

PRO-POOR SERVICES

Pro-poor services include those publicly provided services that reach out to the poor and that disproportionately benefit the poor. A classic example is primary education. If poor families are compelled, for reasons of access and affordability, to send their children to government schools–as opposed to the more expensive and higher quality private schools–then expenditure on expanding the coverage and quality of public schools is of greater benefit to the poorer segments of the population.

Among the large array of social and economic services provided by the government, which are more pro-poor? Unfortunately, there is insufficient research in developing countries on the incidence of different forms of public expenditure according to household income levels. Some services, such as primary education, are clearly pro-poor. But in the case of others, the incidence of benefits depends on the extent that poor households have access to the services. For example, the development of water supply systems in cities and towns may commonly be perceived as being a pro-poor investment. But whether they are indeed pro-poor depends on the nature of the water distribution system. If piped water connections are provided primarily to housing units in more affluent neighbourhoods, or if water supply is regulated in such a way that a higher level of service is provided to larger consumers, then any subsidies inherent in such facilities are largely pre-empted by the more well-off households.

During recent years there has been a retreat by the government from the provision of pro-poor services.

For the purpose of identifying the more pro-poor services, we have studied major initiatives such as the Five Point Programme and the Social Action Programme. These were launched in Pakistan with the avowed intention of reducing the incidence of poverty, especially in the rural areas of the country where poverty is spatially concentrated. The designers of these programmes must have had some notion as to which public investments are more likely to be effective in alleviating poverty.

The comprehensive Five Point Programme, launched by the Junejo government in 1985-86, envisaged a wide-ranging public investment programme that would expand the coverage of both economic and social services. If anything, the programme was more oriented towards economic services, accounting for just over half of the overall proposed investment outlay. Interestingly, the place of pride in the Five Point Programme was given to village electrification, which had the highest sectoral priority and accounted for over one fourth of the overall size of the programme. Other priority investments in economic infrastructure were drainage (to reduce waterlogging and salinity) and rural roads, essentially at the level of farm-to-market roads. The social sectors were collectively accorded second priority, with a combined share of approximately 40 per cent of the programme. Rural education received the largest allocation within the social services (about 23 per cent of total programme funds), followed by rural water supply and sanitation, rural health, and rural housing (the Seven *Marla* [about 30 square yards] Scheme). While it may argued that some of the priorities were misplaced–such as the emphasis on rural housing, which failed miserably due to lack of demand–the overall design and priorities of the programme probably accurately reflected the preferences and needs of the majority of the rural population, which had been articulated in elections held prior to the induction of the Junejo government.

The Social Action Programme, which was introduced some seven years later, essentially focused on the social services component of the Five Point Programme, while continuing to target only rural areas. This approach was based on the realization that, until the end of the 1980s, Pakistan's economic growth had been more than satisfactory compared to other developing countries with similar income levels. However, social indicators, such as the country's literacy rate, infant mortality rate, life expectancy, and contraceptive prevalence rate, all lagged behind. There was a growing realization that the process of growth, as well as improvement in the quality of life, would be retarded unless adequate emphasis was given to human resource development. Hence, the key social services focused on during the first phase of the Social Action Programme (1992-93 to 1996-97) included primary education, primary health care, population welfare, and water supply and sanitation. The programme focus of the second phase of SAP (until 2001-02) has been broadened to include middle schools, non-formal education, *tehsil* (sub-district) level referral hospitals, tuberculosis and nutrition in the health sector, and water supply and sanitation in urban *katchi abadis* (squatter settlements) and slums.

Research undertaken by Ghaus (1989) has identified pro-poor services within the functions performed by Pakistan's municipal and provincial governments **(see box 7.1)**. She finds that services such as primary and secondary education, urban transportation, public and curative health care, and intra-urban roads have a strong pro-poor bias. In contrast, benefits from higher education (colleges), law enforcement (police) and water supply are more often pre-empted by the upper-income groups.

Using the above information, we can identify, based on the principle of exclusion, services that cannot be classified as pro-poor and which should, therefore, be accorded relatively low priority in any national poverty reduction strategy. This list includes defence and police protection. Within education, low-priority services include higher education. Within economic services, telecommunications, highways (and motorways) and airports should receive less emphasis. Services for which there remains some degree of ambiguity are water supply and sanitation,

BOX 7.1

WHICH SERVICES ARE PRO-POOR?

Ghaus (1989) uses various allocation bases for distributing public expenditure among households with different income levels, as shown below.

Services	Allocation Base to Household	Suits Index
PROVINCIAL		
Primary and Secondary Education	90%: Number of children enrolled in government schools 10%: Externalities	-0.492
Colleges	Number of children enrolled in colleges	0.035
Transportation	Expenditure on public transportation	-0.466
Health Care	90%: Utilization of government health facilities 10%: Externalities	-0.396
Law and Order	Marginal utility of income	0.106
MUNICIPAL		
Water Supply	Cost of water consumed minus payment of tariff	0.343
Public Health (garbage disposal)	Number of times garbage is collected per week	-0.378
Roads	Commuting distance of household (adjusted for axle load of vehicle used)	-0.343

The Suits Index is used to determine whether a service is pro-poor. The value of this index ranges from -1 to +1. A negative value implies that the service is pro-poor (i.e., the closer the magnitude is to -1, the more pro-poor the service). In contrast, a positive value indicates that the service is pro-rich.

A caveat to her findings is that her research is based on a sample of urban households and may not be readily applicable to rural areas.

irrigation, agricultural extension, and gas distribution, since the benefits from these could be pre-empted by the rich and influential segments of society. One of the goals of public expenditure reform **(see chapter 4)** is to institutionalize the process of sectoral allocations in such a way that there is a diversion of resources towards pro-poor services.

LEVELS OF COVERAGE

Primary Education

We now focus on the coverage level of some of the key pro-poor services identified in the previous section. The first service considered is primary education, for which the most reliable enrolment estimates have been generated by the Pakistan Integrated Household Survey (PIHS). This survey also includes coverage by the private sector, which is generally under-reported in other government estimates. The most recent estimates are for 1996-97.

The PIHS reveals that the gross enrolment rate (GER) at the primary level in 1996-97, for the country as a whole, was 72 per cent. Contrary to expectations (in view of the rapid expansion of schools under the Five Point Programme and SAP), the GER has been falling. This is the first indication that increasing levels of poverty are preventing children from attending school. There are also large variations in enrolment rates by gender and location. The 1996-97 GER for boys was 80 per cent, and for girls, 64 per cent. In urban areas, the GER was 93 per cent, while in rural areas, it was 64 per cent. Provincially, the highest GER was observed in Punjab (75 per cent) and the lowest in Sindh (62 per cent).

Based on the assumption that the GER has not fallen significantly since 1996-97, we estimate that out of Pakistan's approximately 21 million school-aged children, as many as 6.5 million are currently not attending school. This figure includes 4 million girls and 2.5 million boys.

An even more striking conclusion can be reached based on the pattern of school attendance according to household income level, as shown in **table 7.1**. Poor households are concentrated in the first quintile and partly in the second quintile. It appears that only about 60 per cent of children from poor families are able to attend school, compared to over 80 per cent from upper-income households. As such, almost 3 million of the

TABLE 7.1

SCHOOL ATTENDANCE BY INCOME LEVEL OF HOUSEHOLD (% OF CHILDREN 10-19 YEARS HAVING ATTENDED SCHOOL)

Income Quintile[a]	Male	Female	Total
First	72	41	56
Second	81	53	67
Third	86	59	73
Fourth	90	63	77
Fifth	93	73	84
Total	85	57	72

[a]Quintiles in ascending order of income
Source: PIHS (1996-97)

As many as 6.5 million children are currently not attending school.

country's 6.5 out-of-school children are from poor households. This finding has important implications for the intergenerational consequences of poverty, and for its tendency to perpetuate over the long term. Children from poor families are unable to attend school, largely because of poverty. Either their families cannot afford the cost of education, or the children are compelled to find some form of work to augment their families' incomes. This implies that when such children grow up, they are likely to form poor households because they lack sufficient income-earning capacity due to inadequate human capital. This is how poverty transmits itself from one generation to the next. Somehow or other, this vicious cycle of poverty has to be broken.

How can primary school enrolment be enhanced? It is sometimes argued that there is a basic problem of demand and that private returns are low, especially given the low quality of education provided in government schools. Also, there may be social, cultural and religious barriers to attaining formal education, especially for girls. Most studies have found, however, that the private returns from primary education are relatively high in Pakistan. Khan and Irfan (1985) and Pasha and Wasti (1989) demonstrate that the return ranges from 12 to 15 per cent, and is substantially higher than that from secondary education. The latter authors show that the premium on primary education (in terms of the earning differential with respect to illiterate workers) may be small at first, ranging between 4 and 7 per cent, but that it rises rapidly, approaching 24 per cent by middle age, and over 40 per cent by the end of one's working life. This increase demonstrates that the basic ability to read and write makes workers more trainable and thus enhances the rate of accumulation of human capital over a lifetime.

We must ask, then, can enrolments be enhanced by operating on the supply side? Will enhanced public expenditure induce higher enrolment? The answer to both questions is yes. Research undertaken by SPDC reveals that enrolments are responsive, but to different inputs. In the case of girls, there is a large increase in enrolments as the availability of schools improves **(see box 7.2)**. This indicates that proximity to schools is an important consideration for girls. For boys, however, enrolment can be raised not so much by increasing the number of schools, but by enhancing quality and supervision by means of

Almost 3 million of the country's 6.5 out-of-school children are from poor households.

BOX 7.2

WHAT DETERMINES PRIMARY LEVEL ENROLMENT?

SPDC's ISPM model **(appendix A.5)** estimates national school enrolment functions based on data for 1972-73 to 1998-99. From these functions, elasticities of enrolment have been derived, with respect to different determinants. These elasticities are shown in the table below.

For example, the elasticity of female primary school enrolment with respect to the number of schools is 1.03. This indicates that a 1 per cent increase in the number of schools will increase girls' enrolment by 1.03 per cent. It may also be noted that the elasticity of male primary enrolment with respect to the number of teachers is relatively high, at 0.67.

The results indicate that female enrolment, in particular, is sensitive to changes in per capita income. Therefore, if the economy goes into a recession, the first children to be withdrawn from the schooling system are girls. However, the case for promoting female literacy is strengthened by the fact that educated mothers appear to be important in raising the enrolment rate, especially of boys.

With respect to	ELASTICITIES OF PRIMARY ENROLMENTS	
	Male	Female
School-age population	0.13	0.10
Schools	0.19	1.03
Teachers	0.67	0.19
Per capita income	-	0.42
Female literacy rate	0.27	-

There are serious questions concerning access to and quality of services provided by government facilities.

improved teacher-student ratios and improved skill endowment of the teachers. Therefore, a strategy for increasing the coverage of primary education enrolment would emphasize expenditure on more schools for girls, and more and better teachers for boys.

The problem of primary education coverage is exacerbated by the number of enrolled children who drop out of school prior to completion of grade five. If the withdrawal is early (the highest dropout rate is for grade one) then such children do not acquire sufficient education to become literate. Dropout rates are high in Pakistan, as shown in **table 7.2**. According to the latest estimates, over 60 per cent of boys and girls who begin primary school do not complete grade five. It also appears that the dropout rate increased during the 1990s, whereas it had been falling in the 1980s. This is probably a reflection of the increase in the incidence of poverty in the nineties. PIHS estimates that the school dropout rate among children from poor households is over three times that of children from upper-income households.

All told, we have a situation wherein over 40 per cent of the children from poor families are unable to enrol in primary school, and of those who

TABLE 7.2

DROPOUT RATE[a] IN PRIMARY EDUCATION

	Boys	Girls
1980	53	62
1985	51	63
1990	49	60
1995	59	59
1997	60	64

[a]The percentage of children starting primary school who do not complete grade 5
Source: Social Sector Development Indicators (see back of book)

A strategy for increasing the coverage of primary education enrolment would emphasize expenditure on more schools for girls, and more and better teachers for boys.

do enrol, over 60 per cent do not complete primary school. Consequently, only about 24 per cent of children from poor households successfully obtain a primary school education. As emphasized earlier, this perpetuates the cycle of poverty from one generation to the next. It also indicates that, even if the increase in poverty is temporary in character, it may impose permanent social costs if children are compelled to withdraw from school during a period of economic adversity. Once a child leaves school, s/he is unlikely to go back after a long absence. Countries such as Thailand and Indonesia, for example, witnessed sharp drops in school enrolment rates in the aftermath of the 1997 financial crisis.

Health and Population Welfare

Indicators of the coverage of curative health facilities in Pakistan are given in **table 7.3**. There have been major improvements in this area, especially during the 1980s. The availability of doctors has increased dramatically, reflecting rapid expansion in the capacity of medical education institutions. However, the majority of doctors continue to congregate in the large cities, and availability of qualified doctors in the rural areas remains a problem. The number of beds in government hospitals increased in the 1980s, in relation to the population, but has barely kept pace with population growth in the 1990s. And while there has been a relatively rapid expansion in recent years in the network of hospitals run by the private sector, it is not clear how much access the poor have to these facilities. Also, there are serious questions about the quality of service provided by government facilities, especially in the rural areas (Rural Health Centres [RHCs] and Basic Health Units [BHUs]), in the presence of the rampant absenteeism of doctors and the severe shortages of paramedical personnel, equipment and medicines.

Progress in preventive health care remains limited. A key indicator is the coverage of children by immunization services. The PIHS reveals that, for the country as a whole, only about half of the children were fully immunized in 1996-97. Coverage was especially poor in the province of Sindh (at 35 per cent). As shown in **table 7.4**, only about 40 per cent of children belonging to households in the lowest income quintile used the immunization services. Altogether, Pakistan's immunization programme

TABLE 7.3

COVERAGE OF CURATIVE HEALTH FACILITIES AND PERSONNEL

	POPULATION[a] SERVED PER		
	Doctor	Hospital Bed	Rural Health Facility
1975	11.1	1.9	385
1980	7.4	1.7	221
1985	3.1	1.6	99
1990	2.1	1.5	64
1995	1.7	1.4	61
1998	1.5	1.5	62

[a]Population given in thousands
Source: Social Sector Development Indicators

TABLE 7.4

COVERAGE OF IMMUNIZATION BY INCOME LEVEL OF HOUSEHOLD (%)

Income Quintile	Rural Areas	Urban Areas	Total
First	36	50	41
Second	45	52	47
Third	48	62	53
Fourth	53	66	57
Fifth	56	71	61
Total	**48**	**60**	**52**

Source: PIHS (1996-97)

failed to reach over 9 million children out of the country's total population of about 19 million children aged 5 years and under in 1996-97.

The population welfare programme has also had limited success. PIHS (1996-97) reports that only about 17 per cent of then-married women aged 15 to 49 years of age used family planning methods. The Pakistan Fertility and Family Planning Survey's estimate for the same year is somewhat higher, at 24 per cent. **Table 7.5** shows a wide divergence in the contraceptive prevalence rates between rural and urban areas, and between households in the lowest and highest income quintiles. The resulting higher fertility rate of women in poorer households implies both larger families and larger dependency ratios, which is a contributing factor to poverty.

Water Supply

The proportion of the population with access to piped water connections remains low. According to the 1998 population census, the overall extent of coverage is 27 per cent (58 per cent in urban areas, and 13 per cent in rural areas). While an acceptable standard of service is provided to a large number of rural households (especially in Punjab)—by access to groundwater through handpumps—almost 42 per cent of households in urban areas depend largely on communal sources or purchase water from the informal market at three to five times the municipal costs. In effect, the urban poor pay significantly more for drinking water than do upper-income households with access to piped connections.

TABLE 7.5

USE OF FAMILY PLANNING METHODS BY INCOME LEVEL OF HOUSEHOLD (%)

Income Quintile	Rural Areas	Urban Areas	Total
First	11	21	14
Second	10	24	15
Third	13	28	18
Fourth	13	30	19
Fifth	12	39	21
Total	**12**	**28**	**17**

Source: PIHS (1996-97)

The higher fertility rate of women in poorer households implies both larger families and larger dependency ratios, which is a contributing factor to poverty.

Over 35 million people in rural areas live without electricity.

It is also significant to note that investments in urban water supplies decreased considerably during the 1990s. According to an FBS housing survey, 60 per cent of the urban population had access to piped water in 1989; the proportion declined to 58 per cent by 1998. Rural coverage improved somewhat during the corresponding period, from 9 to 13 per cent–probably as a result of the impetus provided by SAP to the rural water supply and sanitation sector.

Village Electrification

Village electrification has been identified as a key pro-poor service. It not only improves the quality of life of rural households, but also enhances income-earning opportunities in the agriculture sector and cottage industry, and leads to significant cost savings in lighting fuel. Village electrification proceeded at a rapid pace during the 1980s, especially in the second half of the decade, with rural coverage increasing from only 15 to 50 per cent **(see table 7.6)**. This is due to the high priority it received in the Five Point Programme. Since then, the momentum of the programme appears to have faltered, coverage having increased by only another 10 percentage points between 1989 and 1998, in comparison with 36 percentage points in the nine years leading up to 1989. It is likely,

TABLE 7.6

EXPANSION IN COVERAGE OF ELECTRICITY (% OF POPULATION)

	1980	1989	1998
Rural Areas	15	51	61
Urban Areas	71	92	93
Total	31	64	71

Sources: Population Censuses (1981 and 1998)
Housing Survey (1989)

however, that the more accessible villages have already been covered, and so the cost of electrifying the remaining uncovered villages is higher. It is currently estimated that over 35 million people living in rural areas do not have access to electricity.

In summary, it is evident that there are wide gaps in the coverage of key pro-poor services such as primary education, preventive health care, and village electrification. Efforts were made in the 1980s to expand the coverage of most services, but the pace of expansion seems to have slowed down perceptibly during the 1990s. This at least partly explains why the incidence of poverty fell in the 1980s and increased rapidly during the 1990s.

PUBLIC EXPENDITURE ON SERVICES

The trend in public expenditure on the social sectors during the 1990s is shown in **table 7.7**. At its peak in 1995-96, public expenditure aggregated to over 4 per cent of the GDP. In the second half of the 1990s, there was a sharp cutback and the level of expenditure declined to 3.4 per cent of the GDP by 1999-2000.

As expected, education is the largest single sector in terms of outlays. However, the pro-poor component of primary education accounts for only about 45 per cent of this expenditure; the rest goes to higher education, which differentially benefits upper-income households in Pakistan.

Expenditure on education peaked during 1995-96, at about 2.5 per cent of the GDP. Since then, it has fallen to just over 2 per cent of the GDP. The education policy announced in 1997 by the former government called for total allocations to education of 4 per cent of the GDP in order to achieve its ambitious targets, including an increase in the literacy rate to 60 per cent by 2002-03. Currently, the country is able to meet only half of this expenditure target.

Health sector expenditure has remained constant at about 0.7 per cent of the GDP. The big decline is in allocations to other social sectors, consisting primarily of water supply and sanitation, population welfare,

TABLE 7.7

PUBLIC EXPENDITURE ON SOCIAL SECTORS (% OF GDP)

Year	Education	Health	Others[a]	Total Social Sectors
1990-91	2.1	0.7	1.0	3.8
1991-92	2.2	0.7	1.0	3.9
1992-93	2.2	0.7	1.0	3.9
1993-94	2.3	0.7	0.8	3.8
1994-95	2.4	0.7	0.9	4.0
1995-96	2.5	0.7	0.9	4.1
1996-97	2.3	0.7	0.8	3.8
1997-98	2.2	0.7	0.7	3.6
1998-99	2.1	0.6	0.8	3.5
1999-2000	2.1	0.7	0.6	3.4

[a] Others include physical planning and housing (mostly water supply and sanitation), human resources and social welfare, social security, sports, culture, religious affairs, and population welfare
Sources: Federal and provincial annual budget statements

TABLE 7.8

REAL PER CAPITA EXPENDITURE[a] ON SOCIAL SECTORS, AT 1998-99 PRICES (RS.)

	Recurring Expenditure	Development Expenditure	Total	Inter-governmental Transfers[b]
1990-91	551	197	748	659
1991-92	567	243	810	1103
1992-93	595	211	806	1114
1993-94	582	217	799	1179
1994-95	603	247	850	1207
1995-96	631	280	977	1336
1996-97	604	217	821	1226
1997-98	580	195	775	1063
1998-99	559	188	747	1010
1999-2000	580	169	749	1106

[a] By both federal and provincial governments
[b] From the federal government to the provincial governments
Source: SPDC estimates

human resources, and social welfare. These declined from 1 per cent of the GDP in the early nineties to 0.6 per cent of the GDP by the end of the decade.

What has been the consequence of the cutbacks on real per capita recurring and development expenditure on the social sectors? **Table 7.8** indicates that real per capita recurring expenditure was down by almost 8 per cent in 1999-2000, in relation to the peak allocation in 1995-96. This has had negative implications for the quality of services provided. With regard to education, the availability of teaching materials has been affected. In the area of curative health care, there is an even greater shortage of medicines, largely because governments have tried to protect salary budgets in the face of the cutbacks.

The fall in development expenditure is steeper. It was down by almost 40 per cent in 1999-2000, in relation to the peak level attained in 1995-96. This has meant that the expansion rate of facilities has declined sharply and that the large gaps in coverage have acquired a permanent character. **Table 7.9** presents the annual rate of expansion in major pro-poor services during the 1990s. The slowing-down process is clearly visible, especially in the second half of the decade. In the early nineties, there was a rapid increase in the number of primary schools as the first phase of the SAP got underway. At the peak in 1992-93, over 7,500 new primary schools were constructed. The number is now down to less than 1,700. In 1992-93, over 4,800 hospital beds were added; that figure was reduced to about one quarter by 1998-99.

In the area of pro-poor economic services, government cutbacks have been even more pronounced. The number of newly-electrified villages is down to one fifth of the peak attained in 1994-95. Construction of farm-to-market roads is proceeding at less than one third the expansion rate achieved in the mid-nineties.

What explains the government's large-scale retreat from the provision of pro-poor services? Is this a reflection of the general fiscal constraint or has the priority of providing such services fallen? Both factors have apparently contributed to the slowdown. The provision of social services, in particular, is the responsibility of provincial governments, and over 80 per cent of the expenditure is incurred by them.

The fall in development expenditure has meant that the expansion rate of facilities has declined sharply and that large gaps in coverage have acquired a permanent character.

TABLE 7.9

RATE OF EXPANSION IN PRO-POOR SERVICES IN THE 1990s

	Primary Schools (no.)	Hospital Beds (no.)	Villages Electrified (no.)
1990-91	3157	2808	2453
1991-92	4235	1133	3649
1992-93	7511	3109	4824
1993-94	5232	4836	5283
1994-95	7175	922	6243
1995-96	5504	2649	4957
1996-97	3728	1475	2441
1997-98	1514	730	1383
1998-99	1807	1260	1232
1999-2000	1668	n/a	1152

Source: Pakistan Economic Survey (various issues)

The fiscal position of the provinces and their ability to spend depends directly on the amount of transfers received from the federal government. Provincial transfers constitute over 80 per cent of total provincial resources. As shown in **table 7.8**, the transfers increased sharply in real per capita terms in 1991-92, following the promulgation of the 1991 National Finance Commission (NFC) award, which was favourable to the provinces. During the tenure of this award, they continued to show growth until 1995-96 because tax revenues–especially the divisible pool of taxes–grew rapidly during this period. The 1996 NFC award effectively led to a contraction in the provinces' share of revenue. Simultaneously, import tariff reforms and sharp cuts in income tax and GST rates, which were announced in the initial days of the Nawaz Sharif government as part of a supply-side strategy for economic revival, led to a large once-and-for-all decline of almost 13 per cent in real per capita transfers in 1997-98. In 1998-99, transfers declined even further due to a stagnation in tax revenues. In 1999-2000, there was some improvement due to the broad-basing of the tax system and the consequential expansion in the divisible pool.

The pattern of real per capita expenditure on social services mirrors the trend in intergovernmental transfers. The former continued to show growth until 1995-96, in line with the increase in transfers. In 1996-97 and 1997-98, when transfers fell cumulatively by 20 per cent, expenditure also declined by about 15 per cent. Since then, as transfers have stabilized, so has expenditure. Therefore, a major contributing factor to the decrease in real social sector expenditure has been the worsening fiscal position of the provinces, caused largely by the sharp decline in real transfers after 1995-96.

Beyond this, have social services been able to retain their priority in expenditure allocations? This is examined in **table 7.10**, which gives expenditure on the social sectors as a percentage of total public expenditure. The social sectors received increasingly higher priority during the first half of the 1990s, especially because of the rapid growth in allocations to the SAP. In the mid-nineties, the share approached 16 per cent. But since then, priorities appear to have changed and the overall share has fallen to about 12 per cent.

It is now clear that in an environment of resource limitations and changing priorities, expansion in the coverage of pro-poor services will have to come through higher efficiency and cost effectiveness in the

A major contributing factor to the decrease in real social sector expenditure has been the worsening fiscal position of the provinces, caused largely by the sharp decline in real transfers after 1995-96.

TABLE 7.10

PRIORITY TO SOCIAL SECTORS (% OF TOTAL PUBLIC EXPENDITURE)

	Recurring Expenditure	Development Expenditure	Total
1990-91	12.0	28.4	14.2
1991-92	12.0	33.5	14.9
1992-93	11.9	32.8	14.3
1993-94	11.7	42.9	14.6
1994-95	12.8	35.1	15.7
1995-96	12.3	39.0	15.6
1996-97	12.4	50.2	15.4
1997-98	11.6	50.9	14.4
1998-99	11.6	48.1	14.3
1999-2000	10.8	22.7	12.4

Source: Federal and provincial annual budget statements
Pakistan Economic Survey

delivery of services. Fortunately, there appears to be a significant margin for improvement in delivery, by the reallocation of funds among inputs and by institutional and policy reforms. Greater cost-effectiveness can be achieved by focusing expenditures more on outputs and impact, improving prioritization, eliminating areas of wastage, undertaking better investment planning, experimenting with alternative delivery mechanisms, and promoting greater participation by the private sector. **Box 7.3** provides the results of SPDC research on the optimal mix of inputs needed for maximizing the output of public school and health systems.

Beyond getting greater value from outlays on pro-poor services, the government will also have to demonstrate its commitment to poverty reduction by improving the availability of finances for upgrading the quality and expanding the coverage of such services. A new NFC has

In an environment of resource limitations and changing priorities, expansion in the coverage of pro-poor services will have to come through higher efficiency and cost-effectiveness in the delivery of services.

BOX 7.3

COST-EFFECTIVENESS IN PUBLIC EDUCATION AND HEALTH

Policy recommendations (derived from a 1994 SPDC study) indicate that if a *cost-efficient* approach is adopted with regard to public education and health, then even with the same available resources, a big increase in enrolment rate can be achieved for female students, compared to the present rate of 57%. Such a cost-effective strategy will require an expanded and accelerated school construction programme for girls, and a simultaneous deceleration in the growth of boys' schools. An *alternative optimization approach* has been proposed, wherein, once a relatively modest participation rate for boys' secondary schools is achieved, the bulk of the resources should be diverted towards female institutions. It needs to be emphasized that, prior to the formulation of an accelerated school construction programme (as in the one under SAP), policy makers should ensure the steady inflow of recurring outlays.

Another SPDC study on the determinants of the output of health facilities indicates that expansion in urban areas should be slowed down in the short term (i.e., for two to three years), with some of the resources being reallocated towards the rural sector. Not only should attractive wage policies be formulated for rural health facility personnel but, as with the armed forces, the status of nurses should be elevated by giving them higher Basic Pay Scales (BPSs).

While a generous amount has already been spent on SAP, access to basic services like potable water remains low.

recently been constituted. In deciding on the provinces' overall share of the revenue, the next award must consider the fact that most pro-poor services (especially social services) are delivered by provincial governments. Their share, therefore, must be large enough to enable expansion in these services. Clearly, the decrease in public expenditure on pro-poor services, observed especially in the second half of the nineties, has to be reversed. As part of the national poverty reduction strategy, the government may target expenditure on social sectors to increase to 20 per cent of total public expenditure. Allocations to pro-poor economic services such as village electrification should simultaneously be raised.

THE SOCIAL ACTION PROGRAMME

A Programme in Jeopardy

In 1991, Pakistan, in cooperation with donors, launched the SAP with great expectations. Since then, cumulative expenditure on SAP has been Rs. 323 billion **(see table 7.11)**, including Rs. 96 billion of development expenditure. But the impact on key social indicators has been mixed.

1. The gross enrolment rate in primary schools has not improved. In fact, there is evidence from the PIHS that it is falling despite the rapid construction of schools in the early to mid-nineties. The timing of this investment was not propitious since it coincided with rising poverty, which deterred families from sending their children to school and also contributed to a higher dropout rate. The literacy rate increased at a modest rate of about 1.5 percentage points per annum during the 1990s, reaching 47 per cent by the end of the decade.

2. Health investments have possibly done better due to SAP. The infant mortality rate fell sharply from 105 deaths of children under one (per one thousand live births) in the early nineties, to 86 by 1996. Life expectancy, which did not show any significant improvement during the eighties, increased by six years from 1992 to 1996. The overall death rate consequently showed a significant decline.

TABLE 7.11

SAP EXPENDITURES

	LEVEL (Rs. Billion)			AS % OF GDP			SAP as % of Total Public Expenditure
	Current	Development	Total	Current	Development	Total	
1992-93	15.6	7.2	22.8	1.2	0.5	1.7	6.3
1993-94	19.1	7.1	26.2	1.2	0.5	1.7	6.4
1994-95	23.4	12.0	35.4	1.2	0.6	1.9	7.5
1995-96	29.8	14.5	44.3	1.4	0.7	2.1	7.8
1996-97	30.0	12.4	42.4	1.2	0.5	1.7	7.1
1997-98	31.1	18.1	49.2	1.2	0.7	1.8	7.4
1998-99	34.6	12.6	47.2	1.2	0.4	1.6	6.7
1999-2000	33.6	9.8	43.4	1.1	0.3	1.4	6.2

Source: Federal SAP Secretariat

3. The population welfare programme began yielding positive results. The total fertility rate declined from 6.2 to 5.5 within six years, and the natural population growth rate–which had remained close to 3 per cent for a long time–began to fall visibly and was down to 2.6 per cent by 1996. Some government estimates are that it is currently as low as 2.2 per cent, however this may not be due so much to the population welfare programme as to the incipient process of demographic transition which is now occurring in Pakistan.

Provincial governments, the principal executing agencies of SAP, are becoming increasingly worried about the financial sustainability of the programme. Earlier investments have led to big increases in recurring expenditure liabilities at a time when federal transfers have become stagnant. This has tended to *crowd out* expenditure on economic services such as irrigation, agricultural research and extension, and roads, which are considered important in the short term for promoting economic revival.

The consequence is a significant cutback in the allocation of resources to the SAP, and a scaling-down of its priorities. At its peak, in 1995-96, SAP outlays exceeded 2.1 per cent of the GDP. These have since been reduced to 1.4 per cent of the GDP, with a major slashing of the development component. Expenditure on SAP, which had risen rapidly to 7.8 per cent of public expenditure by the mid-nineties, is now down to 6.2 per cent. Even in nominal terms, SAP expenditure in 1999-2000 was below the level attained in 1997-98.

Following the launch of the poverty alleviation programme, there is a new source of competition for SAP development funds. Within the provincial Public Sector Development Programmes (PSDPs), the new Integrated Small Public Works Programme (ISPWP) has been allocated Rs. 15.7 billion in 2000-01. Simultaneously, the allocation for SAP has been cut from Rs. 16 billion in 1999-2000 to Rs. 10.3 billion in 2000-01. The government has revealed a preference for short term poverty alleviation measures, rather than focusing on building the human capital endowments of the people in order to better equip them to fight against poverty on a sustained basis.

The fact that SAP is in crisis is also demonstrated by the sharp cutbacks it has experienced in relation to the outlays agreed upon with donors. In 1997-98, the shortfall was 32 per cent. By 1999-2000, it had increased to 55 per cent. Development and non-salary budgets have been disproportionately cut. This has not only affected the flow of donor funds, but has also adversely affected the effectiveness of the programme.

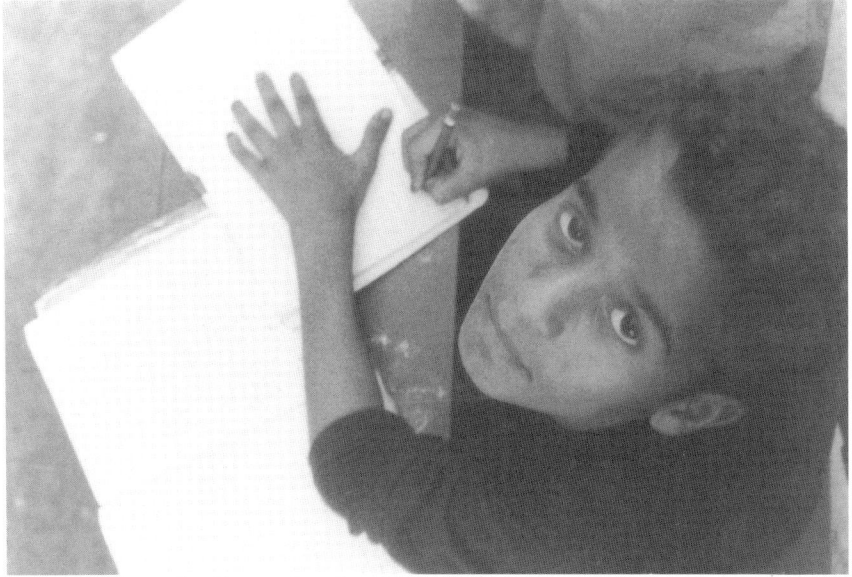

Services such as education must continue to receive priority attention in the allocation of resources.

A point has been reached where Donors (2000) have been compelled to make the following observation:

The government is developing several new initiatives which are closely related to delivery of basic social services. These include the poverty reduction strategy, including the Poverty Alleviation Programme (PAP), and the proposed devolution programme. It is important that SAP, a major ongoing government programme, designed to improve delivery of basic social services which are especially important for the poor, be seen as a core element of the government's poverty reduction strategy, and be provided the managerial and financial resources to have this central role.

The PAP is now under implementation throughout the country. It is important that the activities financed through PAP should complement, and not be in conflict with, SAP. Consideration should also be given to use PAP funding flexibly to meet critical needs in the delivery of social services (such as non-salary budgets). In addition, PAP implementation needs to be closely coordinated, especially at the district level, with the SAP sector line departments, as these departments are already involved in ongoing program implementation. Education and RWSS [Rural Water Supply and Sanitation] sector schemes, financed through PAP, should maintain the government's established site selection criteria and key sector policies, such as the unified policy of community participation in the RWSS sector.

Revamping the SAP

It is generally felt that SAP will have to be revamped if it is to continue receiving priority attention in the allocation of resources. Following are key problems that have been identified with the current institutional arrangements and implementation modalities of SAP.

It is important that SAP be seen as a core element of the government's poverty reduction strategy.

Lack of decentralization. There has been no decentralization within the line agencies themselves, nor a devolution to local governments and communities. In addition, there is a lack of capacity building, no focus on quality improvement and consolidation, and no change in the power structure within the SAP line departments. Implementation of the government's devolution plan **(see chapter 6)** provides a real opportunity for decentralizing the provision of SAP-related services to the district, *tehsil* (sub-district) and union council levels.

Lack of community involvement. Little decision-making capacity in the planning, building or running of services has yet been given to or developed in communities. This is contrary to both SAP's philosophy and its sector strategy. It was anticipated that SAP would be supported by the Participatory Development Programme (PDP), which unfortunately lacks a proper institutional framework. No project has yet been undertaken within the framework of the PDP, owing to prolonged and complex processing mechanisms. The PDP will have to be streamlined and the process of selection of NGOs made more transparent.

Inadequate monitoring and evaluation. Monitoring and evaluation is lagging behind. The Auditor General began surveying process parameters such as procurement and recruitment, but in a way which is strictly administrative and narrowly focused, and is not truly independent. Line departments are being encouraged to set up management information systems, but nearly all are unreliable since they are based on administrative information with no independent field verification. Projects that exist only on paper, absenteeism, and poor performance are common and go unreported. The PIHS is upgrading its sampling and survey methods, but falls short of highlighting regional disparities and measuring service quality or impact. There is an urgent need to establish a minimum set of critical monitoring indicators, and to develop appropriate information systems that can be tracked more frequently and at less cost.

Lack of value engineering. No attempt has been made to measure the value for the money, or cost-effectiveness, of SAP. The programme is being critically constrained by a lack of adherence to the criteria for site selection, staff recruitment, and procurement. Further, there is a serious lack of understanding of SAP-II at all levels. This may be due to a lack of communication. Also, progress is being severely jeopardized by weaknesses in institutional capacity and staff capability, and the rapid, indiscriminate and disruptive transfer of key managers in all SAP departments. In order to ensure better value for the money, the emphasis must shift from the construction of new facilities to the consolidation and improvement of existing facilities, and to a realignment of current expenditure towards the non-salary component.

Altogether, reforms to improve the workings of SAP must include the following:
- identification of core pro-poor social services such as primary education and preventive health care, which will remain the responsibility of the government and will be protected from any expenditure cutbacks;
- implementation of institutional reforms that will increase cost-effectiveness and impact, as well as use innovative approaches that ensure sustainability;
- greater involvement of NGOs, the private sector and beneficiaries;

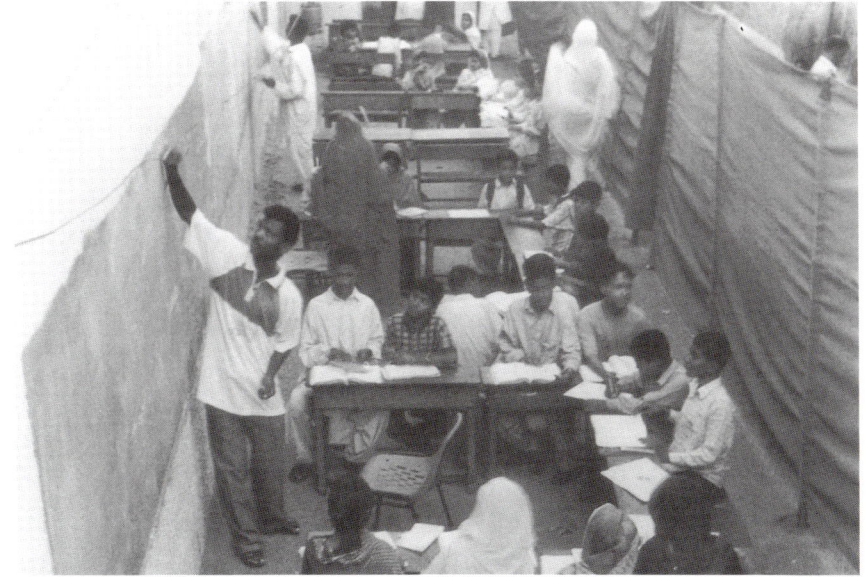

Communities should operate and manage local facilities such as schools, whereas standards and codes should be established by higher levels of government.

- use of independent and effective monitoring and evaluation systems.

ROLE OF NGOs AND THE PRIVATE SECTOR

NGOs

In recent years, as the quality and rate of expansion of public sector services has fallen, the NGO sector has risen to meet the growing demand for social services. This is evident in education and family planning, and to some extent in health. Given stagnant revenues, rising deficits, and lower cost-recovery by the government, social services will continue to fall increasingly into the domain of NGOs. This should help make the delivery of these services more efficient, cost-effective and sustainable.

To gain the maximum benefit from community-based organizations, an appropriate mix of horizontal and vertical relationships needs to be established among the stakeholders. For instance, communities are often best placed for operating, managing and monitoring local facilities, such as schools or clinics. They should not be burdened with tasks that are better suited to higher tiers of government, such as the establishment of standards and codes. These can be best handled regionally at the state or provincial level, and overall national goals and objectives should be handled centrally or federally. When community involvement is partnered with local government, the likelihood of gaining benefits increases substantially. In Pakistan, even in the absence of local governments, such examples have been tried and some success attained in the area of elementary education **(see box 7.4)**. Implementation of the government's devolution plan will greatly increase the scope for such partnerships.

Another significant role that NGOs have played in Pakistan is in the struggle against poverty. Various rural support programmes have drawn on lessons learned from the Comilla Rural Development Programme, which was first replicated in Pakistan by Dr. Akhtar Hameed Khan, with

BOX 7.4

SCHOOL MANAGEMENT COMMITTEES (SMCs) IN THE PUNJAB

One of the major changes advocated in the implementation of SAP was the involvement of beneficiaries in the management of the facilities. In elementary schools in the Punjab, this has manifested itself in the establishment of School Management Committees (SMCs). After some initial hiccups, the experiment proved to be so successful that vested interests were being severely affected. The reason for success lies in the close involvement of the beneficiaries in both the operations and management of the facilities.

The SMCs initially comprised 12 nominated members, of whom civil society representatives included 1 elected parent, 3 local influential persons, and 3 retired government officials. After the initial trial period of one year, the size of the SMCs was diminished to 9 members: 3 nominated teachers, 3 local influential persons or social workers, and 3 elected parents. Because of the real fear that the people nominated from outside the school (the local elite) could overwhelm the parents (the disadvantaged), plans were approved to change the composition to include only teachers and parents (in a ratio of 1:3). The parents were to be elected, thereby ensuring true beneficiary participation. The mandate of the SMCs was to increase enrolment; decrease and eliminate dropouts; improve the quality of education; check teacher absenteeism; purchase instructional materials; undertake repairs and maintenance; construct buildings for shelterless schools; purchase furniture; raise funds locally; manage school affairs, including finances; involve the community, particularly parents, in school activities; and collect school-based data.

Each of the SMCs had its own bank account and received a grant (of Rs. 1,500 for teaching supplies and Rs. 1,500 for repairs and maintenance per classroom per year) directly from the finance department. These accounts were operated by the president of the committee and one elected parent, thus ensuring transparency. At least two members from each of the SMCs were trained in the maintenance of accounts, and were given a manual for purchasing standardized furniture and instructional materials. The finance committee reported quarterly to the SMC on the utilization of funds, thereby ensuring accountability. Local procurement of goods and services ensured least cost, and committee supervision of work ensured adherence to quality and standards.

Because teacher attendance and performance was monitored by the SMC, the quality of teaching improved to some extent. The SMC often met monthly to discuss plans for the future and to review operations, thereby ensuring the continuity of true beneficiary participation. Most SMCs were also able to raise funds locally for improvements and supplementary reading and teaching materials. The major thrust for change was brought about because of the political will to implement changes that had been advocated for some time. However, just as plans were afoot to empower the SMCs with the authority to debit pay based on performance, the Punjab Teachers' Association filed a suit in the courts to have the SMCs declared illegal entities. They argued that SMCs were operating without legal cover and were, therefore, non-juridicial. The courts upheld this petition, and government since then has not redressed the problem.

Source: Ismail, McGarry, Davies, and Hassan (2000)

---

the implementation of the Orangi Pilot Project (OPP) in Karachi. These programmes propound the philosophy of community-based self-help. By encouraging savings to be diverted to income-generating activities, and providing access to supervised microcredit for further expansion and consolidation of livelihoods, they utilize the social capital available to the poorer segments of society. These NGO-operated social safety nets have reached such a level of success that partnerships between them and the public sector are beginning to develop. Examples include the link between the Habib Bank Ltd. (a public sector bank), and the OPP and NRSP, which respectively operate microcredit programmes in the urban heartland of Karachi's largest slum, Orangi, and in the rural areas of 13 districts. Attempts are also being made by the Pakistan Poverty Alleviation Fund and the new Microfinance Bank to bond with NGOs, either directly or through local government institutions, to fight poverty. Among the greatest advantages of these pro-poor alliances are an increase in cost-effectiveness and targeting efficiency, and a substantial reduction in the diversion of benefits to the undeserving.

The private sector can also play a significant role in partnership with the public sector in the revitalization of underutilized facilities. One such example is the partnership between a private medical college in the city of Abbottabad and a government district hospital in the city of Mansehra in NWFP, the benefits of which have largely favoured the poorer segments of society in terms of access to better curative health facilities **(see box 7.5)**. This example demonstrates that successful partnerships can evolve in the presence of synergy between the partners, strong leadership, shared objectives, successful coalition building, appropriate changes in the structure of governance, a proper legal framework, built-in safeguards, and outside support.

Another mechanism for improving the delivery of services is through the privatization of public facilities, particularly those from which the state is retreating as a consequence of redefining its role. Privatization could take the form of public-private partnerships, an outright sale, or the contracting-out of management to the private sector.

The Private Sector

The general perception is that the profit-oriented private sector caters largely to the upper-income end of the market and, therefore, is unlikely

---

BOX 7.5

A PUBLIC-PRIVATE PARTNERSHIP IN THE HEALTH SECTOR

The private sector partner is the Frontier Medical College (FMC), located in Abbottabad, a divisional headquarter in the province of NWFP. The public sector partner is the government of NWFP, which owns the District Headquarters Hospital (DHH) in Mansehra, located in close proximity to Abbottabad.

As specified in the legal agreement between the partners, the basic objective of the government of NWFP is to upgrade and improve the healthcare facilities at the DHH in Mansehra, while FMC desires clinical training facilities for its medical students at this hospital. The FMC is expected to pay a capitation fee of Rs. 50,000 per student per year for providing these facilities.

A number of safeguards have been built into the agreement related to the ownership of assets (new construction at the hospital financed out of the capitation fees), rights of beneficiaries, status of hospital employees, matching budgetary commitments by the government of NWFP, and establishment of a hospital fund. As part of the new governance structure to manage the partnership, a Hospital Management Board has been established with full operational autonomy and representation from both partners.

A *synergy* in the partnership has been created by benefits to both partners. Benefits to the DHH in Mansehra include greater access to development funds and enhancement in status as a teaching hospital. For FMC, benefits consist of lower start-up costs and immediate recognition of its degree by the Pakistan Medical and Dental Council.

The prime indicator of success is the completion of the new wing of the hospital, financed by the capitation fees paid by the FMC and matching funds from the government of NWFP. Also, clinical training of FMC students has commenced successfully at the hospital, which is now endowed with better facilities.

The lessons learned from this case study are that a successful partnership can evolve in the presence of synergy between partners, strong leadership, shared objectives, success in coalition building, appropriate changes in the governance structure, a proper legal framework, the building-in of safeguards, and outside support. Already, other public hospitals in Pakistan are seeking to replicate this model by searching for partners among private medical colleges.

Source: Pasha and Nasar (2000)

Successful partnerships can evolve in the presence of synergy between the partners.

to get involved in the provision of pro-poor services where the majority of consumers do not have the ability to pay. But in Pakistan, because of the failure of public services and a high willingness to pay for services such as primary education and curative health services–even by low-income households–the private sector has carved out an important and growing niche in the delivery of social services.

Today, private sector involvement in primary education is extensive, having increased rapidly during the last decade. As shown in **table 7.12**, almost half of the urban enrolment is in private schools, and private education is even emerging in the rural areas. What is striking is the significant penetration of private schools into low-income urban households. By now, over 30 per cent of children from poor households attend private schools. This testifies to the high willingness to pay for education, even though surveys reveal that at the lower end of the market private schools are only marginally better in quality than the typical public school.

The resort to privately-provided services is even more pronounced in the area of curative health. According to the PIHS, for example, private practitioners handle 63 per cent of the cases of diarrhoea among children in urban areas, and 60 per cent in rural areas. Also, with regard to childbirth, private facilities are used for over half of all cases of non-home deliveries.

Policy issues with regard to private sector involvement in social services relate primarily to regulation. There is a need to ensure at least a minimum quality of school instruction and medical care, especially where the clientele consists primarily of poor households. Also, in view of the vast and growing network of private schools, clinics and hospitals, possibilities exist for rationalizing the presence of public schools and hospitals in large cities. As mentioned earlier, many of these facilities could be contracted out to the private sector on the basis of a mutually beneficial public-private partnership. The resulting cost-savings could be diverted to other pro-poor services.

In conclusion, we have demonstrated in this chapter that the government retreated significantly from the expansion of pro-poor services during the 1990s (especially in the second half), primarily due to emerging fiscal constraints and changing priorities. This is possibly a major contributing factor to an increased incidence of poverty, and will limit the scope for implementation of a successful poverty reduction strategy in the long run. The SAP also appears to be in jeopardy, and will

TABLE 7.12

SHARE OF PRIVATE SCHOOLS IN PRIMARY ENROLMENT (%)

Income Quintile	Rural Areas	Urban Areas	Total
First	7	26	13
Second	7	35	16
Third	6	45	19
Fourth	12	54	26
Fifth	20	75	38
Total	**10**	**47**	**22**

Source: PIHS (1996-97)

Female schooling, a major poverty reducing factor must be the nation's priority.

require substantial revamping through better prioritization, along with an emphasis on cost-effectiveness and institutional reform.

We believe that a reversal of policy, in order to promote greater coverage of pro-poor services, will have to be a key element in the national poverty reduction strategy. For this, the federal government must commit itself to allocating 20 per cent of total public expenditure to social services, and also make adequate financial arrangements, through transfers to sub-national governments, to ensure the attainment of this target. Simultaneously, development allocations to basic economic services, such as village electrification and farm-to-market roads, will have to be increased, and an appropriate environment will have to be created for greater participation of NGOs and the private sector in the struggle against poverty, especially through the formation of public-private partnerships.

The federal government must commit itself to allocating 20 per cent of total public expenditure to social services.

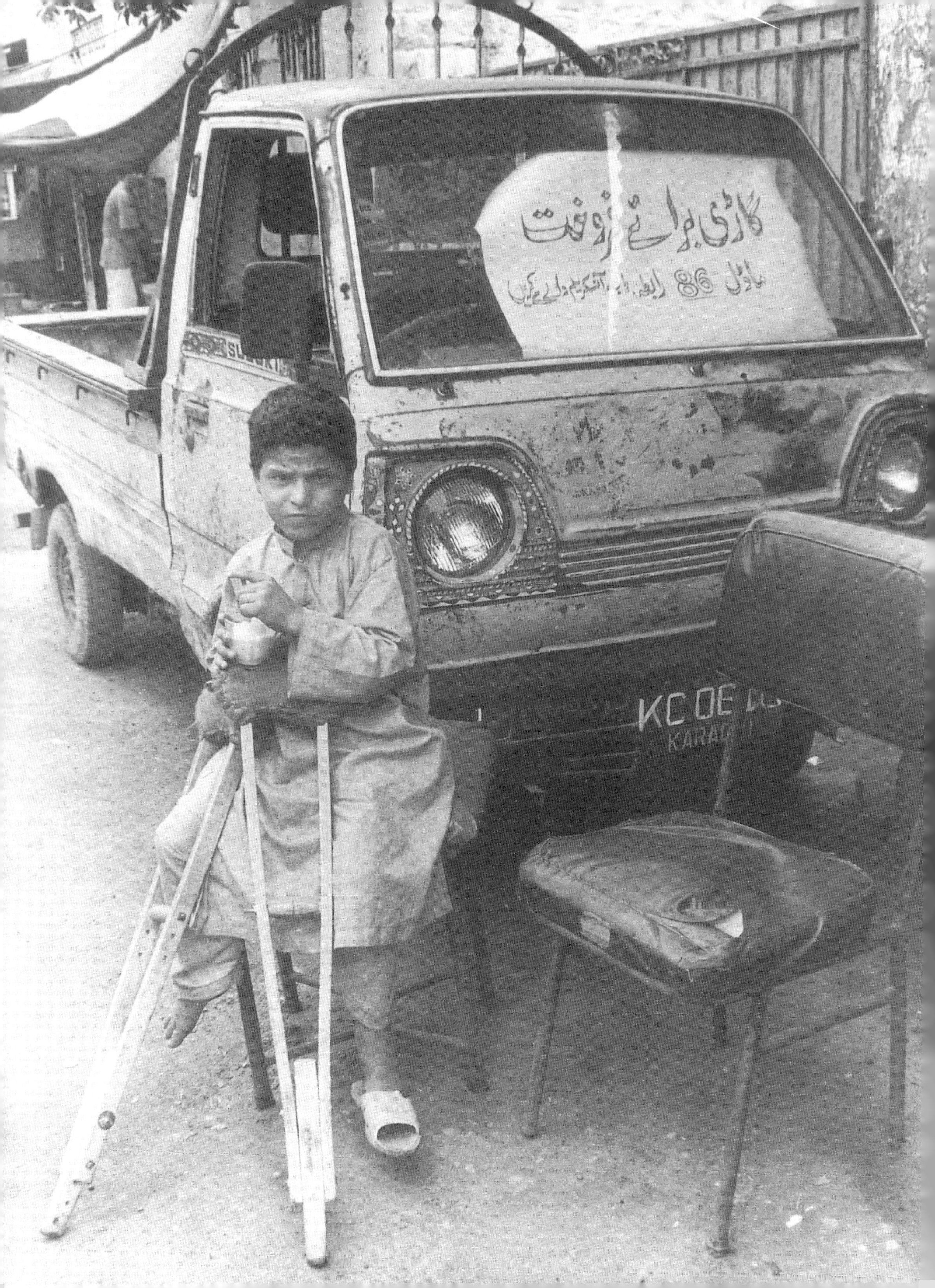
گاڑی برائے فروخت

TARGETING THE POOR

CHAPTER 8

"The development of adequate social safety nets will be a natural complement, but not a substitute, to the other elements of the poverty reduction strategy."

TARGETING THE POOR

The previous chapters have highlighted the grim prospects for poverty in Pakistan. We have already described the key elements of the poverty reduction strategy, including an aggregate demand stimulus; the supply-side incentivization of particular sectors to promote pro-poor growth; improvements in governance to make state institutions more responsive to the needs of the poor; economic reforms to change public expenditure priorities in favour of the poor; reforms to make the tax system more productive and progressive; empowerment of the poor through a redistribution of assets, especially agricultural land; and greater access to basic services.

Even so, there will continue to be large pockets of hard-core poverty that cannot be effectively targeted through the above initiatives. Therefore, the development of adequate social safety nets will be a natural complement, but not a substitute, to the other elements of the poverty reduction strategy.

The present military government has articulated a poverty reduction strategy for the first time. This was initially outlined in the Economic Revival Plan, announced by the Chief Executive on December 15, 1999, and subsequently presented in more operational terms in the federal budget for 2000-01. Due recognition must be given to the government for beginning to address the problem of growing poverty in Pakistan. The objective of this chapter is to evaluate the social safety net component of the government's poverty alleviation strategy.

We begin this chapter by describing possible social safety nets. We then proceed to describe and evaluate the interventions proposed by the government, deriving the likely impact of the government's efforts and suggesting ways in which these efforts can be strengthened. Finally, the potential role that donors can play in supporting the national poverty reduction strategy is discussed.

TYPES OF SOCIAL SAFETY NETS

To be effective, social safety nets must be designed on the basis of an understanding of the extent and nature of poverty. They must respond to the needs of those most affected by the prevailing economic conditions. As such, there are generally at least three types of programmes. The first is long-term financial assistance to those who are more or less permanently unable to provide for themselves through work; that is, those who are chronically poor. This group includes such people as the handicapped and disabled, orphans, and widows. The second type of programme is designed for those who are able to work, but whose incomes are low and irregular. The goal here is to compensate for low income, and ensure adequate consumption, during slack seasons.

Of great importance in Pakistan's current context is a third type of programme. It is for people who are normally capable of earning adequate incomes, but who are temporarily unable to earn a living because of shocks or downturns in the economy (e.g., Pakistan's prevailing

The government's poverty alleviation strategy must adequately provide for the most vulnerable.

recession). Recent estimates **(see chapter 4)** are that over 40 per cent of new entrants to the labour force, including those with relatively high levels of education, are unemployed even after almost a year of job searching. These programmes provide short-term assistance (e.g., unemployment benefits), promote employment through public works programmes, and offer microcredit for income generation.

Transfers to people living in poverty can take various forms. *Cash transfers* are the traditional form of support. They include private, charitable contributions, and are considered to be a fairly efficient transfer method because they do not distort consumption or production choices. However, the need for a means test, which has targeting problems and the scope for leakage (i.e., benefits being pre-empted by higher income groups), makes them difficult to administer by governments. They also tend to create a state of permanent dependence on the part of the beneficiaries.

In-kind transfers are designed primarily to provide basic food security to poor households. The transfer mechanisms for in-kind transfers include quantity rationing (along with a price subsidy), food stamps, and food for work. If well designed, in-kind transfers can be an effective equivalent to cash transfers, but are usually more complex to administer. Related to these are generalized price subsidies for food items or for other basic commodities and services. The disadvantage of in-kind transfers is that they can distort consumption choices and do not specifically target poor people. They are, however, easy to administer.

In Pakistan, the principal form of cash transfers to the poor is through the publicly administered *Zakat* system (along with private charitable contributions). The *Ushr* system is also designed to subsidize poor people, primarily those in rural areas, but it has floundered due to inadequate collections. Cash transfers have more recently acquired importance by the launching of the cash *Atta* (wheat flour) Subsidy

Scheme (ASS) through the *Bait-ul-Maal* (which provides assistance to those in need who are not covered by *Zakat*, e.g., minorities). Another traditional social safety net has been the generalized wheat subsidy, a primary source of expenditure by both federal and provincial governments. However, it has been criticized for problems of targeting and leakages, and has largely been phased out.

Within the realm of social security, the federal government operates an employees' old age benefits insurance scheme through a semi-autonomous institution, the Employees' Old Age Benefits Institution (EOBI). The coverage of workers under this scheme remains limited. There are, however, proposals for more elaborate private pension schemes with matching employer contributions and tax breaks by government. The House Building Finance Corporation (HBFC) continues to operate a subsidized housing finance scheme but it, too, has problems. It has been accused of having an urban and middle class bias, loans are not being paid back, and in recent years, access to funding has become a serious problem.

Ambitious microcredit schemes for self-employment, by commercial banks and other institutions such as the Small Business Finance Corporation (SBFC) and the Pakistan Poverty Alleviation Fund (PPAF), have also been launched. This is considered pivotal in the creation of opportunities, especially for educated youth at a time when employment prospects have significantly worsened. However, experience with such schemes (such as the Yellow Cab scheme) has not been encouraging because of poor targeting and high default rates in the repayment of loans. Perhaps the largest operational microcredit scheme is the joint venture of the commercial bank, Habib Bank (HBL), and a large non-governmental organization, the National Rural Support Programme (NRSP). HBL provides the bulk credit line and NRSP undertakes retail lending operations.

An overall appraisal of social safety nets in Pakistan demonstrates the low priority that the government has historically assigned to direct interventions for poverty alleviation. Most schemes have weak institutional structures. Their funding is uncertain, their targeting inefficient, and their coverage very limited. Even the current low level of transfers is proving to be unsustainable in the face of fiscal constraints and in view of the Supreme Court judgement against compulsory deductions of *Zakat*. The limited coverage of social safety nets at least partly explains the growing incidence of poverty in the country.

The government has announced that it will focus on four direct anti-poverty interventions: the Integrated Small Public Works Programme (ISPWP), the Food Support Programme, establishment of a new microfinance bank, and improvements in the *Zakat* system. The crucial question is: Do these initiatives have the appropriate scale, design features and implementation modalities to have a large enough impact on poverty?

Appraisal of social safety nets in Pakistan demonstrates the low priority that the government has historically assigned to direct interventions for poverty alleviation.

PUBLIC WORKS PROGRAMME

The government has announced a budgetary allocation of Rs. 21.2 billion in 2000-01 for the ISPWP, to be implemented largely by the provincial governments. It aims to create employment and income-generating activities for both the rural and urban populations, in addition to improving their living conditions. Local communities will also be involved in the identification of schemes to be funded under the

Labour will need to be utilized effectively to build infrastructure for increased growth.

programme. A targeting mechanism has been evolved that is meant to "allow greater application of funds to areas facing extreme backwardness." The army monitoring system will act as a third-party audit to ensure the maximum and efficient utilization of funds.

Of the 5,500 projects being undertaken this year, there are 1,600 projects involving farm-to-market roads, 1,600 water supply projects, 1,200 projects for the construction, renovation and expansion of schools, 150 electrification projects, and 40 health projects. All of these projects will be supervised by the civil district administration, army monitoring teams, and the local people. It is estimated that 0.5 million people will gain employment next year through the ISPWP.

Internationally, public works programmes have been an important *counter-cyclical* intervention in both developed and developing countries. During the Great Depression (in the 1930s), developed countries implemented such programmes; recently, many developing countries have adopted public works programmes in one form or another. They have acquired the status of a key social safety net in many developing countries, having conferred direct transfer and/or stabilization benefits to the poor. At the same time, they use people's labour to build infrastructure for growth, thereby indirectly influencing poverty levels, as well.

The central issues in the design and management of a public works programme are figuring out how to direct the programme specifically to the poor, in order to increase both transfer and stabilization benefits; identifying what the institutional arrangements for cost-effective delivery should be; and determining how the secondary benefits can be maximized.

The best way to ensure that the programme reaches the poor is to build in appropriate self-selection features **(see box 8.1)**. This can be achieved by maintaining programme wages at a lower level than the ruling market wage for unskilled labour. This practice not only helps keep costs down, but ensures that the non-poor and the already-employed are kept out of the programme. Moreover, in addition to keeping wages lower than market levels, the programme could have other features that restrict participation to only the poor and the unemployed. For example, payment

Public works programmes use people's labour to build infrastructure for growth, thereby indirectly influencing poverty levels, as well.

BOX 8.1

PUBLIC WORKS IN PRACTICE

In 1987, the outreach of Chile's public works programme was vast, covering almost 13 per cent of the labour force with the creation of 40-45 million person days of employment. The programme wage was maintained at approximately 70 per cent of the minimum wage, facilitating self-targeting for the poor. Although the finances were provided by the central government, the work was organized by municipalities in a decentralized way. Even though the programme had desirable features, it suffered from some weaknesses (e.g., absenteeism from work was high, at 12 per cent). This weakness could have been prevented, however, by better supervision or by building appropriate incentives into the programme design.

A renowned state-run programme in **India** is the Maharashtra Employment Guarantee Scheme (MEGS). The resources for this programme were raised by an employment tax, supplemented by additional funds from the state budget. Until 1988, it provided a guarantee of employment to all those who needed it–within a 5 km radius from the place of residence, and at the going market wage. The emphasis was on much-needed rural and agricultural infrastructure. The programme's effectiveness as a guarantor of employment was considerably eroded after 1988, when the programme wage was raised to reach the (high) level of the minimum wage. A high wage meant fewer person days of employment, which in turn led to a rationing of jobs. In spite of this, MEGS remains a good example of how to target benefits to the poor, having created 100-180 million person days of employment.

Source: Datt and Ravallion (1992)

---

of 50 per cent of wages in-kind (e.g., food) may attract more women than men (as it did in Zambia and Lesotho).

In most programmes, wages account for between 30 and 60 per cent of total programme costs. While a higher share is desirable, in that greater transfer benefits would then be conferred directly on the poor, many factors determine this ratio–including the nature of the assets to be created, the duration and timing of the work, and the availability of technically and economically feasible labour-based production techniques. For most road construction activities, for example, wages account for 40 to 50 per cent of total costs.

The delivery mechanism used to carry out the programme is important in order to ensure cost-effectiveness, efficiency, and proper targeting. Essentially, there are three basic types of delivery mechanisms for carrying out public works in developing countries. These are either direct execution by line departments, themselves (in which public agencies supervize, manage, and control machines and labour), or through registered and pre-qualified contractors, or through small, local petty contractors. The issue of what mechanism should be adopted is important considering the level of corruption, weak governance and political intervention in the use of public funds.

Public works programmes are highly visible, which means that they are especially susceptible to political influence. Political pressure can affect the wage rate offered by such programmes, the choice and location of projects, and the programme size. Public works are often manipulated for electoral purposes, there being overwhelming evidence that new public works programmes have been introduced just prior to elections.

A number of interest groups are usually involved in the design and execution of public works programmes: politicians and bureaucrats, who influence the size and design of the programme; the poor, who benefit from the programme; and politically important groups, who may or may not benefit from the programme (e.g., private contractors, large farmers). The interests of these groups are often in conflict, affecting the programme's design and sustainability (e.g., farm hands demanding

Public expenditure needs to be concentrated on the rehabilitation of facilities that are for the poor.

higher wages when land owners want lower wages can complicate the politics of implementing a rural employment programme). These group conflicts may result in the inefficient allocation of resources. Interagency politics and competition for resources might result in institutional support being given to inefficient programmes, ultimately decreasing the benefit for the target group.

If public works programmes are sectorally concentrated on the development or rehabilitation of facilities that are pro-poor (e.g., agricultural land, reforestation, primary schools, or rural dispensaries), then the secondary benefits from the assets that are created can also contribute to raising the living standards of the poor. However, since these schemes usually produce economic assets such as roads, they may have significant second-round effects on income inequality and growth. It is claimed that in Maharashtra, India, a disproportionate share of the secondary benefits has benefited the rural rich, and that this has been an important factor in achieving political support for the employment-generation scheme. Such a programme may also result in wages being multiplied/intensified (especially if construction activities overlap with peak periods of agricultural demand), ultimately having an adverse affect on agricultural production.

Whether stabilization benefits successfully even out the income of the poor depends very much on the timing of the programme. For instance, if the timing of a programme coincides with the agricultural slack season, when the demand for labour is low, then workers who would otherwise be temporarily unemployed are most likely to gain from the resulting income stabilization. Such income stabilization pre-empts acute distress and rising indebtedness, thereby reducing distress-selling of productive assets like land.

The design features of the programme can also be used to minimize transaction costs to the poor. Locating a project close to where the poor live, for example, will minimize transportation costs. Also, if the implementing agency is prone to corruption and leakages, the poor who participate in the programme may have to pay part of their wages to officials, contractors, or politicians, or incur other transaction costs—all of which may reduce the transfer of benefits from the programme. As such, transparency in delivery and project design must be ensured in order to minimize transaction costs within the programme.

Overall, the following features are important for maximizing the poverty alleviating impact of a public works programme:

- The wage rate should be set at a level that is lower than the prevailing market wage, to ensure self-selection among unskilled manual labour.
- Restriction on eligibility should be avoided; in fact, a worker's willingness to work at a lower wage rate should be the only requirement for eligibility.
- The programme should target areas with a heavy concentration of people living in a state of poverty. To this end, a credible poverty map should be prepared for efficient and effective targeting. The poverty map can be developed with the help of household surveys and the mapping of infrastructure and other facilities.
- The labour intensity (i.e., wages as a percentage of total costs) should be as high as possible.
- Public works programmes in rural areas should be synchronized with the timing of agriculturally slack seasons.
- In order to encourage female participation, appropriate forms of wages are important. Women can benefit from piece-rate or task-based wages; sometimes wages in the form of food have attracted more women to work sites. Also, the provision of childcare or preschool services can increase the participation of women.
- Transaction costs to the poor should be kept to a minimum. One important way of accomplishing this is by locating project sites close to the villages or slum areas where the project participants live.
- Appropriate mediation by NGOs should be ensured, in order to protect the rights of the poor and to ensure a degree of transparency and accountability.

Based on the above requirements for the success of public works programmes, a number of problems can be identified with the design features and implementation modalities of the Integrated Small Public Works Programme. First, although the government has announced a budgetary allocation of Rs. 21 billion for ISPWP, this funding appears to have been largely diverted from allocations to other, related sectors, such as rural development, the *Tameer-e-Watan* programme, and physical planning and housing. As such, it is not clear to what extent additional resources are actually being committed, over and above the level of previous years, for the purpose of employment generation. With wages constituting about 30 per cent of costs, and a wage rate of Rs. 100 per day, ISPWP will generate about 60 million person days of employment. But much of this employment would have been created anyway through the execution of the sectoral programmes from which ISPWP has been carved out. Also, since the major part of the ISPWP is to be implemented by the provincial governments, it is not clear how they will find the additional resources to finance this programme.

Second, the issue of budgetary resources aside, it is not yet clear whether the institutional framework for implementation has been changed to ensure local involvement in the programme design (e.g., planning, design, site selection) in order to ensure proper targeting, minimization of leakages, cost-effectiveness, and increased use of labour. Details are not yet available. Third, one must ask whether spatial targeting is a feature of the programme. Given the regional differences in the incidence of

Women and children are worst affected by proverty. Has the government adequately focussed on them?

poverty, will the distribution of scarce funds be sensitive to considerations of relative backwardness?

Besides this, there is the issue of determining the wage rate. The daily wage set by the government is Rs. 100 per day. In general, the prevailing market wage rate is significantly lower than this, especially in the rural areas. This negates the programme's key feature of automatic self-selection, enhances the probability of participation by the non-poor and already-employed workers, and increases the susceptibility of the scheme to political/vested group interference. Finally, the programme is biased in favour of men. The participation of women is likely to be severely constrained given the nature of the programme activities and cultural practices.

In conclusion, even though ISPWP appears to have desirable objectives, some of the key features of a good public works programme are either missing or not adequately addressed. As discussed above, the design features, especially the wage rate, the timing of activities, the nature of the implementing agencies, and the institutional framework, will determine the programme's efficacy as an anti-poverty intervention. Doubts remain about the amount of extra employment created by the programme.

MICROFINANCE

A key component of the government's poverty alleviation strategy is microfinance for the poor. This is reflected in the recent establishment of a new microfinance bank. The Microfinance Bank (MFB), named the *Khushali* Bank, has been established under the Microfinance Bank Ordinance of 2000. The objective of this institution, according to the ordinance, is "to mobilize funds and to provide sustainable microfinance services to poor persons, particularly poor women, in order to mitigate against poverty and promote social welfare and economic justice through community building and social mobilization."

Poor persons have been defined in the ordinance as those whose

A key component of the government's poverty alleviation strategy is microfinance for the poor.

Will any secondary benefits filter out to this generation of future hopefuls?

total income during a year is less than the minimum taxable limit set for income tax. The MFB has the following key functions:

- to provide credit, with or without collateral security, in cash or in kind, for such terms and subject to such conditions as may be prescribed, to poor persons for all types of economic activities, including housing;
- to accept cash deposits;
- to invest in shares of any corporate body whose objective is to provide microfinance services to poor persons;
- to borrow and raise money, and open bank accounts;
- to mobilize and provide financial and technical assistance and training to microfinance institutions (MFIs).

The MFB shall not be deemed to be a banking company for the purposes of the Banking Companies Ordinance of 1962.

The authorized capital of the MFB shall be Rs. 5 billion, to be subscribed to by such banking companies, financial, and other institutions as the State Bank of Pakistan (SBP) may determine. A member who has subscribed to the capital of the MFB shall be free to sell his/her share after a period of five years from the date of subscription, provided the intending buyer has received prior approval from the SBP.

The MFB's Board of Directors will consist of a minimum of seven directors, as determined by the SBP, at least two of whom will be women. The directors shall be elected by the members and will, to the extent possible, be persons having knowledge and experience in the fields of banking, microfinance and poverty alleviation. The President shall be the Chief Executive of the MFB, and shall serve for a period of three years, extendable for another three years by the SBP.

The MFB shall create and maintain a reserve fund to be called the General Reserve Fund, to which shall be credited an amount which is not less than 20 per cent of its net annual profit. The MFB shall at all times maintain liquid assets at a level determined by the SBP. It shall also maintain, by way of a cash reserve in a current account opened with the

SBP, a sum equivalent to not less than 5 per cent of its time and demand liabilities.

An important provision under the ordinance is that the MFB shall not, for such a time period as the federal government may specify, be liable to pay taxes on its income, profits or gains provided that the income subject to tax exemptions is used as a capital investment. The profits, if any, and any other income of the MFB, shall not be used to pay any dividends to the members, but shall be used to promote the objectives of the MFB.

An interview with the President of the MFB has revealed the following:

- the bank will make both individual and group loans;
- the loan size will range from Rs. 3,000 to Rs. 30,000;
- the interest rate will range from 18 to 20 per cent, similar to the NRSP scheme;
- community mobilization for group loans will be undertaken by the partner organization, NRSP;
- special microfinance counters will be established in the bank branches of government-owned banks;
- the first phase of the MFB will start in October 2000 as a pilot project in four districts, one in each province.

The MFB recently signed a loan agreement for US$150 million with the Asian Development Bank, under the proposed Microfinance Sector Development Programme (MSDP).

The government's effort in microfinance follows many successful experiments worldwide, such as the Grameen Bank in Bangladesh. In practice, as shown in **table 8.1**, a range of practices has been adopted by different major microfinance institutions. Most engage in retail lending, and in some cases, like the Grameen Bank, the clientele exceeds 2 million. Loan sizes are generally small, at less than US$200, although

TABLE 8.1

CHARACTERISTICS OF SELECTED LEADING MICROFINANCE PROGRAMMES

	Grameen Bank, Bangladesh	Banco-Sol, Bolivia	Bank Rakyat, Indonesia	Badan Kredit Desa, Indonesia
Membership (000)	2400	82	2000	766
Average Loan Balance (US$)	134	909	1007	71
Typical Loan Term (months)	12	4-12	3-24	3
Group Lending Contracts	yes	yes	no	no
Collateral Required	no	no	yes	no
Voluntary Savings Emphasized	no	yes	yes	no
Progressive Lending	yes	yes	yes	yes
Regular Repayment Schedules	weekly	flexible	flexible	flexible
Target Clients for Lending	poor	non-poor	non-poor	poor
Currently Financially Sustainable	no	yes	yes	yes
Nominal Interest Rate on Loans (% per year)	20	47-50	32-43	55

Source: Murdoch (1999)

there are notable exceptions like the Banco-Sol, in Bolivia, and the Bank Rakyat, in Indonesia, where the average loan size approaches US$1,000. Most MFIs lend on a short-term basis with a maximum tenure of up to 24 months. Both individual and group lending contracts are possible, with the Grameen Bank, in particular, relying on the latter approach. Most MFIs do not require physical collateral, although the Bank Rakyat of Indonesia does, probably because of relatively large loan amounts.

Some MFIs emphasize voluntary savings, while others, like the Grameen Bank, do not. The common practice is to engage in progressive lending, with successively larger loans as the borrower builds up a successful credit history. Repayment schedules can be flexible, although the Grameen Bank insists on weekly payments to maintain discipline on the part of the borrower. Some MFIs only target the poor, while in other cases the non-poor also have access.

The important point to note, however, is that some MFIs, including the Grameen Bank, are not sufficiently financially sustainable to be able to access market-based sources of funding. Rather, reliance is frequently placed on subsidized credit lines, including those established by foreign donors. This lack of financial sustainability exists despite the relatively high interest rates charged on loans. The Grameen Bank, for instance, charges 20 per cent, while in some MFIs the annual interest rate even exceeds 50 per cent. Such high interest rates are a reflection of the relatively high overhead costs associated with managing loans, including the costs of social mobilization and preparation of the communities. Most MFIs are successful in keeping default rates low, however, even in the presence of high interest rates.

What are the advantages of microfinance? First, group-based lending reduces the transaction cost of credit delivery and mitigates problems of adverse selection. Also, peer monitoring within the group reduces the risk of default and moral hazard. For instance, in group lending, it is not the individual, but the community who is responsible for repayment of the loan. An incentive for all members to oblige is that, if a member defaults, the whole group's creditworthiness is adversely affected.

Second, microcredit schemes enable substitution of physical collateral. Unlike conventional banks, physical collateral is often substituted with social collateral, or the pledge of a fixed proportion of the loan as collateral to the organization.

Third, microfinance provides dynamic incentives. To secure high repayment rates, microfinancing programmes begin by lending small amounts and then increase the loan size upon satisfactory repayment. The repetitive nature of the interaction, and the threat of cutting off a loan in the case of default, are used to overcome problems of asymmetric information, and improve lending efficiency. In this way, these incentives motivate a high recovery rate. The recovery rate for the Grameen Bank, for example, is over 90 per cent.

Fourth, the cost of borrowing is lower for the clients of microfinance schemes because no physical collateral or other requirements are involved in the loan procedure. Similarly, it is believed that the rate of interest paid by the borrower in these schemes is lower than the interest rate charged by local moneylenders.

However, microfinancing is not without shortcomings. International evidence suggests that microfinancing is probably not well suited to all segments of the poor. Microfinance schemes are limited with regard to targeting efficiency, financial and economic sustainability, and potential for growth in the economy. Even the minimal collateral requirements

Outside the formal economy, workers in hazardous home-based industries are largely excluded from the formal credit system.

potentially exclude the poorest from the scheme. In Bangladesh, for example, only one fourth of all microfinance clients are among the *hard-core poor*. The main reason for this is that the poorest people tend to be less visible and very shy, and often live outside the mainstream economy. The recently released UNDP report (2000) claims that "the hard-core poor, having few assets, are reluctant to take on the risks of credit, and when they do, it is usually for emergencies and consumption, not for production."

According to Murdoch (1999),
> the promise of microfinance should be kept in context. Even in the best of circumstances, credit from microfinance programmes helps fund self-employment activities that most often supplement income for borrowers rather than drive fundamental shifts in employment patterns. It rarely generates new jobs for others, and success has been especially limited in regions with highly seasonal income patterns and low population densities. The best evidence to date suggests that making a real dent on poverty rates will require increasing overall levels of economic growth and employment generation. Microfinance may be able to help some households take advantage of those processes, but nothing so far suggests that it will drive them.

The experience of microfinancing in Pakistan is not that different from other countries. It is generally recognized that the present microfinancing framework is characterized by low coverage (an inability to reach the poor), targeting inefficiency (the poorest are left out), inadequacy of support (insufficient loan sizes), a low degree of ease of access (there are problems in joining the community organization), and lack of self-financing (dependence on donors). For instance, the largest microfinance scheme in Pakistan (NRSP), with total disbursements of Rs. 2 billion, covers only 52,000 borrowers **(see box 8.2)**.

To examine the effectiveness of microfinancing in Pakistan, and to get borrowers' views regarding access, problems, and the impact of

Credit from microfinance programmes helps fund self-employment activities that most often supplement income for borrowers rather than drive fundamental shifts in employment patterns.

> ### BOX 8.2
>
> ### HBL-NRSP: A KEY MICROCREDIT INITIATIVE
>
> The National Rural Support Programme (NRSP) was registered in November 1991 as a non-profit public company under the Companies Ordinance of 1984. Replicating the successful programmes of the Aga Khan Rural Support Programme (AKRSP) in the northern areas, and the rural microcredit programmes of the Grameen Bank, it operates in 13 rural areas within Pakistan.
>
> The programme aims to reduce poverty among small farmers and landless labourers through microfinancing with community participation. The Government of Pakistan has provided a Rs. 500 million grant to set up an endowment fund and, since July 1997, NRSP has obtained access to a credit-line facility with the Habib Bank Limited (HBL).
>
> NRSP's partnership with HBL is a breakthrough in the rural microcredit history of Pakistan. In less than a year and a half, credit disbursement has increased from Rs. 0.1 billion to almost Rs. 2.0 billion, and the number of borrowers has gone up from 23,000 to 52,000, representing almost 4,000 community organizations.
>
> Peer pressure and social reputation of the individual and the community organization are effectively used as a collateral tool. Even though the annual rate of interest is 18 to 20 per cent, the recovery rate is high. This has been achieved by developing an effective credit disbursement procedure.
>
> The initiative has had a positive impact on development (given its focus on employment and income generation through crop and livstock activities in agriculture). It has a degree of financial sustainability (because a minimum savings contribution of 25% is required), and positive incentive effects (it encourages saving, as well as greater community organization and participation). However, while its targeting efficiency (ability to reach the poor) is high, the mandatory requirement that contributions be matched with savings results in the poorest communities being precluded. Also, given the small number of borrowers, the degree of programme coverage is still limited.

microfinancing, SPDC conducted focus group discussions with recipients of the two leading schemes, NRSP and the Orangi Pilot Project (OPP). The former is rural-based, while the latter involves microfinancing in urban squatter settlements in Karachi. Seven group discussions were conducted among the former (covering Mirpurkhas and Badin, in Sindh, and Rawalpindi in Punjab), and four group discussions (two specifically for women) were conducted among the latter. Detailed interviews were also conducted, from which case studies were developed. The key findings are as follows:

- The programmes are inefficient in terms of targeting the poorest households, since no mechanism is available for identifying the poor, and the poorest are restricted from joining the borrowing communities because of the perception that they are a higher risk.
- Access to credit is denied if a person has no repayment capacity, implying that the neediest are not eligible for loans.
- Although access to credit for women is encouraged, cultural practices impede their involvement and so women generally do not borrow.
- To the extent that women get access to credit, there is improvement in their status within the household.
- The programmes are inadequate due to small loan sizes, which are insufficient to fulfil the minimum cash requirements for cultivation, livestock or business.
- Borrowers are compelled to repay the loans within a very short time period, especially in the case of urban micro-entrepreneurs. This repayment schedule creates problems, such as the need to sell assets, or to take out further loans for repayment.
- The mark-up rates are higher than for formal sector loans, but lower than in informal borrowing.
- There is no organizational mechanism to verify whether a loan is used for the stated purpose, particularly in the urban areas.

- The savings mechanism is not very strong, and the microcredit programmes are not working as real financial intermediaries.
- Technical guidance and assistance from microcredit programmes is either insufficient or non-existent.
- The preference for lending to existing borrowers encourages dependence on the loans.
- There is no marketing assistance for selling off the output of the funded enterprise.
- In general, borrowers perceive positive changes in terms of income-generating activities, improved cash flows, and lower dependence on informal money lenders.

The first government microfinance initiative was the Pakistan Poverty Alleviation Fund (PPAF), which was established in 1997 under the Companies Ordinance of 1984. A key element of PPAF's strategy is its role as a small, decentralized organization that reaches out to the poor mainly through partner organizations (POs). Besides offering bulk credit to POs for onward lending to the poor, PPAF also supports the development of small-scale community infrastructure and capacity building within local communities.

The PPAF governance structure includes a general body, with three fourths of its members representing civil society and one fourth from government. There is also a twelve-member Board of Directors, including eight members representing civil society and three from government. The fund's Chief Executive is the twelfth member. All directors are selected from the general body.

PPAF's partner organizations are limited to making loans of between Rs. 700 and Rs. 35,000. The rate of interest charged by POs is to be based on market principles, while the fund charges 7 per cent interest to the POs. The main eligibility criteria for POs are a sound track record, transparent financial and management systems, and gender sensitivity. The fund received Rs. 100 million in initial equity from the federal government, and is expecting an additional grant of Rs. 400 million, as well as US$100 million from the World Bank and other donors, for establishing a credit line. The fund has received 300 applications since its inception, of which 62 were shortlisted and 11 approved. To date, 6 NGOs have been selected as POs, with a total allocation of about Rs. 500 million. These include the Aga Khan Rural Support Programme (AKRSP), the National Rural Support Programme (NRSP), the Kashif Foundation, the Taraqee Trust, the Strengthening Participatory Organization (SPO), and the Family Planning Association of Pakistan (FPAP).

A comparison of the characteristics of PPAF and the Khushali Bank (i.e., the Microfinance Bank) highlights their key similarities as well as significant differences **(see table 8.2)**. Both have the mandate to reduce poverty through microcredit. Both focus on rural areas, and lend money to finance income-generating activities, infrastructure development, and institutional capacity building. The main financiers in both cases are multilateral donor agencies. The World Bank is to provide funding for PPAF, while Khushali Bank is to have a line of credit from the Asian Development Bank. Also, their key partner organization is the same: the NRSP.

The major difference between the two initiatives is the nature of lending. While PPAF is essentially a wholesale lender, the Khushali Bank focuses on retail lending. The former lends to NGOs (referred to as partner organizations [POs]), who then lend to individuals and groups within the communities. The loan collateral and responsibility for repayment therefore belong to the PO and the community.

TABLE		8.2

KEY CHARACTERISTICS OF PPAF AND KHUSHALI (MICROFINANCE) BANK

	PPAF	Bank (KB)
Regional Focus	Mostly rural	Mostly rural
Programme Components		
Microcredit	✔	✔
Infrastructure Development	✔	✔
Institutional Capacity Building	✔	✔
Level of Lending	Wholesale (to POs/NGOs)	Retail (to individuals)
Loan Collateral	PO's reputation/ physical[a]	Social/physical[c] (individual's reputation)
Nominal Interest Rate (per year)	6-8%	18-20%
Typical Loan Term	12 months	6 to 12 months
Frequency of Disbursement	Quarterly	Lump sum
Progressive Lending	Yes	Yes
Voluntary Saving Encouraged	Yes	Yes
Gender Focus	Yes[b]	Yes
Main Financier	Multilateral donor agency (WB)	Multilateral donor agency (ADB)
Major Collaborator/Partner	NRSP	NRSP

[a] Property, if any, owned by PO
[b] Preference for female POs and borrowers
[c] One fourth of the loan amount

The Khushali Bank has a number of advantages. First, it is likely to obtain cheap (perhaps forced) equity for commencing operations from Pakistani commercial banks. As per the ordinance, the Bank is not under any obligation to pay dividends to its members (the shareholders). Second, it has the major advantage of enjoying complete tax exemption on its income, profits, or gains, and can use these savings to increase its capitalization. Third, the Bank is exempt from the Banking Companies Ordinance of 1962, and is therefore not required to follow the normal reserve requirements, nor SBP's prudential regulations. Fourth, the Bank has been promised a large and subsidized line of credit from the Asian Development Bank. Fifth, the Bank has already been able to develop a partnership with NRSP which, as pointed out, has substantial experience organizing group-based borrowing among communities in Pakistan. Sixth, the Bank is being provided with specialized institutional support from the nationalized commercial banks, in the form of access to their extensive network of branches where microfinance counters can be set up at low cost.

This combination of favourable factors represents a unique example in the Pakistani setting. The fact that tax laws, regulations, and the institutional framework have been consciously oriented towards supporting a pro-poor initiative testifies to the government's and donors' commitment to poverty reduction in Pakistan. With such a head start, the general expectation is that the Khushali Bank will quickly make inroads into the field of microfinance, and become a major player in the market over the next few years.

The general expectation is that the Khushali Bank will quickly make inroads into the field of microfinance.

FOOD SUPPORT PROGRAMME

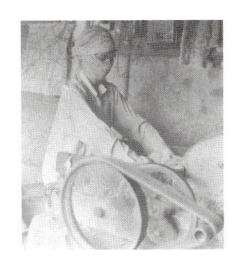

The Food Support Programme (FSP) has been granted Rs. 2.5 billion in the 2000-01 federal budgetary allocations, and is anticipated to benefit an estimated 1.2 million people. The objective is to target households whose income is Rs. 2,000 per month or less. Government employees and those engaged with semi-autonomous organizations are not included in this target group. Furthermore, households already receiving the *guzara* allowance under the *Zakat* system are also not eligible for this programme.

The federal government will administer the FSP. *Bait-ul-Maal* offices have been directed to ensure that at least 3 per cent of the total allocation is reserved for minority families, while women will be given *preference*. At the district level, FSP steering committees will be constituted, each committee comprising a deputy commissioner, a *Bait-ul-Maal* district in charge, a social welfare assistant director, a district chief postmaster, a district *Zakat* and *Ushr* chairperson, and a representative of minority communities. Army monitoring teams will independently scrutinize the selection of beneficiaries, as per the lists prepared by the deputy commissioners, and also oversee disbursement of the cash subsidies.

Under the programme, a cash subsidy of Rs. 2,000 per year will be given to the listed people, in biannual installments. Application is free of charge, and limited to one person per family. Applicants are asked to enclose a copy of their national identity card with their completed application forms. The forms must then be attested to by the chairperson or a member of a local *Zakat* committee, or a retired or in-service army or government official. The approved beneficiaries will be asked to open accounts with a minimum of Rs. 5 at their nearest post office, through which their cash subsidies will subsequently be made available.

The launch of the Food Support Programme demonstrates clear recognition by the government of the need to provide basic food security to poor households. The timing of the launch coincides with the significant increase in the price of wheat flour, which occurred following the 25 per cent increase in the procurement/issue prices of wheat. For most poor households, wheat flour is the staple food and the primary source of calories. A rise in the price of this food item therefore has a major impact on the cost of living. The cash subsidy is expected to act as a compensatory mechanism.

A number of developing countries have adopted various forms of food support programmes to increase the real incomes of beneficiaries and provide basic food security. Such programmes take the form of general subsidies, quantity rationing, or food stamps. A general, untargeted subsidy is provided by food rationing, in which the subsidized commodities are restricted in quantity but not in coverage. In contrast, a general price subsidy on a particular food item enables the supply of unlimited amounts of the subsidized food to anyone who wishes to buy it. The advantages of these programmes reside in their relative simplicity and the limited demands on administrative resources. The main disadvantage lies in their targeting inefficiency, since the benefits are not limited to the poor.

As such, there is now a greater emphasis on targeted initiatives, which include:

- self-targeting through geographic location;
- self-targeting through the subsidization of low-quality or inferior commodities;
- targeting by income.

The launch of the Food Support Programme demonstrates clear recognition by the government of the need to provide basic food security to poor households.

An example of geographic targeting would be the placement of ration shops or distribution outlets only in areas where the poor live. This is, in effect, a form of self-targeting by location; it has the advantage of administrative simplicity, though a certain degree of leakage is inevitable.

An alternative method of self-targeting is by commodity. Empirical studies of consumption patterns have confirmed that lower income groups tend to consume *inferior* goods, or "poor people's food," which are not found in the consumption basket of upper-income households. Subsidizing such food items tends to benefit only the poor.

An example of targeting on the basis of income is the distribution of food stamps, or coupons, to the poor. However, problems arise with regard to administering a proper *means* test for such subsidies. In most low-income countries, information on household income is scarce or even non-existent, thereby making it difficult to target beneficiaries. This problem is compounded by the fact that households move both physically, thus creating the danger of being lost to the administering authorities, and in and out of income brackets. Effective and continuous monitoring is necessary for the success of any coupon system, not only for initial identification, but also because the poorest of the poor are the most itinerant.

A review of international experience with food support programmes **(see box 8.3)** reveals that the following design features are important in determining the success of such a programme:

- target commodities should be primarily consumed by the poor;
- programme outlets should be easily accessible to the poor;
- purchase requirements should not be imposed on rations or food stamps (these affect the ability of the poor to purchase required items, particularly in times of constrained cash);
- programmes should not be implemented where markets are not functioning (or where poor households are mostly subsistence producers);
- in the case of rations or food stamps, the design should minimize transaction costs (especially in the form of queues) that may limit access to the poor;
- to avoid incentive costs, the value of the transfer should not be too large in relation to the total amount spent by households on food;
- eligibility should be reviewed periodically.

Pakistan also has some past experience with food support programmes. Established in 1992, the Pakistan *Bait-ul-Maal* programme has been operating a Food Subsidy Scheme (FSS), renamed the *Atta Subsidy Scheme*. Its limited coverage is one of its main problems. With only 240,000 people receiving the *atta*, or wheat flour subsidy (SPDC 1999), it is quite clear that interventions by the *Bait-ul-Maal* make only a minor contribution to poverty alleviation in Pakistan. Further, given that the programme has no identifiable source of income, its exclusive reliance on budgetary support makes it particularly vulnerable to changing fiscal conditions, as can be seen from the steep fall in grants from Rs. 300 million in 1998-99 to Rs. 225 million in 1999-2000. A food stamp programme has also been implemented in the province of Punjab, specifically oriented towards the purchase of wheat flour.

The Pakistani government traditionally provided a generalized wheat subsidy. It engaged in a complex wheat procurement, acquisition, transport, storage and distribution operation, such that wheat reached the flour mills at less than full cost. This resulted in a subsidy to registered mills, which got their quotas from the provincial governments. Thus, the

> **BOX 8.3**
>
> **FOOD SUPPORT PROGRAMMES IN SELECTED COUNTRIES**
>
> **Sri Lanka**
> A food stamp scheme was introduced in 1986 to enable the transition from a generalized ration system to a more targeted intervention, and thereby reduce costs. Potential beneficiaries were subjected to a means test, which was not rigorously applied. Consequently, almost 50 per cent of the population was covered by the scheme. There is evidence that the scheme increased per capita calorie consumption, especially of pre-school children. However, entitlement to food stamps was not indexed to inflation, and their value eroded over time.
>
> **Honduras**
> Honduras provides a good example of self-targeting by the distribution of stamps through education and health centres. Under the maternal child coupon programme, the target group was children under five years of age belonging to low-income families, and pregnant and lactating women. This programme was more cost-effective in comparison with other nutrition programmes.
>
> **Jamaica**
> A food stamp programme was implemented in 1984, with a means test used to determine eligibility. Poor relief officers and community members could name beneficiaries in the "elderly, handicapped and impoverished" category. The programme eventually reached about 12 per cent of all Jamaican households, with almost 40 per cent of households in the lowest income quintile gaining access to food stamps. By and large, the programme was successful in targeting the poor.
>
> **Source:** Ezemenrai and Subbarao (1998), Edirisinghe (1987)

subsidy intended for the low-income consumer was, in effect, channelled through the flour mills. Zaman (1996) suggests that because the bulk of the subsidy was being pre-empted by the millers, it had no significant impact on reducing the retail price. As such, a strong case existed for withdrawing the generalized subsidy and moving to a more targeted intervention, like the food support programme launched by the government.

However, the food support programme announced by the government also has a number of potential problems. First, if the *Bait-ul-Maal's* existing lists of beneficiaries are used for the identification of recipients of the cash subsidy, then there is a danger of serious mistargeting. Funds allocated to the *Bait-ul-Maal* have been notoriously prone to leakage and corruption, a former Chief Minister of Punjab having already been indicted on the charge of misuse of *Bait-ul-Maal* funds.

Second, Pakistan's FSP is unique in that support is being provided in the form of a cash subsidy, and not only as stamps or coupons for the purchase of basic food items. Therefore, even if a poor household is correctly targeted, there is no guarantee that it will use the subvention largely to improve its nutritional standards and not divert it to other uses. Also, the prospect of being able to obtain a cash subsidy will increase the likelihood of the non-poor finding ways of accessing the programme.

Third, the choice of beneficiaries from among the poor is also an issue of concern. The food support programme is small in size, with only 1.2 million beneficiaries. Currently, it is estimated that there are over 8 million poor households in the country, the bulk of which have been affected by the increase in wheat flour prices following the government's withdrawal of the generalized wheat subsidy. The intent of FSP was to target all Pakistani households with an income of Rs. 2,000 or less per month, implying that any household that could prove it met this income criterion should have been made eligible for receiving the subsidy. Instead, the programme has restricted numbers. This raises the problem of serious horizontal inequity, with otherwise eligible households not gaining access to the programme.

With an effective social safety net system, this should be a rare sight.

The programme explicitly recognizes the need to support minorities, proposing a 3 per cent quota for them. It also demonstrates a preference for women. The latter consideration, however, could have been more effectively incorporated by requiring that the accounts be opened in the name of a female member of a household who would then make the cash withdrawals. Alternatively, preferential access to the programme could have been given to pregnant or lactating women who attend government facilities for maternal and child care (as in the case of Honduras). Coverage by the programme should also be oriented more towards wheat-deficient areas of Pakistan, especially in the three smaller provinces (NWFP, Balochistan and Sindh), where one of the significant contributing factors to higher poverty is the relatively high price of wheat flour.

Fourth, there is concern about the fiscal sustainability of the programme. Allocations to the *Bait-ul-Maal* have been progressively cut in recent years in response to growing fiscal constraints, and there is no guarantee that the FSP will not meet the same fate. A better option would have been to earmark a portion of revenues from a particular source for continued financing of the programme. This is, in fact, what the Chief Executive indicated in his statement on the Economic Revival Plan on December 15, 1999. He had promised that a certain percentage of revenues from the general sales tax would be earmarked for the FSP. This has not been implemented. As such, if the budget deficit target proves to be elusive this year, then the allocation of Rs. 2.5 billion to the programme may be scaled down. It is recommended that, in line with the Chief Executive's policy statement, 5 per cent of revenues from the federal share in the GST should henceforth be allocated to the FSP. This will raise the allocation to about Rs. 4 billion, ensuring not only that more households are reached, but also that the annual cash subsidy of Rs. 2,000, which appears inadequate, is enhanced somewhat.

Altogether, at this initial stage of implementation, the FSP appears to be fraught with a number of serious problems, including the mechanism chosen for targeting poor households, inadequate coverage and the likelihood of horizontal inequity, uncertainty about the nature of use of the cash subsidy by recipient households, and lack of fiscal sustainability. The programme will therefore need to be carefully monitored during the implementation process in order to identify the degree of success in both targeting beneficiaries and in improving the nutritional standards of poor households.

ZAKAT

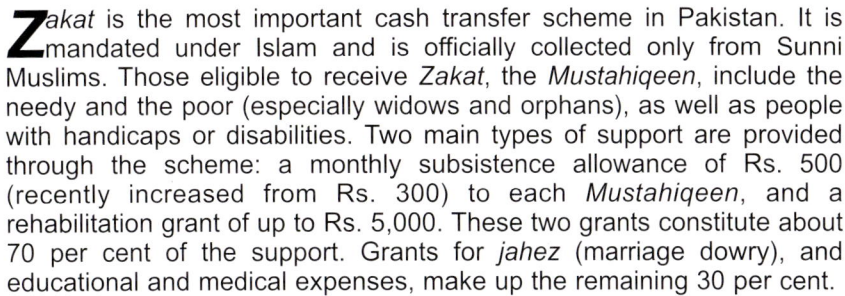

Zakat is the most important cash transfer scheme in Pakistan. It is mandated under Islam and is officially collected only from Sunni Muslims. Those eligible to receive *Zakat*, the *Mustahiqeen*, include the needy and the poor (especially widows and orphans), as well as people with handicaps or disabilities. Two main types of support are provided through the scheme: a monthly subsistence allowance of Rs. 500 (recently increased from Rs. 300) to each *Mustahiqeen*, and a rehabilitation grant of up to Rs. 5,000. These two grants constitute about 70 per cent of the support. Grants for *jahez* (marriage dowry), and educational and medical expenses, make up the remaining 30 per cent.

An autonomous *Zakat* council administers the Central *Zakat* Fund, which is maintained by the State Bank of Pakistan (SBP) but does not form part of the federal consolidated fund. This council is supported by the *Zakat* and *Ushr* wing of the Ministry of Religious Affairs. Disbursement in the provinces is regulated by the provincial *Zakat* councils. The most important tier is the local *Zakat* committee (LZC), which identifies the *Mustahiqeen*. It is estimated that there are about 1.5 million *Mustahiqeen* at present. These committees, of which there are about 39,000, have seven elected, non-official, unpaid members, including two women. Each committee may spend up to 10 per cent of its allocated funds on administration.

Zakat has traditionally been a compulsory, annual deduction paid by Sunni Muslims at the rate of 2.5 per cent on the value of specified financial assets. Collections in 1997-98 were estimated at Rs. 4.1 billion, a drop from the peak of Rs. 4.7 billion in 1993-94. More than 50 per cent of the revenue comes from a tax on savings bank accounts and about 16 per cent from fixed deposits. A judgement by the Supreme Court, however, has allowed all sects to file a declaration seeking exemption from payment of *Zakat* on financial assets. This puts in jeopardy the mechanism of compulsory deductions and thus, the level of contributions.

The Central *Zakat* Fund retains a portion of the proceeds, which it invests on a non-interest basis. The outstanding cash balance as far back as January 1997 was almost Rs. 11 billion. Provincial disbursements are based on population, although this criterion is not strictly followed. Distribution of funds by the provincial *Zakat* councils is formula driven, with 60 per cent going to the local *Zakat* committees and 40 per cent to institutions (e.g., *deeni madaris*, or religious schools; public hospitals; vocational training institutions). Those eligible to receive *Zakat* receive payments through the banks.

Zakat performs well on a number of the criteria of a *good* social safety net. The support, provided in the form of a subsistence allowance, appears to be adequate (especially after its recent enhancement) and non-distortionary (since the allowance is in cash). Administration costs, as a whole, are low, primarily because of voluntary inputs provided by members of the local committees. One of the strongest points in favour of *Zakat* has been its access to an earmarked source of revenue. Reliance on a specific source not only ensures sustainability, but the nature of the

Zakat is the most important cash transfer scheme in Pakistan. One of the strongest points in favour of Zakat has been its access to an earmarked source of revenue.

tax (i.e., being based on financial assets) is such that the burden falls mostly on upper-income households. Therefore, *Zakat* has the potential of playing a strong redistributive role.

Problems with *Zakat* include its degree of targeting efficiency. There is conflicting evidence on this. According to the World Bank (1995) and Jehle (1995), only about half of the benefits went to the lowest quintile of households in 1991. Therefore, the other half went to households which cannot be considered poor. However, latest estimates from HIES (1996-97) show that 68 per cent of *Zakat* (official and private) was received by poor families **(see chapter 3)**.

Access to the benefits is another problem. A number of stages are involved in being declared a *Mustahiqeen*, and there is inevitably some patronage involved at the local level. The number of *Mustahiqeen* has grown slowly despite a significant increase in the number of people living below the poverty line. With only 1.5 million *Mustahiqeen*, it is clear that the programme covers only a small proportion of poor households. This demonstrates problems of access to *Zakat*, as well as inadequate programme coverage.

Being a recurring cash transfer, *Zakat* runs the risk of creating a state of dependency among recipients, and reducing the incentive to search for productive work. However, most of the *Mustahiqeen* are disabled people and widows who are not in a position to join the labour force, anyway.

Also at issue is the interaction with private transfers. To the extent that *Zakat* is deducted at source, there is the possibility that private transfers may be correspondingly reduced. This has been the basis for the argument that *Zakat* payments should be largely voluntary.

The Supreme Court judgement has cast doubts about the financial sustainability of *Zakat* funding. There has not yet been a decrease in the amount of *Zakat* collected, however this may be primarily due to confusion over the mode of claiming exemption, for which a form must be filled in and submitted 30 days before the deduction date–a fact of which many are unaware. It can therefore be expected that *Zakat* funds will decrease as more people gain exemption from compulsory payments.

Given the possibility of a decline in *Zakat* funding, the question that arises is, how will the additional *guzara* allowance of Rs. 200 per month be financed? With a beneficiary population of about 1.1 million, the rise in the *guzara* allowance implies an additional annual outflow of Rs. 2.6 billion. In the absence of firm government fiscal commitment, it will be unfortunate if the increase in the size of the allowance results in a reduction in the coverage of *Mustahiqeen* which, as already mentioned, is low.

The LZC is responsible for disbursing the funds it receives from the District *Zakat* Committee. While the selection of the beneficiaries is done by the LZC, the number of beneficiaries entitled to receive the *guzara* allowance (who, incidentally, tend to be mainly widows), is set by the District Committee. Monitoring by the District Committees is irregular, which leaves us with the question, how can a committee determine the number of beneficiaries without knowing the extent of poverty in a community? Furthermore, the funds from the District Committees, are irregularly disbursed, causing delays of up to 6 months in the disbursement of the *guzara* allowance to recipients. As the *guzara* allowance is an income support payment to the poor, particularly those unable to work or without a regular source of income, the delay in disbursement is a serious shortcoming of the system. The poor simply cannot be expected to limit their expenditure on basic food items to that extent **(see box 8.5)**.

The Zakat system continues to be criticized for its inability to target the neediest of the poor.

BOX 8.4

WIDOW TURNS TO *ZAKAT* FOR ASSISTANCE

The *Zakat* system has been criticized for its inability to accurately target the neediest members of the poor. As widow Nasim Akhter explains, she has had a mixed experience with *Zakat*, which she turned to in recent years to supplement her family's meagre resources.

"I am a fifty-one-year-old woman. I live in the *katchi abadis* (squatter settlement) of Sultanabad, in a two-room house with gas, electricity and water connections. I have four sons and six daughters, of whom five are married.

All my daughters have studied up to the Matric level, while my eldest son studied up to Class VIII, two others up to Class V, and my youngest son still goes to school. My eldest son is a driver and earns Rs. 2,000 per month. Two of my sons are jobless. They are not interested in their studies nor do they try to find any employment. They spend their time with the bad boys in our area, and honestly, I am extremely worried about them.

My husband died nine years ago. He was a peon in the Public Works Department and died of cancer. Because of our limited resources, he could not get better medical treatment, even though I borrowed money for his medical expenses. After his death, I worked as a domestic maid in order to pay off the debts. I used to earn Rs. 500 per month. Besides that, I received a pension of Rs. 200 per month. The mistress of the house where I used to work helped me in more ways than one, making it possible for me to run my household, and get five of my daughters married, despite my meagre income.

Two years after the death of my husband, when our circumstances got worse, I made an application to the *Zakat* Committee, in which I narrated my problems. I myself was ashamed of asking for such help, and while some good people helped me, others mocked and scorned me. But then no one ever helps anyone else under such circumstances—only God comes to one's rescue.

After the acceptance of my application, I began receiving Rs. 300 per month from the *Zakat* Committee, and the amount was sufficient for fulfilling our several smaller needs. After three years, though, the money suddenly stopped. Upon inquiry, I was told that since my sons had grown up, I was no longer entitled to any help. It was irrelevant that only one of my sons earned Rs. 2,000, an insufficient amount for our needs. Since I am also getting old, I am unable to work and whenever I am sick, I am taken to the government hospital. I assure you, we do not have enough money for medicine.

Some of the residents of our locality have requested that the *Zakat* Committee restore my monthly stipend, but so far it remains suspended. I hope they will restore my monthly income because it is the only hope I have in my present circumstances."

BOX 8.5

ZAKAT AT THE LOCAL LEVEL: INSIGHTS FROM THE FIELD

In order to understand the dynamics of the local *Zakat* process in the urban context, SPDC conducted interviews of *Zakat* recipients and officials in two *katchi abadis* (squatter settlements) in Karachi. The communities each have a population of between 30,000 and 50,000, and are located in different districts of the city. Case studies of over a dozen recipients were compiled. Following are some of the key findings from the field.

- The subsistence allowance, which is supposed to be disbursed monthly, is highly irregular and not being paid for up to 6 months or more in some cases.
- Recipients face major difficulties opening up bank accounts. Many banks do not wish to keep the deposits of *Zakat* recipients, and others insist on a minimum balance that is too high given the small amounts being received as *Zakat*. It is often through the personal intervention of the chairperson that recipients are able to open a bank account. Women, in particular, face problems going to the bank.
- One form of fraud mentioned by officials is that of recipients applying from two adjoining localities as a means of obtaining more money; the officials try to prevent this by checking with the neighbouring committees.
- Monitoring is highly irregular. In one locality, the *guzara* records, which should be checked every 6 months by the Sub-*Tehsil* and District *Zakat* Committees, had been examined only once in two years.
- Since anonymity is supposed to be preserved in the *Zakat* process, the barriers to access may actually be lower than if this were not the case. However, there are still a few indigent people who will not apply for *Zakat* due to the stigma it carries. Those who do apply say that the lack of an ID card, which all applicants must possess, is a major barrier.
- One of the major drawbacks of the *guzara* allowance is that it does not take into account the number of dependents; the same allowance is given to all households, irrespective of size.
- *Zakat* is largely spent on food, although some of the seemingly better-off families use it to pay their children's school fees.
- The average length of time recipients had been receiving *Zakat* is 1 to 2 years.
- The beneficiaries of the *guzara* allowance are mainly widows, with one third being disabled men.
- Among the rehabilitation allowance cases, in the locality where there is no female representation on the LZC, more men than women have received the benefit.
- People who have set up small businesses report higher incomes (e.g., Rs. 4,000 per month) than those who receive the *guzara* allowance (who report monthly incomes of Rs. 1,500-2,000).

As far as the adequacy of the payment is concerned, while Rs. 500 for a person whose monthly income is between Rs. 2,000 and 2,500 may seem reasonable, it does not fare too well when one takes into account the number of dependents in a household. A widow with two children is much better off on such a payment than one with six. This calls for the government to consider giving each additional dependent an income supplement, and correspondingly reducing the basic payment itself.

A fundamental concern is that the *guzara* allowance breeds dependency among its recipients. One solution would be for the government to use the money to set up income-generating projects for the *Mustahiqeen*, provided these people have the capacity and capability to engage in such activities. In fact, this seems to be the direction the government is pursuing, as mentioned by the Chief Executive in his speech of August 14, 2000. An annual *guzara* allowance comes to Rs. 6,000, while a one-time rehabilitation allowance is Rs. 5,000. However, some people, such as the severely ill and the elderly, are unable to use the rehabilitation allowance to set up a business. Also, some income-generating activities require the acquisition of skills (e.g., embroidery). This may further stretch the already limited finances of the poor since, not only would their earnings be forgone, but money would also have to be spent on learning these skills.

There is also a clear need for better monitoring of the *Zakat* process.

Zakat runs the risk of creating a state of dependency among recipients, and reducing the incentive to search for productive work.

BOX	8.6

ZAKAT HELPS HANDICAPPED ACHIEVE BETTER LIFESTYLE

"My name is Mohammad Arshad and I am twenty years old. I have two sisters and a brother. We live in a three-room house in Qayyumabad. Both my parents are alive. My father works at a milk shop. My mother used to work as a *masi* (sweeper) in a school, but since her eyesight has weakened, she passes her time at home. My sister teaches in a *madressa* (Islamic school) and my brother owns a food stand from which he sells burgers and cold drinks. I am the youngest member of the family. Our total monthly income is Rs. 4,000. In my childhood, I fell victim to polio. Both my legs suffered, resulting in my inability to walk properly. While I studied until Class V, my brother and two sisters are illiterate because of our parents' meagre income that was hardly able to meet our daily requirements.

My main weakness is that I am a cripple. I cannot do any job that has to be performed while standing up. However, I did work alongside my brother, and I applied for *Zakat*, which I now receive as a *guzara* allowance of Rs. 300 per month.

But lately, I realized that I could not sustain myself on this small allowance for long, and made a fresh application to the *Zakat* Committee, asking them to provide me with some money under the permanent restoration programme. The *Zakat* Committee responded with a Rs. 5,000 grant that I invested in my brother's cold drink shop. I began working there as well, and now I earn an additional Rs. 50 to Rs. 60 daily.

I feel happy that I am no longer a burden on anyone, and seeing my ability to earn money, I want to work hard and spend the rest of my life in a better way."

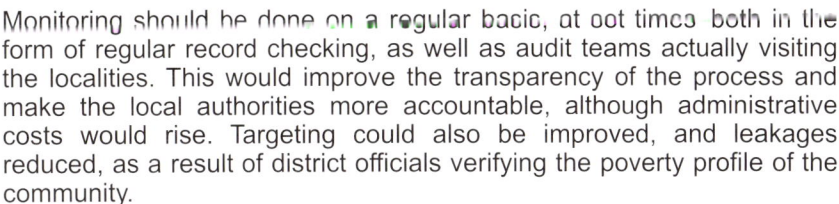

Monitoring should be done on a regular basis, at oot times both in the form of regular record checking, as well as audit teams actually visiting the localities. This would improve the transparency of the process and make the local authorities more accountable, although administrative costs would rise. Targeting could also be improved, and leakages reduced, as a result of district officials verifying the poverty profile of the community.

Ease of access is a major issue, since *Zakat* requires that all applicants possess an ID card. Illiteracy can also be a hindrance to applicants, both in terms of filling out required forms and dealing with bank officials; usually, however, illiterate people are helped out by neighbours, relatives and officials. Women do face problems going to banks without male escorts. There is also the fear of a social stigma being attached to *Zakat*, which may deter some of the needy from applying for this form of assistance.

To sum up, there needs to be a review of the *Zakat* system, which suffers from relatively low coverage, targeting problems, low ease of access, and possible financial unsustainability. Apparently the government has set up a committee for this purpose. While the increase in the *guzara* payment is a step in the right direction, it will only work in the overall context of a more efficient and transparent system. Also, the implications of the announcement that the government plans to expand the rehabilitation allowance at the cost of the *guzara* allowance must be examined. It is important to realize that some of the *Zakat* recipients may always need income-supplementing transfers. Furthermore, the disbursement criteria and modalities will also have to be made more responsive to considerations of greater backwardness and poverty in some parts of the country.

OVERALL EVALUATION

Based on the previous sections, we find that, despite the new-found commitment to poverty reduction in Pakistan, the total of overall transfers under the various social safety nets remains limited. As such, they are likely to have only a small impact on the incidence of poverty in the country. About 3 million people are potentially likely to be reached, even if we make the favourable assumptions of no mistargeting or overlapping of coverage. This includes approximately 1 million people through *Zakat*, 1.2 million through the new Food Support Programme, 0.5 million through the Integrated Small Public Works Programme, and a maximum of 0.3 million through other initiatives, including EOBI and microfinance. Even if we were to assume that the support is adequate for entire households, still fewer than 40 per cent of the country's poor households will be reached by some form of social safety net.

Table 8.3 indicates that the total value of public transfers, in the absence of any fiscal cutbacks, will aggregate to approximately Rs. 20 billion in 2000-01, equivalent to about 0.6 per cent of the GDP. Pasha (1999) estimates that the value of transfers required for substantial mitigation of poverty is about 2 per cent of the GDP, or Rs. 70 billion–which demonstrates the inadequacy of the social safety nets in place.

In **chapter 3**, private transfers to the poor are quantified as being close to 2 per cent of the GDP. If we consider that public transfers represent less than one third of private transfers, we have some indication of the extent to which the people of Pakistan have had to rely on their own resources to get their compatriots out of the poverty trap. Even with due recognition of fiscal constraints, it seems reasonable to argue that the government must commit itself to ensuring that total transfers from the federal budget to the poor are increased to a minimum of 1 per cent of the GDP (from the current amount of about 0.3 per cent of the GDP). This will require additional allocations of over Rs. 20 billion annually for the poverty alleviation programme. It is important that these allocations not be financed by the printing of money, but by progressive

TABLE 8.3

TOTAL VALUE OF TRANSFERS UNDER DIFFERENT SCHEMES, 2000-01

	(Rs. million)
Cash Transfers	**9,100**
Zakat	6,600
Bait-ul-Maal (food support)	2,500
Micro-Credit Programmes[a]	**2,500**
NRSP	1,000
PPAF	500
Microfinance Bank	2,000
Public Works	**6,300**
ISPWP[b]	6,300
Social Security	**1,500**
EOBI	1,500
Housing Finance	**300**
HBFC[c]	300
Total Value of Transfers	**19,700**[d]

[a] Assumed income multiplier of 1
[b] Assumed share of labour costs of 30 per cent
[c] Assumed income multiplier of 0.2
[d] Total value of transfers equals 0.6% of the GDP
Source: SPDC estimates

The total value of public transfers will aggregate to approximately Rs. 20 billion in 2000-01, equivalent to 0.6 per cent of the GDP.

taxation of the type described in **chapter 5**. Otherwise, the resulting higher inflation will adversely affect the poor and at least partially neutralize the benefits of the poverty alleviation programme.

What should be the priorities in the higher allocations? Clearly, the government must give first priority to performing its basic welfare or humanitarian role, which is to support, on a continuing basis, those who are permanently incapacitated and unable to work. These are primarily the *Mustahiqeen*. If the *Zakat* system is unable to reach out to the bulk of the *Mustahiqeen* in the country due to lack of revenue, then the government must develop other means to reach this target group.

Two other sections of the population also deserve special support. The first category is that of elderly and retired low-income workers. The EOBI is a potentially useful mechanism for providing social security to such workers, and the government has recently announced a pension increase from Rs. 425 to Rs. 630 per month. But the EOBI's coverage is very limited and access is difficult. It currently covers fewer than 20 per cent of workers in urban areas. The scheme could be improved by having employers pay a flat rate contribution per worker, and ensuring that a matching contribution is made by the government. In addition, the scheme should be opened up to the self-employed, as well as to employers in establishments with fewer than ten workers. Receipts from the Workers' Welfare Fund, which currently accrues to the federal consolidated fund, could be earmarked as part of government's matching contribution to EOBI.

The other category is that of households which suffer a loss of assets or life due to natural calamities or disasters. The ineffectiveness of the present government system to respond quickly and effectively to emergencies has been amply demonstrated by the inadequate response to the recent drought in Pakistan which, in some remote parts of the country, even affected lifeline water supplies. Institutional arrangements, including the involvement of NGOs, will need to be strengthened in order to respond effectively to future calamities or disasters. In addition, the government must establish a permanent Disaster Relief Fund, to which contributions are made annually. The fund would provide support to poor families, particularly to resurrecting their economic lives in the aftermath of a disaster. Such a fund could also become the focal point for private charitable contributions.

Beyond this, the government's next priority in its poverty alleviation programme should be to provide employment opportunities to adult members of poor households who are capable of working but have become poor because of lack of opportunities. This would primarily imply upscaling the Public Works Programme, subject to the development of adequate institutional capacity and proper implementation modalities. The present ISPWP is highly skewed towards rural areas, whereas urban poverty is also high and increasing rapidly. The additional allocations should be used for starting a *Katchi Abadis* and Slum Areas Improvement Programme, involving the provision of basic infrastructure such as roads, water supply, sewerage and sanitation. Not only will this provide employment opportunities to construction workers in urban areas, a high proportion of whom are currently unemployed, but it will also provide significant secondary benefits to the urban poor, who generally live in *katchi abadis* and slum areas.

Finally, the government must concentrate on empowering the poor by improving access to basic services like education and health. Welfare initiatives of the government must not come at the expense of programmes like the Social Action Programme. This is important if the people (especially the future generation) are to be equipped to break out of the vicious cycle of poverty and not become permanently dependent on handouts from well-off households or the government.

Welfare initiatives of the government must not come at the expense of programmes like the Social Action Programme.

Basic welfare strategies must reach the poorest of the poor to mitigate against rising distress among children.

ROLE OF DONORS

Both globally and in the context of Pakistan, donors have increasingly placed poverty reduction as one of the principal objectives governing their assistance. There have long been concerns about the impact on poverty of the typical structural adjustment and stabilization programmes implemented by the IMF in various countries. In recent years, these concerns have heightened considerably as a result of the impact that IMF conditionalities have had on poverty in countries (especially Indonesia) that were severely affected by the East Asian financial crisis. Leading intellectuals, NGOs, and civil society groups in the West have increasingly questioned the policies of the World Trade Organization (WTO), the World Bank and the IMF. These concerns have been manifested in major public demonstrations.

Consequently, there has been a process of fundamental rethinking. The IMF has replaced its conventional extended structural adjustment facility (ESAF) with a new poverty reduction and growth facility. The Asian Development Bank has recently finalized its long-term lending strategy (up to 2015), which envisages 40 per cent of future lending to member countries being directly for poverty reduction. Many of the bilateral donors and UN agencies, which have traditionally had a greater concern for social development, have further increased their focus on poverty alleviation. There is now a universal commitment to reduce global poverty by half by the year 2015.

The promotion of poverty reduction from being a residual item in the development assistance agenda to the focal point among lending operations is beginning to create a potentially new set of problems. Countries such as Pakistan, which have large concentrations of poverty, are increasingly being confronted by a multitude of donors, both multilateral and bilateral, talking primarily of poverty reduction and proposing initiatives largely in this area. This has raised the likelihood of duplication and the overlapping of efforts towards poverty alleviation. Clearly, if this process is to be handled efficiently, there will have to be much greater coordination of the role of donors and adequate recognition of the limits of institutional capacity of recipient governments, especially given the fact that, in countries like Pakistan, poverty alleviation programmes, including the establishment of social safety nets directly targeting the poor, have traditionally been accorded low priority.

Who should perform this coordination of poverty reduction initiatives? What should be the key directions and programmes of funding by donors in the area of poverty reduction? Can and should countries like Pakistan borrow internationally, even on concessional terms, to finance programmes/projects aimed primarily at poverty alleviation? These are some of the important issues and questions that arise in the context of the role of donors in the area of poverty reduction.

As far as the issue of coordination of the role of donors is concerned, this clearly has to be the responsibility of the national government. Such coordination must be undertaken within the overall framework of a national poverty reduction strategy, which clearly articulates the objectives, targets, instruments and modalities, and highlights the government's own priority initiatives. This strategy must be developed on the basis of a participatory approach that recognizes the importance of the involvement of the poor in deciding on their own priorities for support. NGOs and civil society groups can play a useful role in articulating these preferences.

Once the national poverty reduction strategy is developed, and the space for the participation of donors has been identified, then it will be possible for individual donors to carve out niches of assistance based on their own comparative advantages and preferences. The task of donor coordination in the area of poverty alleviation could possibly be performed by the Planning Commission, for which purpose a separate Poverty Alleviation Programme (PAP) wing should be created. This wing should act as the secretariat for a PAP national steering committee, which should preferably be chaired by the Chief Executive (to signal the priority) and meet at least quarterly. Both federal and provincial governments should sit on this committee, along with representatives of NGOs and civil society.

On the road to a better future?

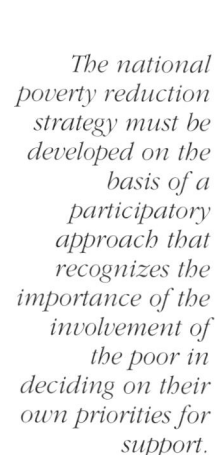

The national poverty reduction strategy must be developed on the basis of a participatory approach that recognizes the importance of the involvement of the poor in deciding on their own priorities for support.

Government, donors, civil society and people at large will all have to work together with great determination to improve the future for them.

Regarding the nature of support from donors for implementation of the national poverty reduction strategy, it needs to be emphasized that, given Pakistan's current economic problems, this role has to be initially at the macro level in order to have the maximum impact. We have already highlighted that Pakistan potentially has a severe balance of payments problem, which will become virtually unsustainable after the expiry of the current period of debt relief in December 2000. Therefore, the first priority has to be given to finalizing a medium-term poverty reduction and growth facility with the IMF and other donors, which ensures enough balance of payments support (including a second round of debt relief) to create the necessary space to pursue a programme of structural reforms along with sustained efforts at poverty alleviation. This could be perhaps the greatest contribution that donors can make to ensure that poverty does not rise exponentially in Pakistan. A short-term standby facility, of the type which has been offered by the IMF to Pakistan, will primarily focus on macroeconomic stabilization and may even have deleterious consequences on poverty.

Beyond this, it is our view that the basic welfare role must be performed by government in the form of transfer payments to the hard-core poor, although NGOs could provide assistance in this area. Donors can assist financially and otherwise in the employment-generation and empowerment components of the poverty alleviation programme, while smaller bilateral donors can contribute to special initiatives related to the development of a database and research on poverty, and to monitoring the poverty impact of different programmes/projects. The microfinance component of the employment-generation strategy has already been promised large-scale financial assistance by both the World Bank and the Asian Development Bank. Other donors could provide additional resources for the Public Works Programme. More importantly, it is essential that the donor commitment to the Social Action Programme be sustained at a time when the government is beginning to retreat from this area **(see chapter 7)**. This programme is vital for empowering the poor

The first priority has to be given to finalizing a medium-term poverty reduction and growth facility with the IMF.

> **BOX 8.7**
>
> ### SUICIDE AS AN ESCAPE FROM POVERTY
>
> On June 27, 2000, twenty-four year old Abid Sheikh, a resident of Korangi, committed suicide by drinking insecticide. Trying to control the ceaseless flood of tears issuing forth from her eyes, Abid Sheikh's mother manages to explain between sobs, "It was the fear and dread of unemployment that made my son embrace death. With great difficulty he managed to secure a job in which he was earning Rs. 3,500 a month, but after only fifteen days, his employer fired him. Abid confronted his renewed unemployment with silence, and it was with the same silence that he took his own life. His act has destroyed my family and the sanctity of my home."
>
> "I had ten children, out of whom three have already passed away. My husband is also deceased, and I live with my children in my own home."
>
> "I have managed to marry off my three daughters to respectable families. Abid was my youngest son. He always dreamed of joining the police force, but ended up working in the construction industry instead. This work was inconsistent and inefficient. He would only get work fifteen days of the month, and would earn around Rs. 3,000 to Rs. 3,500, if anything at all. Occasionally, he would not get work in an entire month, in which case he would remain at home, and have no earnings. It was this irregular, low-paying work that made managing the household and purchasing necessities almost impossible. Resources were always insufficient in our home. Once he found regular employment, Abid hoped his circumstances would improve, and it was just after he secured a job that he was engaged to be married to a girl from within the community. But once Abid lost his job, the girl's father demanded that the engagement be broken off, on the grounds that since Abid was unemployed, he would not be able to adequately support his daughter. It was in the wake of this unemployment, and his broken engagement, that Abid committed suicide."
>
> Abid was a victim of the uncertainty and despair that accompany unemployment and financial instability.

and increasing their capacity to get out of the poverty trap. Donors will need to exercise enough leverage to ensure that the badly needed institutional and policy reforms are implemented in this programme. Also, there will have to be greater reliance on grant assistance rather than loans (however soft) for poverty alleviation programmes, as these programmes are unlikely to contribute directly to enhancement in debt repayment capacity.

In conclusion, we want to reiterate that Pakistan is perilously placed. There is the likelihood of a rapid increase in poverty in coming years, which could lead to a systemic breakdown and shake the foundations of the state. Government, donors, civil society and people at large will all have to work together with great determination and commitment to avert this outcome.

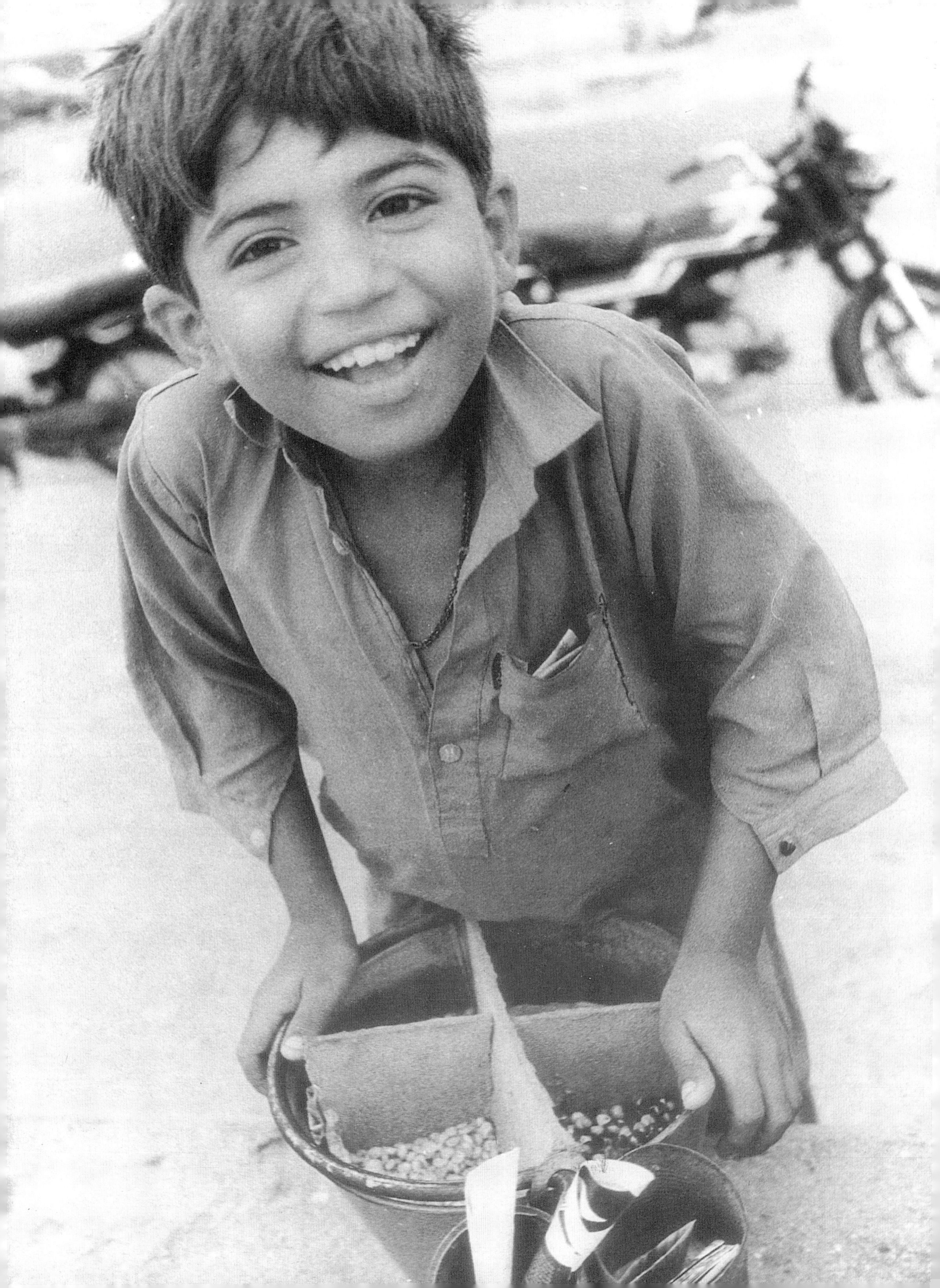

# APPENDICES

A.1

CHRONOLOGY OF KEY EVENTS IN THE SOCIAL SECTORS - 1999

EDUCATION

January 14	The Sindh Education Department establishes a task force to identify ghost teachers as well as absent and illegally appointed teachers.
February 15	The Sindh Education Department identifies 7,244 (7 per cent) ghost primary teachers from a total of 102,246 primary teachers.
March 22	A study released by Oxfam reveals that South Asian countries have 56 million out-of-school children despite legislative efforts for universal primary education (UPE). This high dropout rate can be attributed to the dismal quality of education **(see box A1.1)**.
May 3	The Sindh Education Management Information System (SEMIS) report for the last year reveals that 3,941 (9 per cent) of government schools–out of a total 41,896–are not functioning.
May 6	The Sindh Finance Department agrees to provide funds to contribute to the establishment of community schools under the Social Action Programme (SAP), following the World Bank's refusal of further funding.
May 11	UNICEF agrees to provide Rs. 30 million, in collaboration with the Government of Punjab, to launch a literacy programme in three districts.

BOX A1.1

OXFAM INTERNATIONAL'S EDUCATION REPORT, 1999

According to Oxfam's 1999 report, *Education Now: Break the Cycle of Poverty*, 150 million primary school age children worldwide, primarily girls, drop out of school before completing the crucial first four years needed to attain basic literacy. Of these, 56 million are in South Asia. In Pakistan alone, almost 5 million children (i.e., half of those enrolled) leave school before completion–mostly in grades one or two. According to the report, by the year 2005, 40 per cent of the region's dropout children will be from Pakistan–up from 27 per cent in 1995. Furthermore, the increase in girls' enrolment has been slow compared to that for boys; had it been comparable, there would be an additional 1.5 million girls in school.

Generally speaking, the infant mortality rate (IMR) is 36 per cent higher in households where a mother has not received formal education than in households where a mother has some level of schooling. Pakistan's IMR is 34 per cent higher among the poorest 20 per cent of households than among the richest 20 per cent. Furthermore, it is estimated that about one third of school children are without safe water and over two thirds are without toilets.

Without an increase in public funding for primary education, improvement in such social indicators as universal primary education (UPE) is unlikely. Pakistan's National Education Policy targets are ambitious, containing platitudes about the merits of education, yet lacking crucial details about goals and how to achieve them, as well as information on administrative and financial measures. According to Oxfam's report, significantly more resources are allocated to the military budgets in Pakistan and India than to the education sector, Pakistan's military expenditure being about 25 per cent higher than the combined education and health budgets. The international Education Performance Index (EPI)- which is based on performance in enrolment, completion, and gender equity, and which shows the degree of educational deficit–ranks Pakistan only 99th among 104 countries.

August 3	The Punjab government decides to establish 50,000 non-formal basic education (NFBE) community schools in the province.
August 6	The Pakistan government allocates Rs. 500 million for establishing 200 (of 2,000 planned) *smart* (i.e., computer-based) schools in the rural areas of the country during 1999-2000.
November 5	According to a national survey by Gallup Pakistan, more than 60 per cent of parents in urban areas opt for English medium schools.
November 9	Two international donor agencies, the Department for International Development (DFID) and the World Bank, suspend funding for the government's educational projects in Sindh.
December 14	UNICEF selects Kohat as a model district to attain optimal literacy during the next two years, and expects to extend this programme to other districts. A financial incentive would be offered to parents to convince them to send their children to school.
December 28	Balochistan government statistics claim girls' enrolment in schools has increased between 1990 and 1999 by 190 per cent, compared to a 29 per cent increase in boys' enrolment.
December 30	The Asian Development Bank (ADB) suspends aid of Rs. 400 million to an education project in Balochistan due to reports of misappropriation.

HEALTH

January 3	The World Health Organization (WHO) states that 64,000 adults and children in Pakistan are suffering from AIDS/HIV.
January 29	Integrated Health Services (IHS), a voluntary non-governmental organization (NGO), introduces a health awareness campaign for Hepatitis A and B—focusing on its prevalence, prevention measures, symptoms, and other relevant information about the disease.
February 25	A seminar on "Rising Costs of Health Care" observes that it is becoming difficult to provide medical facilities free of cost or at a nominal charge at public hospitals. It recommends full cost recovery.
March 12	The WHO states that Pakistan will have 15 million diabetics by the year 2025, ranking 4th highest in the world.
May 13	According to the National Health Survey, about 9 million children below five years of age are anaemic in Pakistan. The causes of anaemia, besides nutrient deficiency, include malaria, intestinal parasites, and genetically-determined haemoglobin deficiencies **(see box A1.2)**.

May 14	Sindh proposes to lease 200 non-operational public health centres to unemployed doctors or NGOs, with preference given to the latter.
June 14	The Punjab government extends the Primary Health Programme to the year 2003.
October 1	The WHO announces *Vision 2020: The Right to Sight*, a programme aimed at eliminating blindness throughout the world by the year 2010.
October 3	In their report, the European Union and the United Nations Fund for Population Activities (UNFPA) state that Pakistan has one of the highest total fertility rates in Asia (2.8 per cent) and only 55 per cent of its population have access to basic health facilities.
October 28	Polio Day is marked with the administration of polio drops to 25 million children under the age of five in Pakistan.
November 1	The WHO declares that there are approximately 3.2 million newborns per year in Pakistan, based on the statistic that every 10 seconds a child is born in the country. Furthermore, every 40 seconds a newborn dies because of the non-availability of required medical facilities.
November 9	The WHO states that the infant mortality rate in Pakistan is 9.1 per cent, and that 128 per 1,000 children under the age of five die due to various diseases. It also reports that while the fertility rate in Pakistan is 5.6 per cent, only 18 per cent of births are attended by trained personnel.
December 10	The WHO declares Pakistan to be one of the most TB-affected countries in the world, more than half the world's cases being found in Pakistan, India, Bangladesh, China and Indonesia.

BOX A1.2

NATIONAL HEALTH SURVEY OF PAKISTAN

The National Health Survey's assessment of the population's nutritional status indicates large urban-rural differentials. As many as 62.9% of children under the age of five, 41.8% of those aged 5-14 years, and 41.4% of pregnant women are anaemic. The prevalence of anaemia is most common in Balochistan, followed by Sindh, Punjab and NWFP.

Diarrhoea is the most common cause of infant mortality in Pakistan. While mothers are aware of the immunization schedule, only 73% have had their children immunized (about 76.3% in the urban areas and 72% in the rural areas). Punjab ranks the highest with an immunization rate of 73%, followed by Sindh at 68.2%. Urban area ranking shows NWFP having the highest percentage of immunized children at 82.5%, followed by Sindh at 79.8%.

In all the provinces, particularly in rural areas, the majority of children (90%) are born at home. Among home deliveries, about 79.2% are assisted by a *dai* (traditional birth attendant). In the urban areas, NWFP has the highest proportion (39.1%) of hospital deliveries, followed by Sindh (30%), Punjab and Balochistan (with about 10%, respectively).

A strong majority (98.1%) of mothers have breastfed their children, with the highest practice being reported in NWFP (98.7%).

EMPLOYMENT

January 6	Under the Prime Minister's Self-Employment Scheme, Rs. 1,240 million is disbursed among 7,434 unemployed youth by the eight banking and financial institutions.
July 13	Rs. 5 billion is allocated for the Self-Employment Scheme. Fifty thousand people will benefit in the first year.
July 14	The government lifts the ban on jobs between grades 11 and 15. It also approves a 10 per cent job quota for the poor, needy and disabled.
July 14	The Economic Survey of Pakistan states that the unemployment rate has remained 6.3 per cent for the last three years. There are 2.4 million unemployed people in the labour force.
December 15	The Chief Executive announces a relief package for workers: an ad hoc increase in the salary of low-paid employees and a 48 per cent increase in old age pensions.

POVERTY

March 16	A Poverty Alleviation Programme of Rs. 1.2 billion is launched in Balochistan. The programme is intended to create 250,000 job opportunities for youth and bring about socio-economic changes in the province. Task forces have been set up in various sectors to execute the programme.
May 5	The Punjab government is expected to extend the food stamp scheme to the province as a whole, covering approximately 1.2 million poor families.
June 19	The World Bank announces US$90 million to support the Pakistan Poverty Alleviation Fund (PPAF) for a five-year programme to provide microcredit to poor individuals and community-based projects.
October 29	The Executive Board of the World Food Programme approves US$10 million for Pakistan.
December 11	The federal government approves the economic reforms package, which places special emphasis on poverty alleviation **(see box A1.3)**.
December 16	The Chief Executive announces an Economic Revival Plan emphasizing poverty alleviation. The plan includes: Rs. 15 to 20 billion through budgetary readjustment for small public works for the poorest and low-income workers; a voluntary cut of Rs. 7 billion in defence expenditure, to contribute towards poverty alleviation; establishment of a microcredit bank; and a comprehensive reappraisal of the *Zakat* and *Ushr* system.

> **BOX** A1.3
>
> **PAKISTAN POVERTY ALLEVIATION FUND**
>
> The Pakistan government announced a special package for poverty alleviation in its recent Economic Revival Plan. The Rs. 15 billion Poverty Alleviation Fund is directed towards people who are extremely poor as well as those whose are susceptible to falling below the poverty line. The programme, which is intended to curb escalating poverty levels, envisages measures such as basic food security, enhancement of the livelihood of the poor, provision of employment and business opportunities, and reduction in malnutrition among children. It places special importance on decentralizing the process of identifying and implementing projects to the district level, through the establishment of district development departments, and encourages the involvement of the local community in the need-based identification of projects through a transparent selection method. It is also planned that a district advisory board will be established to identify problems within the districts and to recommend development schemes for the allocation of funds. Army monitoring teams will be established to supervise proper utilization of the funds, and efforts will be made to complete the schemes at minimum cost.

WATER AND DRAINAGE

May 13	The ADB agrees to provide 91 per cent of the total Rs. 3 billion loan needed for Rawalpindi's Water and Sanitation Agency (WASA). Eighty-seven percent is allocated for water supply projects and 13 per cent for sewerage schemes.
October 6	The NWFP government decides to launch a Rs. 740 million Rural Water Supply and Sanitation (RWSS) project to improve water and sanitation facilities in the rural areas of the province. This four-year project is to be carried out with financial assistance from the United Kingdom.
October 22	The ADB refuses to extend further assistance for the Rawalpindi WASA.
November 8	UNICEF proposes to launch a Rural Sanitation Programme in Punjab, where one million toilets will be constructed.

WOMEN

January 31	A seminar on "Violence against Women: Techniques to Counteract," organized by the Progressive Women's Association (PWA), outlines a strategy to curb violence against women.
February 4	The Minister of State for Women's Development, Social Welfare and Special Education states that the government is planning to further increase the women's job quota, which is currently 5 per cent.
March 16	The ADB agrees to provide a US$47 million loan for a project to reduce maternal and infant mortality. It intends to expand community-based health care and family planning services, and to develop 20 women-friendly district health facilities.
August 29	The Pakistan Agricultural Research Council (PARC) decides to establish

	a gender and development directorate in their Social Sciences Division, intended to fortify agricultural development through the equitable utilization of women's skills.
October 22	A Pakistani businesswoman is awarded the first "Asian Women's Achievement Award."
October 29	The federal Ministry of Law announces the establishment of executive committees, assisted by the provincial governments, for legal and monetary assistance to female prisoners.
October 30	The 1999 *State of Human Rights in Pakistan* report is released, highlighting the plight of women **(see box A1.4)**.
December 14	The World Bank agrees to assist with women's development projects, providing technical and other relevant assistance to facilitate these projects. This includes setting up women's crisis centres to provide legal and medical aid to female victims.

CHILDREN

September 2	The Punjab government and UNICEF agree to spend Rs. 9.6 million on the elimination of child labour in the province (Rs. 1.4 million and Rs. 8.2 million, respectively).
September 6	UNICEF launches "Education as a Preventive Strategy against Child Labour": a 29-nation plan to fight against child labour, including pilot projects to provide schooling for working children.
November 24	The United Nations Economic and Social Commission for Asia and the Pacific (UNESCAP) agrees to launch a four-year programme worth

BOX A1.4

STATE OF HUMAN RIGHTS IN PAKISTAN, 1999

The 1999 *State of Human Rights in Pakistan* report highlights the unfortunate, prevalent deprivation of human rights conditions for women. It points to violence against women, as well as the denial of economic and other social rights. According to the report, suicides among women increased to 493 in 1999.

The report claims there were 885 women prisoners in Punjab jails, most awaiting trial, with the majority having already waited for over a year. A major reason for the trial delays is the unavailability of police escorts required to take them to court. Of these women, 40 per cent were jailed under the *Hadood* Ordinance (which applies to adulterers, although has also been known to be applied to rape victims). It was stated that the women in jails were abused and harassed, were living in unhygienic conditions, and were being given unhealthy food.

More than 2,000 rape cases were also reported in the Punjab. Honour killings are on the rise, with 303 having taken place in Punjab and another 271 in Sindh, in 1999 alone. A total of more than 1,000 honour killings were reported during the year, of which more than 15 per cent were carried out on minors.

On average in Pakistan during 1999, more than two women were burnt every three days due to domestic violence, five women were killed daily, and one in every 12,500 women was raped.

	US$1million against sexual abuse of children in 12 countries, including Pakistan.
December 13	UNICEF's annual report, *State of the World's Children 2000*, is released **(see box A1.5)**.
December 14	The United Kingdom's Save the Children Fund reports that besides poverty, large families and low investment in the social sectors are also major contributors to child labour.

MISCELLANEOUS

January 5	Donor assistance of £450 million for SAP-II is agreed to by the World Bank, ADB, European Union, and the Netherlands government.
January 6	The Sindh government decides to abolish the urban-rural quota system in the provincial services.
January 9	The Canadian government agrees to provide Can$6.7 million as a technical assistance grant for the SAP communications project.
February 19	The Government of Japan announces the provision of Rs. 11.9 million to seven Pakistani NGOs for grass-roots assistance.
April 8	The Prime Minister's Programme for Development and Employment is approved, and Rs. 16.5 billion is allocated for farm-to-market roads, rural electrification, and irrigation system.
May 9	The Punjab government reports a Rs. 4.4 billion cut in funds to social sectors in order to contain its recurring expenditures.
May 9	The Punjab government dissolves 1,941 out of 5,967 NGOs working in the province for acting against its charter, being involved in corrupt practices, and misusing funds.
May 17	The Sindh Social Welfare Department cancels the registration of 273 NGOs for not following government rules.

BOX A1.5

UNICEF REPORT, 2000

The latest UNICEF report, *State of the World's Children 2000*, states that, in Pakistan, infant mortality has decreased from 139 (per 1,000 births) in 1960 to 95 in 1998. With regard to under-five mortality, Pakistan is in 33rd position worldwide, with a rate of 136 per 1,000. Approximately 66 per cent of infants under the age of one are immunized against tuberculosis (TB), 59 per cent against DPT (i.e., diphtheria, pertussis [whooping cough], and tetanus), 59 per cent against polio, and 55 per cent against measles. Fifty-eight per cent of expecting mothers are immunized against tetanus.

The primary school enrolment rate for the year was 74 per cent, with net primary school attendance being 71 per cent for males and 62 per cent for females. Secondary school enrolment was 33 per cent for males and 17 per cent for females.

August 4	International donor agencies stop funding the SAP in Balochistan.
September 19	According to a United Nations Development Programme (UNDP) report, corruption accounts for about 5 per cent of Pakistan's gross national product (GNP). The magnitude exceeds Rs. 100 billion per year.
September 20	The Human Development Centre (HDC) launches its annual report, *Human Development in South Asia 1999: Crisis of Governance* **(see box A1.6)**.
October 15	The British government suspends all direct development aid to Pakistan in response to the military coup in Pakistan.
October 26	Pakistan ranks twelfth in the 1999 Corruption Perception Index issued by Transparency International.
December 1	The federal Minister for Environment, Local Bodies and Rural Development announces that the government will help with the legal devolution of the civil bureaucracy in order to bring about such reforms as the introduction of an effective audit system at the district level, and the establishment of an independent election commission.
December 1	The Punjab government decides to strictly enforce the Dowry and Bridal Gifts (Restriction) Act of 1976 in order to curb exorbitant wedding expenditures.

BOX A1.6

HUMAN DEVELOPMENT CENTRE'S REPORT, 1999

The HDC's 1999 Report on *Human Development in South Asia: Crisis in Governance* states that governance in the South Asia region is unfitting and insensitive to the needs and issues of the people. In the case of Pakistan, the report adds that the weak delivery of basic goods by the government is further debilitated by the menace of corruption. It is estimated that, in Pakistan, the cost could be as much as two per cent of the GDP, and that the additional costs of doing business in India and Pakistan are 20 and 28 per cent, respectively.

The report attempts to construct a new concept of governance: *humane governance*. It offers a complete Humane Governance Index (HGI) for 58 industrial and developing countries. A higher number of HGI indicates a higher level of humane governance. The rankings for some South Asian countries are shown in the first accompanying table.

Type of Governance	Pakistan	India	Sri Lanka	Bangladesh
Economic	52	51	47	54
Political	48	31	56	50
Civic	47	41	50	49
Humane	**52**	**42**	**53**	**54**

The HDC quantifies the social costs of the poor system of governance. The report points out that with bad governance, the poor are deprived of social, political and economic opportunities. It reports that over half the world's population living in poverty resides in South Asia.

Gender performance in the region is also poor. Both the gender development index (GDI)[1] and the gender empowerment measure (GEM)[2] compare unfavourably with other developing countries. Figures for some South Asian countries are shown in the second table.

Region	GDI 1995	GEM 1995
Pakistan	0.399	0.179
India	0.424	0.228
Sri Lanka	0.700	0.286
Bangladesh	0.342	0.305
Developing Countries	0.564	n/a

Recommendations for improving governance include the redirection of priorities towards human development, resuscitation of state institutions, and new partnerships between the state and the society.

[1] GDI adjusts the average achievement of each country in life expectancy, educational attainment and incomes in accordance with the disparity in achievement between men and women.
[2] GEM measures the relative empowerment of women and men in political and economic spheres of activity.

A.2

EXTENT AND DEPTH OF POVERTY: ANALYTICAL FRAMEWORK

To analyze the extent and depth of poverty in Pakistan, we pose the following questions: which demographic and socio-economic attributes influence the probability of a household being below the poverty line and, if poor, what determines the depth of poverty? The two-stage Heckman (1976) procedure has been applied to this problem. In the first stage, the probability of the household being poor is analyzed using logic analysis; the dependant variable takes the value of one if poor, and zero otherwise. Once the household has been determined to be poor, we undertake the second stage by analyzing what explains the depth of poverty. Since the analysis concentrates only on poor households there is sample truncation problem, and therefore the Ordinary Least Squares technique cannot be used. The Mills ratio has to be estimated to adjust for sample truncation bias. Specifically, in the first stage, we have:

$$PH_j = bZ_j + \mu_j \quad [1]$$

where:
PH_j = is a dichotomous variable taking a value of one if the jth household is below poverty line
PH_j = 0 otherwise
Z_j = the vector of demographic and socio-economic characteristics that determine poverty
μ_j = a disturbance term

Equation (1) can be used to estimate the Mills ratio, which can then be used (at the second stage) to determine the poverty gap, correcting for the sample bias. That is,

$$PG_j = aX_j + a_j I_j + \mu \quad [2]$$

where:
PG_j = the poverty gap of the jth household
X_j = vector of household attributes that determine the poverty gap
I_j = the inverse of the Mills ratio
m_j = a disturbance term

The above theoretical framework has been applied separately to the rural and urban areas of Pakistan.

Using the HIES (1996-97) database, a number of explanatory variables have been entered into the model. The demographic/social variables include: dependency ratio (age less than 10 years and more than 65 years), age of the head of household (in years) and the square of it, household size, gender of the head of the household (dummy=1 for female, zero otherwise) home ownership (dummy=1 if owner, zero otherwise), and the number of earners in the household. Five levels of educational attainment are represented by dummy variables. The first dummy takes the value of one if the head of the household is educated to primary level, and zero otherwise. The second dummy acquires a value of one if the head has a middle-level education, zero otherwise. Likewise, dummy variables have been created for matric, intermediate and higher education levels.

Similarly, the employment status is indicated by three dummies. If the head of the household is unemployed, the dummy variable acquires the value of one; otherwise zero. If the head of household is underemployed in his main occupation, but makes a living from a secondary occupation, the dummy for unemployment takes the value of one. The phenomenon of self-employment is indicated by the third dummy, which take the value of zero in the case of salary earners.

To analyze the impact of public and private transfers on poverty, four dichotomous variables have been used. The first dummy takes the value of one if the household receives *Zakat* or *Ushr*, otherwise it is zero. To separately quantify the impact of remittances from within and outside Pakistan, two dummies have been created. The first takes the value of one if remittances are received from within Pakistan (zero otherwise), and the second dummy acquires the value of one if remittances are received from outside Pakistan. A dummy for other benefits/gifts/grants has also been used. Lastly, locational dummies have been entered into the model to test for intraprovincial, as well as large versus small city differences, in the incidence of poverty.

A.3

THE POVERTY OF OPPORTUNITY INDEX (POPI)

The Poverty of Opportunity Index (POPI) concentrates on deprivation in three essential dimensions of human life. POPI is the reverse image of the Human Development Index and focuses on human deprivation instead of human achievement. Deprivations in terms of longevity, knowledge and standard of living, are the main components of POPI.

The above three states of deprivation are combined in POPI through the following formula.

$$POPI(a) = [1/a \{(P1)^a + (P2)^a + (P3)^a\}]^{1/a}$$

POPI is a weighted mean of order a of P1, P2 and P3. There is an inescapable arbitrariness in the choice of a. Here the value of a=3 is used to calculate the POPI, which is recommended and used in the Human Development Report (UNDP 1999).

P1 represents the deprivation in health opportunities. Two variables—Life Expectancy at Birth and Child (under 1 year) Mortality Rates—are combined in P1 using equal weights. To capture provincial variations in the index, fixed minimum and maximum values have been established for each of these indicators.

Life Expectancy at Birth (Deprivation)
(Maximum Value - Provincial Magnitude) / (Maximum Value - Minimum Value)
The maximum value is taken as 85 years and the minimum as 25 years.

Child Mortality
(Provincial Magnitude - Minimum Value) / (Maximum Value - Minimum Value)
The maximum value is taken as 120 deaths of children under one in 1,000 live births, and the minimum value as 30.

P2 represents education deprivation. This is a composite of the percentage of adult illiteracy and percentage of primary school-age children who are out of school. P2 is a weighted average of these two percentages. Weights correspond to the ratio of the adult population to primary school-age population.

P3 captures deprivation in terms of standard of living. The percentage of the population which lives below the poverty line is used to represent the state of income deprivation.

Recent estimates from the Household Integrated Economic Survey (1996-97) and Pakistan Integrated Household Survey (1996-97), along with the latest information for Life Expectancy and Mortality rates, are used for the above indicators. POPI is derived for each province of Pakistan.

A.4
AN INTEGRATED SOCIAL POLICY AND MACROECONOMIC PLANNING MODEL

THE NEED FOR AN INTEGRATED MODEL

Historically, Pakistan's development planning models have not explicitly recognized the interdependence between social sector development, intergovernmental revenue-sharing transfers and the macroeconomy. The macroeconometric model of the Pakistan Institute of Development Economics was developed primarily to address the policy issues facing the macroeconomy and was updated in 1992 to include 97 equations. The model, developed by the Applied Economics Research Centre, explicitly incorporates linkages between federal and provincial governments, but its scope is limited to resource mobilization.

Recognizing this reality, the Social Policy and Development Centre (SPDC) has identified a pressing need for Pakistan to develop a macroeconomic model that explicitly incorporates the impact of public expenditure, which is close to 25% of the GDP. SPDC has been working diligently over the past few years to develop just such a model.

STRUCTURE AND LINKAGES OF THE MODEL

The Social Policy and Development Centre has developed a unique economic model which can be used as an effective planning tool for social sector development. This model integrates the social, public finance and macroeconomic dimensions of the economy under one interrelated system.

Called the Integrated Social Policy and Macroeconomic (ISPM) Planning model, the model provides the basic framework for analyzing the implications of SAP and numerous other economic and non-economic policy decisions on the long-term development of Pakistan's social sectors.

The model is highly disaggregated and covers all three levels of government. It is capable of predicting outcomes in great detail, even at the level of individual social service provision. Such a disaggregation of the model at the provincial level in terms of revenues and expenditures on social services (e.g., schools, hospitals, doctors, teachers, enrolments, etc.) is required to analyze the impact of SAP on the macroeconomy.

The model is based on consistent national level data from 1973 onwards and is estimated by single equation regression techniques. It consists of 265 equations, of which 129 are behavioural and the rest are identities. These equations are subsumed into 22 interrelated blocks. All the blocks, along with their size in terms of equations and identities, are listed in **table A 4.1**.

Although the model is broadly Keynesian in spirit, the specification of individual blocks and equations is based on a pragmatic approach. It captures the reality and non-market clearing aspects of Pakistan's economy. Thus, the macroeconomic block is essentially supply driven. In addition, the social sector indicators are also resource determined.

The model is both dynamic and rich in specification. The nature of linkages across the model varies. In some cases, the linkage is simultaneous, in which equations in a block are not only determining equations in another block, but are also determined by them. Examples include the linkages between the macro production and input block, the production and macro expenditure blocks and the fiscal revenues and expenditure blocks. These simultaneous equations may be

TABLE A4.1

INTEGRATED SOCIAL POLICY AND MACROECONOMIC (ISPM) MODEL

		Total Number of Behavioural Equations	Total Number of Identities	Total Number of Equations
A	Macroeconomic Production Block	6	14	20
B	Macro Input Demand Block	7	10	17
C	Macroeconomic Expenditure Block	10	10	20
D	Federal Revenue Block	5	7	12
E	Federal Expenditure Block	9	8	17
F	Federal Deficit Block	1	3	4
G	Provincial Revenue Block	7	5	12
H	Provincial Expenditure Block	12	5	17
I	Provincial and Total Budget Deficit	0	3	3
J	Local Revenue Block	3	4	7
K	Local Expenditure Block	10	6	16
L	Trade Block	5	4	9
M	Monetary Block	1	1	2
N	Price Block	4	5	9
O	Human Capital Index Block	27	27	54
P	Public Health Index Block	12	11	23
Q	Index of Economic Infrastructure Block	0	4	4
R	Index of Fiscal Effort Block	0	4	4
S	Poverty	2	3	5
T	Gender Inequality	1	1	2
U	Educated Unemployment	6	0	6
V	Malnutrition	1	1	2
	TOTAL	129	136	265

behaviourally determined or may just be identities. The broad links **(see chart A 4.1)** of the model can be traced as follows.

Macro → Public Finance

The key link there is that developments in the macroeconomy influence the growth of the tax bases (including divisible pool taxes) and thereby affect the fiscal status of different governments. Also, the overall rate of inflation in the economy affects the growth of public expenditure.

Public Finance → Social Sector Development

The availability of resources, both external and internal, determines the level of development

CHART A4.1

BASIC STRUCTURE OF THE ISPM MODEL

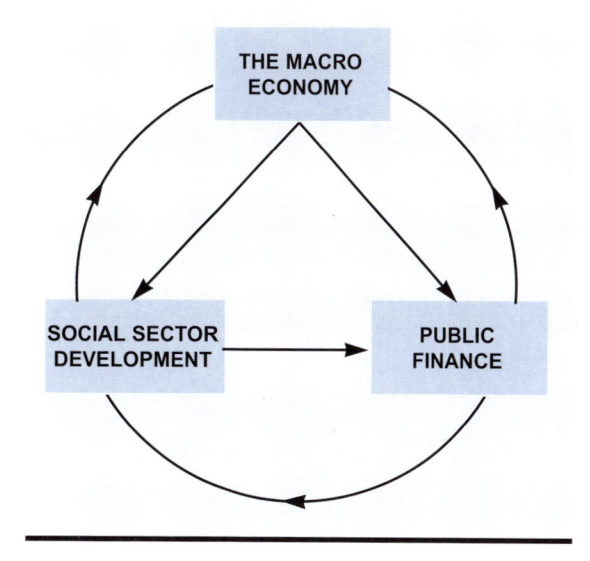

THE MACRO ECONOMY → SOCIAL SECTOR DEVELOPMENT → PUBLIC FINANCE

and recurring outlays to social sectors by different levels of government, especially provincial and local.

Social Sector Development → Macroeconomy

Higher output of educated workers and their entry into the labour force raises the human capital stock and could contribute to improvements in productivity and a higher growth rate of output in the economy. Similarly, an improvement in public health standards may also have a favourable impact on production.

Public Finance → Macroeconomy

The level of government expenditure could exert a demand side effect on national income, while the size of the overall budget deficit of the federal and provincial governments (combined) influences the rate of monetary expansion and consequently the rate of inflation in the economy.

Social Sector Development → Public Finance

A vital link in the model is between the rate of social sector development and the state of public finances, especially of provincial governments, in terms of implications for the level of debt servicing and recurring expenditures.

Macroeconomy → Social Sector Development

Demographic and other socio-economic changes affect the demand for social sector facilities such as schools and hospitals, and thereby influence the level of social sector outputs.

Linkages within macroeconomics, fiscal and social sector blocks

Apart from these broad linkages among different modules, there are also links between different blocks within each module.

An example of a major linkage within the macro module is the two-way linkage to and from the macro production block and macro input blocks. This link is due to the dependence of sectoral value added on the factors of production and input demand functions on the value of production. Macro production determines macro expenditure, as private consumption is influenced by income.

The two-way link between the macro production block and the trade block is due to the fact that the value of imports and exports determines and is determined by economic production activity. The trade gap affects the level of money supply.

Important linkages in the fiscal module consist of the simultaneous dependence of revenues of various levels of government and their expenditures. Non-tax receipts of governments have been made a function of the recurring expenditure on particular services via cost-recovery ratios. Similarly, the level of government expenditure is affected by the government's level of resource generation. Important vertical links between levels of government include fiscal transfers in the form of divisible pool transfers and non-development grants (in line with the feasible level of decentralization) from provincial to local governments. The link between the budget deficits of the federal and provincial governments and their revenues and expenditures is obvious.

FORECASTING AND POLICY ANALYSIS TOOL

Given the richness in structure and the complex web of interrelationships and interactions embodied within it, the ISPM model can be used first as a forecasting tool, both for the medium and long term, and, second, for undertaking policy simulations to analyze the consequences of particular policy actions by the federal or other levels of government.

For example, if the federal government decides to pursue a policy of higher tax mobilization and opts for a rigorous fiscal effort, the model can forecast the impact, not only on federal finances, but also on the fiscal status of the provincial governments. In this scenario, it could also forecast key macroeconomic magnitudes such as growth in the gross domestic product and the inflation rate. With respect to other specific policy issues, the model can also:

- provide projections of the quantum of revenue transfers to the provincial governments by the federal government, both short term and medium term, under different scenarios;

- determine the impact of different rates and patterns of economic growth on provincial tax bases and revenues;

- determine the impact of changes in provincial expenditure priorities on fiscal status, levels of service provision and the overall macroeconomy;

- determine the impact of education expenditures by provincial governments on sectoral inputs (schools, teachers), enrolments, outputs, entry into the labour force and literacy rates;

- determine the impact of health expenditures by provincial governments on sectoral inputs (beds, rural health centres, doctors, nurses, paramedics) and on the health status of the population;

- determine the impact of higher levels of resource mobilization by provincial governments on federal transfers, sectoral levels of expenditure and fiscal status; and

- determine the impact of SAP-type programmes on the level and quality of service provision and on the financial position of provincial governments.

LOOKING AHEAD

The ISPM model is a rich and complex analytical tool for assessing the implications of wide-ranging economic, fiscal and social policy interventions. It was formally introduced to the Planning Commission of Pakistan in January 1997. It has contributed significantly to the development of various planning scenarios for the Ninth Plan. Its completion by the Social Policy and Development Centre is a first step in the evolutionary process of attempts to model and stylize the intricate real-world linkages and working of the Pakistan economy. Work continues on developing the ISPM model further.

A.5

SPDC PUBLICATIONS

INTEGRATED SOCIAL POLICY AND MACRO MODELLING UNIT

RESEARCH REPORTS

Macroeconomic Developments and Poverty
Hafiz A. Pasha
RR 33, April 2000, Price Rs. 70

A Medium-Term Macroeconomic Framework for Pakistan
Hafiz A. Pasha
RR 31, February 2000, Price Rs. 60

Impact of Economic Adjustment on Social Development in Pakistan
Hafiz A. Pasha, Aisha Ghaus-Pasha, Sajjad Akhtar et al.
RR 28, September 1999, Price Rs. 60

Integrated Social Policy and Macroeconomic Planning Model for Pakistan
Hafiz A. Pasha, M. Aynul Hasan, Aisha Ghuas-Pasha et al.
RR 7, June 1995, Price Rs. 360

Specification of Integrated Social Sector Revenue and Expenditure Planning Model
Hafiz A. Pasha, Aisha Ghaus-Pasha, M. Aynul Hasan et al.
RR 3, August 1993, Price Rs. 110

POLICY PAPERS

Statement to the Commonwealth Delegation
Hafiz A. Pasha
PP 17, October 1999, Price Rs. 35

Unsustainability of the Balance of Payments
Hafiz A. Pasha and Zafar H. Ismail
PP 16, September 1999, Price Rs. 40

CONFERENCE PAPERS

An Econometric Evaluation of Pakistan's National Education Policy, 1998-2010
Sajjad Akhtar and M. Ajaz Rasheed
CP 28, July 7-9, 1999, Price Rs. 35

Integrated Social Sector Macroeconomic Model for Pakistan
Hafiz A. Pasha, M. Aynul Hasan, Aisha Ghaus-Pasha et al.
CP 25, December, 1996, Price Rs. 35

Improved Health Status and Economic Growth: Some Co-integration Results from Developing Economies
M. Aynul Hasan, M. Rashid Ahmed, and Aisha Bano
CP 19, July, 1996, Price Rs. 60

Is There a Long-Run Relationship between Economic Growth and Human Development? Some Cross-Country Evidence from Developing Countries
M. Aynul Hasan, Nadeem Ahmed, and Nazia Bano
CP 18, June 1996, Price Rs. 60

Is Public Sector Investment Productive? Some Evidence from Pakistan
Hafiz A. Pasha, M. Aynul Hasan, Aisha Ghaus-Pasha et al.
CP 15, Price Rs. 110

Results of Policy Simulations
Aisha Ghaus-Pasha
CP 13, March 1995, Price Rs. 35

Specification of the Integrated Social Policy Macroeconomic Model
M. Aynul Hasan
CP 11, March 1995, Price Rs. 35

Overview of Integrated Revenue and Expenditure Planning Model for Social Sectors
Hafiz A. Pasha
CP 10, March 1995, Price Rs. 35

Investment Strategy and Expenditure Requirements for Social Development
M. Aynul Hasan
CP 2, April 1993, Price Rs. 35

PUBLIC FINANCE UNIT

RESEARCH REPORTS

Evaluation of the Federal Budget, 2000-2001
Hafiz A. Pasha, Aisha Ghaus-Pasha, Zafar H. Ismail et al.
RR 35, June 2000, Price Rs. 200

Analysis of Provincial Budgets, 1999-2000
Hafiz A. Pasha, Aisha Ghaus-Pasha, Zafar H. Ismail et al.
RR 26, August 1999, Price Rs. 35

Evaluation of the Federal Budget, 1999-2000
Hafiz A. Pasha, Aisha Ghaus-Pasha, Zafar H. Ismail et al.
RR 23, June 1999, Price Rs. 60

Essays on the Federal Budget, 1998-99
Aisha Ghaus-Pasha, Zafar H. Ismail, Sajjad Akhtar et al.
RR 22, July 1998, Price Rs. 110

Fiscal Decentralization: Lessons from the Asian Experience
Hafiz A. Pasha
RR 19, January 1997, Price Rs. 60

Growth of Public Debt and Debt Servicing in Pakistan
Hafiz A. Pasha and Aisha Ghaus-Pasha
RR 17, April 1996, Price Rs. 235

The Provincial Budgets, 1997-98
Zafar H. Ismail, Ajaz Rasheed, M. Asif Iqbal et al.
RR 15, July 1997, Price Rs. 60

An Evaluation of the Federal Budget, 1997-98
Zafar H. Ismail, Sajjad Akhtar, Asad U. Sayeed et al.
RR 14, July 1997, Price Rs. 60

An Evaluation of the Budget, 1996-97
Hafiz A. Pasha, Aisha Ghaus-Pasha, Zafar H. Ismail et al.
RR 13, July 1996, Price Rs. 110

Resource Mobilisation and Expenditure Planning for Social Sectors in Pakistan
Aisha Ghaus-Pasha, M. Asif Iqbal, Rafia Ghaus et al.
RR 12, June 1996, Price Rs. 235

National Finance Commission: 1995 – Intergovernmental Revenue Sharing in Pakistan
Aisha Ghaus-Pasha, Rafia Ghaus, A. Rauf Khan et al.
RR 8, January 1996, Price Rs. 110

A Study on Improving the Efficiency and Effectiveness of Spending in the Social Sectors and Increasing Resource Mobilisation in the Provinces
Hafiz A. Pasha, Aisha Ghaus-Pasha, M. Aynul Hasan et al
RR 2, September 1992, Price Rs. 360 per volume (Rs.1,800 for the full 5 volume set)

Fiscal Policy in Pakistan
Hafiz A. Pasha, Aisha Ghaus-Pasha, and Rafia Ghaus
RR 1, October 1991, Price Rs. 235

POLICY PAPERS

Macroeconomic Framework for Debt Management
Aisha Ghaus-Pasha and Hafiz A. Pasha
PP 19, May 2000, Price Rs. 100

Broad-basing of the GST: The Strategy for Transition
Hafiz A. Pasha
PP 15, July 1999, Price Rs. 35

Provincial Resource Mobilisation
Aisha Ghaus-Pasha, A. Rauf Khan, and Rafia Ghaus
PP 14, June 1998, Price Rs. 35

Financial Sustainability of NGOs: Proposal for 1998-99 Federal Budget
Aisha Ghaus-Pasha and Zafar H. Ismail
PP 13, May 1998, Price Rs. 35

Political Economy of Tax Reforms: The Pakistan Experience
Hafiz A. Pasha
PP 12, February 1997, Price Rs. 60

Fiscal Effort by Provincial Governments in Pakistan
Rafia Ghaus and A. Rauf Khan
PP 10, November 1995, Price Rs. 60

Implication of the TOR of the New NFC
Aisha Ghaus-Pasha
PP 9, June 1995, Price Rs. 35

Provincial Budgets of 1995-96
Aisha Ghaus-Pasha, Rafia Ghaus, and A. Rauf Khan
PP 8, July 1995, Price Rs. 35

Switchover to Ad Valorem Octroi Rates at Dry Ports
Aisha Ghaus-Pasha, M. Asif Iqbal, and Naveed Hanif
PP 7, October 1994, Price Rs. 110

Rationalisation of Octroi Rates
Aisha Ghaus-Pasha, A. Rauf Khan, and Naveed Hanif
PP 6, October 1994, Price Rs. 110

User Charges in Health
Zafar H. Ismail and M. Asif Iqbal
PP 5, August 1994, Price Rs. 110

Sindh Government Budget of 1993-94
Aisha Ghaus-Pasha, Rafia Ghaus, M. Asif Iqbal et al.
PP 4, July 1994, Price Rs. 35

User Charges in Education
Zafar H. Ismail and M. Asif Iqbal
PP 3, June 1994, Price Rs. 110

Sales Taxation of Services by Provincial Governments
Hafiz A. Pasha and Rafia Ghaus
PP 2, June 1994, Price Rs. 110

Rationalisation of Stamp Duties on Financial Assets and Transactions
Aisha Ghaus-Pasha and A. Rauf Khan
PP 1, June 1994, Price Rs. 60

CONFERENCE PAPERS

Issues in Fiscal Decentralization
Aisha Ghaus-Pasha and Hafiz A. Pasha
CP 33, August, 2000, Price Rs. 60

Public Expenditure Reform
Hafiz A. Pasha
CP 32, July 3-4, 2000, Price Rs. 35

Determinants of Rates of Octroi Tax in Pakistan
Aisha Ghaus-Pasha, A. Rauf Khan, and Rafia Ghaus
CP 24, April, 1995, Price Rs. 60

Sustainability of Public Debt in Pakistan
Hafiz A. Pasha and Aisha Ghaus-Pasha
CP 21, July, 1996, Price Rs. 60

Municipal Finance in Small Cities
Hafiz A. Pasha and Aisha Ghaus-Pasha
CP 17, December, 1995 Price Rs. 60

Financial Development of Megacities
Hafiz A. Pasha and Aisha Ghaus-Pasha
CP 16, October 1995, Price Rs. 60

Is the Social Action Programme (SAP) in Pakistan Financially Sustainable?
Hafiz A. Pasha, M. Aynul Hasan, Aisha Ghaus-Pasha et al.
CP 14, April 1995, Price Rs. 60

Development of Property Taxation
Abdul Waheed Khan
CP 9, March 1995, Price Rs. 35

Prospects of Resource Mobilisation by the Provincial Governments
Imtiaz Ahmed Cheema
CP 8, March 1995, Price Rs. 35

Expenditure Planning Issues
Tariq Sultan
CP 7, April 1993, Price Rs. 35

Local Government Resource Mobilisation
Kashif Murtaza
CP 6, April 1993, Price Rs. 35

Local Government Resource Mobilisation
Hafiz A. Pasha and Aisha Ghaus-Pasha
CP 5, April 1993, Price Rs. 35

Problems in Resource Mobilisation in Punjab
Imtiaz A. Cheema
CP 4, April 1993, Price Rs. 35

Provincial Government Resource Mobilisation in Punjab
Hafiz A. Pasha
CP 3, April 1993, Price Rs. 35

POVERTY AND GENDER RESEARCH UNIT

RESEARCH REPORTS

Evaluation of Social Safety Nets in Pakistan
Hafiz A. Pasha, Sumaira Jafarey, and Hari Ram Lohano
RR 32, March 2000, Price Rs. 60

Social Impact of Economic Crisis: Lessons for Pakistan
Aisha Ghaus-Pasha, Hafiz A. Pasha, Sumaira Jafarey et al.
RR 29, December 1999, Price Rs. 110

Modelling Poverty Trends in Pakistan: Some Additional Empirical Evidence
Sajjad Akhtar and Mansoor Ahmed
RR 27, August 1999, Price Rs. 35

The 1998 Population Census
Aisha Ghaus-Pasha, Zafar H. Ismail, Abu Nasar et al.
RR 25, June 1999, Price Rs. 35

Gender Inequality in Developing Countries: A Case Study of Pakistan
Hafiz A. Pasha, Aisha Ghaus-Pasha, and Abu Nasar
RR 24, June 1999, Price Rs. 35

Social and Economic Ranking of Districts of Pakistan
Aisha Ghaus-Pasha, Hafiz A. Pasha, Rafia Ghaus et al.
RR 18, January 1998, Price Rs. 60

The World Summit for Social Development: Its Implications for Social Sector Development in Pakistan
Asad U. Sayeed and Zafar H. Ismail
RR 11, June 1996, Price Rs. 60

Social Development Ranking of Districts of Pakistan
Aisha Ghaus-Pasha, Hafiz A. Pasha, Rafia Ghaus et al.
RR 10, June 1996, Price Rs. 60

CONFERENCE PAPERS

Pakistan's Ranking in Social Development: Have We Always Been Backward?
Aisha Ghaus-Pasha and Naeem Ahmed
CP 29, November 1999, Price Rs. 35

Gender Differentials in the Cost of Primary Education: A Study of Pakistan
Zafar H. Ismail
CP 26, December, 1996, Price Rs. 35

Social Development Ranking of Districts of Pakistan
Aisha Ghaus-Pasha, Hafiz A. Pasha, and Rafia Ghaus
CP 23, December 1996, Price Rs. 60

Has Poverty Returned to Pakistan?
Aisha Ghaus-Pasha and Asad U. Sayeed
CP 20, July 1996, Price Rs. 60

GOVERNANCE, TRAINING, MONITORING AND EVALUATION UNIT

RESEARCH REPORTS

Alternative Delivery Mechanisms for Social Services: Some Case Studies from Pakistan
Zafar H. Ismail, Michael G. McGarry, John Davies et al.
RR 36, June 2000, Price Rs. 90

Public-Private Partnerships in the Health Sector
Hafiz A. Pasha and Abu Nasar
RR 34, May 2000, Price Rs. 65

Elements of Good Economic Governance
Hafiz A. Pasha
RR 30, February 2000, Price Rs. 50

Decentralized Governance of Sindh Katchi Abadis Authority
Hafiz A. Pasha, Aisha Ghaus-Pasha, Zafar H. Ismail et al.
RR 21, May 1998, Price Rs. 110

Review of the Social Action Programme
Aisha Ghaus-Pasha, Micheal G. McGarry, Asad U. Sayeed et al.
RR 16, August 1997, Price Rs. 500

Continuation Rates in Primary Education: A Study of Pakistan
Hafiz A. Pasha, Zafar H. Ismail, and M. Asif Iqbal
RR 9, May 1996, Price Rs. 60

Optimal Enrolment and Cost-Effective Expenditures for Public School System
Hafiz A. Pasha, M. Aynul Hasan, Ajaz Rasheed et al.
RR 6, October 1994, Price Rs. 235

Optimal Mix of Health Sector Expenditure
Hafiz A. Pasha, M. Aynul Hasan, Ajaz Rasheed et al.
RR 5, September 1994, Price Rs. 110

POLICY PAPERS

Revamping the SAP
Hafiz A. Pasha, Aisha Ghaus-Pasha, Zafar H. Ismail et al.
PP 18, May 2000, Price Rs. 60

Ninth Five-Year Plan (1998-2003): Issues Paper
Hafiz A. Pasha, Aisha Ghaus-Pasha, Zafar H. Ismail et al.
PP 11, April 1996, Price Rs. 110

CONFERENCE PAPERS

Issues in Institutional Reform for Devolution
Kaiser Bengali
CP 34, August 2000, Price Rs. 55

Social Sector Policies Under SAP
Zafar H. Ismail
CP 31, October 1999, Price Rs. 40

Impediments to Social Development in Pakistan
Zafar H. Ismail
CP 30, November 1999, Price Rs. 35

Impediments to Improvement of Social Sectors in Pakistan
Zafar H. Ismail
CP 27, March 1998, Price Rs. 35

The City of Karachi: Planning and Managing for Urban Development
Zafar H. Ismail
CP 22, August 1996, Price Rs. 60

The Implementation Environment of the Social Action Programme
Javed Sadiq Malik
CP 1, March 1995, Price Rs. 35

INFORMATION SYSTEMS UNIT

RESEARCH REPORTS

Database Development for Integrated Social Sector Revenue and Expenditure Model
Aisha Ghaus-Pasha, Zafar H. Ismail, M. Asif Iqbal et al.
RR 4, February 1994, Price Rs. 110

CONFERENCE PAPERS

Software Development and Use of the Model
Ajaz Rasheed
CP 12, March 1995, Price Rs. 35

DATABASE REPORTS

Database Report 1997: Education Module
Zafar H. Ismail, A. Rauf Khan, Abu Nasar et al.
DB 3, November 1997, Price Rs. 220

Database Report 1997: Provincial Finance Module
Zafar H. Ismail, A Rauf Khan, Abu Nasar et al.
DB 2, September 1997, Price Rs. 350

Database Report 1997: Federal Finance Module
Zafar H. Ismail, A. Rauf Khan, and Naeem Ahmed
DB 1, July 1997, Price Rs. 120

SPDC BOOKS

Social Development in Pakistan: Social Development in Economic Crisis. Annual Review 1999
Hafiz A. Pasha, Aisha Ghaus-Pasha, Zafar H. Ismail et al.
SPDCB 3, 1999, Price Rs. 395

Social Development in Pakistan. Annual Review 1998
Aisha Ghaus-Pasha, Zafar H. Ismail, Sajjad Akhtar et al.
RR 20, April 1998, Price Rs. 370

Provincial Governments and the Social Sectors in Pakistan
Aisha Ghaus-Pasha, Hafiz A. Pasha, and Zafar H. Ismail
SPDCB 2, 1997, Price Rs. 195

Resource Mobilisation and Expenditure Planning in the Provinces of Pakistan
Hafiz A. Pasha, Aisha Ghaus-Pasha, and M. Aynul Hasan
SPDCB 1, 1996, Price Rs. 395

Proceedings of the Seminar on Prospects and Policies for the Future
CPP 4, January 2000, Price Rs. 50

CONFERENCE PROCEEDINGS

Proceedings of the Launching Ceremony of Social Development in Pakistan. Annual Review 1998
CPP 3, April 1998, Price Rs. 110

Proceedings of the Second Conference on Resource Mobilisation and Expenditure Planning
CPP 2, March 1995, Price Rs. 1,200 for the full 4-volume set

Proceedings of the Conference on Resource Mobilisation and Expenditure Planning
CPP 1, April 1993, Price Rs. 360

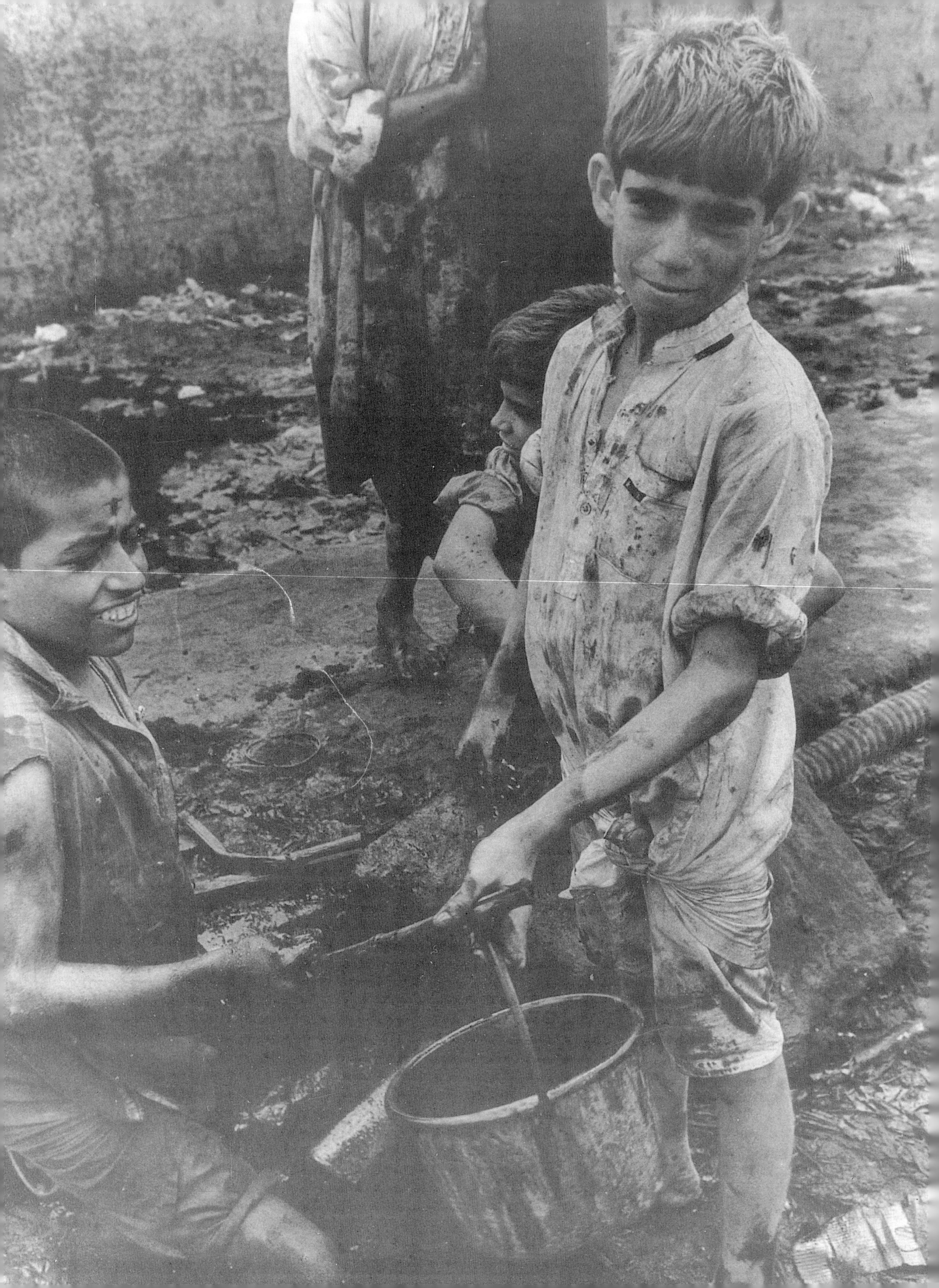

SELECTED SOCIAL DEVELOPMENT INDICATORS

DEMOGRAPHIC PROFILE

	Crude death rate			Crude birth rate			Infant mortality rate			Natural growth rate			Life expectancy
Year	Urban	Rural	Total	Urban	Rural	Total	Urban	Rural	Total	Urban	Rural	Total	(years)
PUNJAB													
1976-79	9.5	11.7	11.1	41.4	42.5	42.2	80	107	100	3.2	3.1	3.1	n/a
1984-86	8.6	12.5	11.0	39.8	44.6	42.7	88	131	120	3.1	3.2	3.2	57.6
1987-89	8.3	11.5	10.6	37.6	43.0	41.4	93	119	105	2.9	3.2	3.1	57.8
1990-92	7.9	11.2	10.2	33.5	41.2	38.9	83	129	110	2.6	3.0	2.9	58.0
1994	7.0	11.2	10.0	31.6	38.8	36.7	54	123	106	2.5	2.7	2.7	n/a
1996	7.1	9.9	9.1	30.9	37.2	35.3	64	100	86	2.4	2.7	2.6	60.0
SINDH													
1976-79	6.1	11.5	9.2	33.7	43.9	39.5	57	83	74	2.8	3.2	3.0	n/a
1984-86	8.5	13.0	10.6	40.2	45.3	42.5	86	138	114	3.2	3.2	3.2	55.1
1987-89	7.8	13.7	10.8	35.4	43.3	39.4	76	145	113	2.8	3.0	2.9	54.4
1990-92	7.1	13.2	10.1	34.7	44.0	39.3	68	138	98	2.8	3.1	2.9	55.4
1994	8.1	13.2	10.6	31.6	43.3	37.3	67	142	110	2.3	3.0	2.7	n/a
1996	7.3	9.9	8.6	32.8	37.9	35.5	54	126	87	2.6	2.8	2.7	55.4
NWFP													
1976-79	9.0	11.1	10.7	41.0	43.6	43.2	100	111	109	3.2	3.3	3.2	n/a
1984-86	10.1	9.8	9.7	38.8	46.3	44.2	146	83	93	2.9	3.7	3.4	58.7
1987-89	7.3	9.7	9.3	38.1	46.9	45.5	67	80	76	3.1	3.7	3.6	59.3
1990-92	7.5	10.1	9.7	34.0	44.7	43.1	74	94	90	2.6	3.5	3.3	59.6
1994	5.1	9.0	8.5	34.3	43.2	41.8	35	60	57	2.9	3.4	3.3	n/a
1996	7.3	8.9	8.6	30.1	36.7	35.6	77	81	80	2.3	2.8	2.7	56.6
BALOCHISTAN													
1976-79	6.4	7.2	7.1	33.1	36.9	36.3	44	69	66	2.7	3.0	2.9	n/a
1984-86	8.4	13.8	12.1	45.4	45.6	45.9	101	166	155	3.7	3.2	3.4	50.4
1987-89	8.7	11.4	11.0	44.4	44.3	44.4	104	117	114	3.6	3.3	3.3	51.0
1990-92	7.9	12.0	11.5	35.5	45.6	44.1	88	128	117	2.8	3.4	3.3	51.5
1994	4.8	9.5	8.8	31.5	41.7	40.2	81	123	118	2.7	3.2	3.1	n/a
1996	4.2	7.5	6.8	25.4	35.1	32.9	81	89	87	2.1	2.8	2.6	57.8
PAKISTAN													
1976-79	8.2	11.4	10.5	38.4	42.7	41.5	74	101	94	3.0	3.1	3.1	n/a
1984-86	8.7	12.2	10.8	40.1	45.1	43.0	92	126	116	3.1	3.3	3.2	56.9
1987-89	8.1	11.6	10.5	37.0	43.7	41.6	85	117	106	2.9	3.2	3.1	57.1
1990-92	7.6	11.4	10.2	34.0	42.5	39.8	77	125	105	2.6	3.1	3.0	57.3
1994	7.0	11.2	9.9	31.7	40.3	37.6	58	116	100	2.5	2.9	2.8	62.0
1996	7.1	9.6	8.8	31.3	37.1	35.2	64	94	85	2.4	2.8	2.6	63.0

DEFINITIONS:
- **Crude birth rate:** The number of live births per thousand population in a year
- **Crude death rate:** The number of deaths per thousand population in a year
- **Infant mortality rate:** The number of deaths of children under 1 per thousand live births in a year
- **Natural growth rate:** ([Crude birth rate]-[Crude death rate])/10
- **Life expectancy:** The number of years a newborn infant would live if prevailing patterns of mortality at the time of birth were to stay the same throughout the child's life

SOURCES:
1. GOP, Pakistan Demographic Surveys, Federal Bureau of Statistics (various issues)
2. Data for 1994 from Pakistan Demographic Survey 1994 (unpublished)

DEMOGRAPHIC PROFILE — 2

Year	Percentage of births in medical institutions Urban	Rural	Total	Fertility rate (per woman) Urban	Rural	Total	Sex ratio (%) Urban	Rural	Total	Dependency ratio Urban	Rural	Total	Contraceptive prevalance rate[a] (%)
PUNJAB													
1976	4.9	0.7	1.8	7.3	7.1	7.1	111	107	108	96	98	98	n/a
1979	4.6	0.6	1.6	7.4	7.3	7.3	110	107	108	96	100	99	9.3
1985	n/a	n/a	8.2	6.3	8.0	7.2	107	104	105	94	101	98	n/a
1990	18.2	4.7	8.2	5.2	6.6	6.1	106	103	104	89	98	95	13.0
1992	22.5	6.1	10.2	4.7	6.1	5.7	105	101	102	85	97	93	n/a
1994	22.5	6.8	10.7	4.5	5.9	5.5	105	102	103	84	99	94	20.0
1996	28.9	9.4	14.3	4.6	5.9	5.4	106	105	105	91	97	95	26.8
SINDH													
1976	33.6	0.6	12.4	5.4	7.3	6.4	112	116	114	87	97	93	n/a
1979	32.4	0.2	11.2	5.1	7.3	6.3	112	117	115	84	98	92	9.6
1985	n/a	n/a	19.1	5.9	7.5	6.6	107	114	110	91	103	96	n/a
1990	41.4	4.1	20.7	5.2	6.9	6.0	109	109	109	87	103	95	12.0
1992	46.3	10.1	26.3	4.8	6.7	5.6	108	107	107	86	105	95	n/a
1994	44.6	8.3	22.9	4.4	6.7	5.5	109	108	109	83	103	92	15.0
1996	48.0	8.8	26.7	4.9	6.2	5.5	108	113	111	87	99	93	23.4
NWFP													
1976	4.6	0.2	0.9	6.6	6.9	6.8	108	101	102	94	108	106	n/a
1979	4.5	0.6	1.3	7.3	6.7	6.7	109	100	101	100	115	112	9.4
1985	n/a	n/a	3.8	7.0	8.4	7.8	107	102	104	99	110	105	n/a
1990	19.5	3.7	5.6	5.0	6.9	6.6	107	102	103	90	113	109	9.0
1992	21.0	5.4	7.2	4.6	6.7	6.4	105	99	100	86	114	109	n/a
1994	28.3	8.9	11.3	4.6	6.8	6.4	104	101	101	85	113	108	15.0
1996	25.1	12.3	13.6	4.4	5.8	5.5	107	102	103	91	114	110	18.7
BALOCHISTAN													
1976	19.8	0.8	2.9	5.9	7.3	7.1	106	108	108	86	91	90	n/a
1979	17.9	0.6	4.1	7.6	4.9	5.2	101	115	113	92	95	94	4.3
1985	n/a	n/a	2.6	6.6	6.5	6.6	114	109	111	105	109	107	n/a
1990	26.2	6.7	9.0	5.2	7.6	7.3	110	105	106	103	115	113	2.0
1992	22.6	4.4	6.3	5.1	8.0	7.5	109	109	109	100	110	108	n/a
1994	15.1	4.8	6.0	4.8	6.8	6.4	112	109	110	96	108	107	4.0
1996	17.6	6.4	7.7	4.0	6.1	5.6	109	115	113	109	108	108	7.1
PAKISTAN													
1976	13.7	0.6	4.1	6.6	7.1	6.9	111	108	109	93	99	97	5.2
1979	13.0	0.5	3.8	6.6	7.1	6.9	110	108	109	92	101	98	n/a
1985	19.8	2.5	10.1	6.2	7.8	7.1	108	106	107	94	103	100	9.1
1990	26.8	4.6	10.6	5.2	6.7	6.2	107	104	105	89	102	98	12.0
1992	31.1	6.6	13.1	4.7	6.4	5.8	106	102	103	85	102	96	n/a
1994	30.6	7.3	13.5	4.5	6.2	5.6	106	103	104	84	102	96	18.0
1996	35.1	9.7	16.4	4.7	5.9	5.5	107	106	106	90	101	97	23.9

[a] For contraceptive prevalance rate, fiscal years are used (eg., 1976-77)

DEFINITIONS:
- **Percentage of births in medical institutions:** The number of births in medical institutions as a percentage of total births
- **Fertility rate:** The average number of children that would be born to a woman if she were to live to the end of her childbearing age and bear children at each age in accordance with prevailing age-specific fertility rates
- **Sex ratio:** The number of males per hundred females
- **Dependency ratio:** The ratio of the dependent population (those under 15 and over 64) to the working-age population (aged 15 to 64)
- **Contraceptive prevalence rate:** The percentage of currently married women aged 15-49 years who are currently using a family planning method

SOURCES:
1. GOP, Pakistan Demographic Surveys, Federal Bureau of Statistics (various issues)
2. Pakistan Contraceptive Prevalence Surveys, Population Welfare Division, Ministry of Planning and Development, Islamabad

LABOUR FORCE AND EMPLOYMENT

Year	Urban Total	Urban Male	Urban Female	Rural Total	Rural Male	Rural Female	Total	Total Male	Total Female	Agriculture (Urban)	Industry (Urban)	Services (Urban)
PUNJAB												
1975	39.8	71.6	4.0	46.1	78.8	9.0	44.6	77.0	7.6	7.4	35.2	57.4
1979	40.0	71.6	5.6	47.9	79.0	14.4	46.0	77.2	12.2	6.4	35.6	58.0
1985	40.0	72.1	4.6	45.7	78.2	11.3	44.1	76.5	9.4	8.6	34.5	56.9
1991	40.1	67.3	10.8	46.1	73.6	17.6	44.3	71.7	15.6	9.4	29.1	61.5
1994	38.2	65.9	9.0	46.2	71.3	20.3	43.9	69.8	17.1	6.0	31.0	63.0
1995	38.1	65.7	8.6	44.9	72.3	16.1	42.9	70.4	14.0	5.7	29.8	64.5
1997	39.9	67.4	10.5	47.8	73.1	20.8	45.2	71.3	17.5	5.6	30.2	64.2
SINDH												
1975	37.6	67.1	3.7	49.1	85.2	6.0	43.1	75.6	4.8	2.4	33.7	63.9
1979	39.4	69.7	5.1	58.9	89.1	24.6	49.9	79.5	15.5	4.3	35.7	60.0
1985	38.2	69.7	3.5	52.1	85.0	13.2	45.1	77.4	8.2	5.2	33.5	61.3
1991	37.9	65.7	5.9	45.7	76.6	9.5	41.6	70.9	7.6	4.9	34.2	60.9
1994	35.9	63.4	5.0	42.9	73.7	6.4	39.5	68.7	5.7	4.3	29.4	66.3
1995	35.9	62.8	5.2	43.1	73.8	6.0	39.7	68.7	5.6	5.2	27.8	67.0
1997	38.0	66.1	5.5	42.5	72.7	6.9	40.2	69.4	6.2	5.1	30.2	64.7
NWFP												
1975	38.4	70.8	3.3	39.9	75.9	3.8	38.6	74.9	3.8	14.0	23.8	62.2
1979	37.3	65.3	5.2	38.8	73.8	4.3	38.5	72.2	4.4	7.3	24.2	68.4
1985	39.7	71.5	4.4	43.9	80.4	6.8	43.3	79.0	4.4	8.7	25.3	66.1
1991	36.2	66.1	5.1	41.0	70.1	10.2	40.2	69.5	9.3	7.9	25.7	66.4
1994	34.5	62.7	4.5	38.9	67.2	11.6	38.2	66.5	10.6	7.8	22.3	69.9
1995	33.7	61.1	4.3	37.2	64.7	11.0	36.7	64.1	10.0	8.1	20.4	71.5
1997	36.4	63.1	5.7	38.5	65.9	10.2	38.1	65.4	9.4	8.6	23.9	67.5
BALOCHISTAN												
1975	37.9	68.2	2.1	45.7	79.4	1.0	44.6	82.5	1.1	22.4	12.8	64.7
1979	36.8	63.3	2.9	47.5	84.1	3.1	45.9	80.3	3.1	6.0	17.7	76.3
1985	37.8	69.3	1.8	45.9	81.4	7.0	44.5	79.4	6.2	8.9	23.2	67.9
1991	36.8	63.1	4.7	43.7	74.3	6.2	42.6	72.7	5.9	11.4	17.7	70.8
1994	35.2	61.8	2.4	41.5	70.8	4.6	40.6	69.5	4.3	8.1	16.1	75.8
1995	34.7	59.8	4.2	41.1	70.0	7.3	40.0	68.3	6.6	11.6	15.9	72.4
1997	34.7	60.6	3.8	40.0	71.0	4.7	38.9	68.9	4.6	10.0	18.8	71.2
PAKISTAN												
1975	38.8	69.6	3.5	45.9	79.8	7.6	43.8	76.7	6.4	6.2	33.6	60.2
1979	39.6	70.3	5.3	48.7	80.1	14.3	46.1	77.3	11.8	5.7	34.5	59.8
1985	39.3	71.1	4.1	46.5	79.8	10.7	44.2	77.1	8.7	7.4	33.3	59.3
1991	39.0	66,6	8.6	45.2	73.6	14.8	43.2	71.3	12.8	7.6	30.7	61.7
1994	37.0	64.7	7.2	44.2	71.0	16.0	42.0	69.1	13.3	5.6	29.6	64.8
1995	37.0	64.3	7.0	43.1	71.3	13.3	41.3	69.1	11.4	5.8	28.3	66.0
1997	38.9	66.5	8.4	45.1	71.8	16.3	43.0	70.0	13.6	5.7	29.6	64.8

DEFINITIONS:
- **Labour force participation:** The number of persons in the labour force as a percentage of the population of 10 years and above

SOURCES:
Pakistan Labour Force Surveys, Federal Bureau of Statistics, Government of Pakistan

LABOUR FORCE AND EMPLOYMENT

Year	Percentage of labour Force in Rural			Percentage of labour Force in Total			Percentage of literates in labour force		
	Agriculture	Industry	Service	Agriculture	Industry	Services	Urban	Rural	Total
PUNJAB										
1975	69.1	15.7	15.2	55.6	20.0	24.4	48.5	19.6	25.9
1979	63.5	19.0	17.5	51.6	22.5	25.9	53.3	26.2	31.9
1985	62.5	18.2	19.3	49.1	22.2	28.7	54.0	28.9	35.2
1991	62.6	17.4	20.0	48.9	20.4	30.7	57.9	31.5	38.3
1994	65.0	14.7	20.3	51.1	18.5	30.4	64.1	32.6	40.0
1995	60.7	16.7	22.6	47.2	19.9	32.9	65.7	34.3	44.7
1997	60.3	15.5	24.2	45.3	19.5	35.2	64.7	37.0	45.9
SINDH										
1975	83.4	5.3	11.3	47.1	18.1	34.9	56.9	23.5	38.4
1979	84.0	6.4	9.6	55.8	16.8	27.4	52.7	19.9	31.5
1985	82.9	6.6	10.5	50.3	17.9	31.8	57.6	22.3	37.1
1991	71.7	10.2	18.1	40.2	21.6	38.3	65.0	34.9	49.1
1994	72.7	9.1	18.2	42.2	18.2	39.6	68.5	33.3	49.0
1995	69.8	11.3	18.9	42.4	18.3	39.4	68.4	30.1	48.2
1997	68.1	9.5	22.3	38.4	19.3	42.3	69.7	30.7	50.3
NWFP										
1975	73.0	10.7	16.3	62.1	13.1	24.8	43.7	18.1	22.8
1979	56.1	17.1	26.8	48.0	18.3	33.8	48.1	25.6	26.0
1985	64.8	14.2	21.0	56.7	15.8	27.4	49.5	20.3	24.5
1991	58.0	14.6	27.4	50.5	16.3	33.3	51.2	28.6	32.0
1994	61.9	12.6	25.4	54.9	13.9	31.3	57.5	28.0	31.8
1995	57.5	12.6	29.9	50.5	13.7	35.8	52.8	30.3	33.8
1997	53.5	15.4	31.1	45.6	16.9	37.5	52.4	31.4	35.2
BALOCHISTAN										
1975	75.4	5.1	19.5	68.8	6.1	25.1	40.5	14.2	17.5
1979	69.9	10.7	19.5	60.6	11.7	27.7	41.6	14.0	18.0
1985	64.4	11.9	23.7	56.7	13.4	29.8	55.5	17.3	22.6
1991	68.1	7.9	24.0	60.9	9.2	29.9	54.8	18.2	22.9
1994	70.5	6.6	22.9	62.7	7.8	29.5	54.7	16.1	21.0
1995	63.1	9.3	27.6	55.5	10.3	34.3	49.1	20.0	25.0
1997	64.4	9.9	25.7	54.6	11.5	34.0	51.4	21.6	27.6
PAKISTAN										
1975	72.1	13.1	14.8	54.8	18.5	26.7	51.2	19.8	28.1
1979	67.4	15.9	16.8	52.7	20.3	27.0	47.2	24.3	31.1
1985	66.7	15.2	18.1	50.6	20.1	29.3	45.0	26.0	33.9
1991	63.8	15.4	20.8	47.5	19.8	32.7	60.2	31.2	39.6
1994	66.0	13.1	20.9	50.0	18.3	31.7	65.1	31.4	40.3
1995	61.9	14.9	23.2	46.8	18.5	34.7	64.3	34.1	43.3
1997	60.8	14.3	24.9	44.2	18.9	36.9	65.2	34.4	44.9

SOURCES:
Pakistan Labour Force Surveys, Federal Bureau of Statistics, Government of Pakistan

LABOUR FORCE AND EMPLOYMENT

Labour force unemployment rate

Year	Total	Urban Male	Female	Total	Rural Male	Female	Total	Total Male	Female
PUNJAB									
1975	3.5	3.5	1.8	2.0	1.7	0.7	2.1	2.1	0.9
1979	6.2	5.5	16.4	4.3	3.0	8.8	3.5	3.5	9.7
1985	6.7	6.8	6.5	4.3	3.7	1.5	4.5	4.5	2.0
1991	10.4	7.3	31.8	7.5	4.6	14.6	5.4	5.4	18.0
1994	8.1	6.6	19.7	5.5	3.8	7.4	4.6	4.6	9.1
1995	8.9	7.0	24.6	6.0	4.3	8.3	5.0	5.0	11.2
1997	9.5	7.0	26.4	5.7	4.4	10.6	6.8	5.2	13.6
SINDH									
1975	1.8	1.8	0.6	1.0	0.4	0.0	1.0	1.0	0.5
1979	4.0	3.5	13.8	1.8	0.6	0.2	1.8	1.8	2.2
1985	4.2	4.3	0.6	2.5	1.5	0.0	2.7	2.7	0.3
1991	4.9	4.0	16.7	3.5	1.3	10.7	2.6	2.6	13.1
1994	4.2	3.7	11.4	3.2	1.5	13.7	2.5	2.5	12.5
1995	3.3	2.6	14.2	2.7	1.2	18.3	1.8	1.8	16.7
1997	3.2	2.1	18.7	2.6	1.0	22.8	2.9	1.5	21.0
NWFP									
1975	2.5	2.4	2.5	2.0	2.0	0.0	2.0	2.0	0.5
1979	4.6	4.4	7.0	3.5	3.0	7.5	3.3	3.3	7.3
1985	6.1	6.2	4.3	3.9	3.8	0.0	4.2	4.2	0.3
1991	7.5	6.0	28.6	6.2	5.1	12.1	5.2	5.2	13.4
1994	6.6	5.2	26.8	5.4	3.8	13.2	4.0	4.0	14.1
1995	8.1	6.1	39.1	7.3	4.3	23.0	4.6	4.6	24.1
1997	6.8	4.7	34.3	9.6	5.2	39.4	9.1	5.1	38.8
BALOCHISTAN									
1975	0.4	0.4	0.0	0.1	0.1	0.0	0.2	0.2	0.0
1979	2.2	2.3	0.8	2.2	1.4	28.3	1.5	1.5	23.5
1985	4.1	4.2	0.0	1.5	1.1	0.0	1.6	1.6	0.0
1991	3.6	2.7	17.4	1.6	1.1	4.7	1.3	1.3	6.0
1994	2.7	2.3	15.1	1.7	1.2	8.3	1.3	1.3	9.0
1995	2.9	1.4	27.2	3.9	2.2	25.7	2.1	2.1	25.8
1997	2.3	1.0	27.8	3.4	1.8	30.7	3.2	1.7	30.2
PAKISTAN									
1975	2.7	2.8	1.8	1.7	1.4	0.6	1.8	1.8	0.7
1979	5.2	4.6	14.6	3.6	2.4	6.4	3.0	3.0	7.6
1985	5.7	5.8	4.1	3.7	3.2	0.8	4.0	4.0	1.4
1991	8.2	5.9	27.7	6.3	3.9	13.7	4.5	4.5	16.8
1994	6.5	5.3	17.8	4.8	3.3	8.5	3.9	3.9	10.1
1995	6.9	5.3	22.6	5.4	3.6	11.7	4.1	4.1	13.7
1997	7.2	5.1	25.2	5.7	3.8	14.6	6.1	4.2	16.8

SOURCES:
Pakistan Labour Force Surveys, Federal Bureau of Statistics, Government of Pakistan

EDUCATION

	Literacy rate			Mean years of schooling			Combined enrolment ratio			Enrolment ratio (primary)		
Year	Male	Female	Total	Male	Female	Total	Male	Female	Total	Male	Female	Total
PUNJAB												
1975	31.6	12.6	22.9	2.0	0.4	1.3	29.6	14.8	22.7	57.8	32.9	46.0
1980	36.4	16.4	27.0	2.5	0.6	1.7	26.7	14.8	21.1	54.5	34.1	44.8
1985	40.9	19.9	31.0	3.1	0.9	2.0	30.4	17.2	24.1	63.1	39.8	51.9
1990	46.9	24.7	36.4	3.1	1.1	2.2	36.1	23.5	30.1	73.9	53.6	64.1
1995	53.7	30.7	42.8	3.7	1.4	2.6	35.8	27.0	31.5	71.1	59.4	65.5
1997	56.8	33.5	45.6	4.0	1.8	2.9	33.7	26.5	30.2	67.4	58.0	62.8
SINDH												
1975	39.3	20.0	30.6	3.1	1.0	2.1	26.9	13.5	20.7	52.5	23.3	38.5
1980	39.7	21.5	31.4	3.1	0.9	2.2	28.9	14.8	22.3	58.2	25.5	42.2
1985	43.4	24.5	34.7	3.8	1.4	2.7	32.4	16.4	24.8	64.0	29.1	47.0
1990	47.8	28.1	38.6	4.2	1.5	3.0	32.8	13.3	23.6	64.5	21.2	43.5
1995	53.2	32.5	43.5	4.7	2.0	3.5	31.6	17.5	24.8	64.6	34.5	50.2
1997	55.4	34.5	45.6	5.2	2.5	4.0	29.8	17.4	23.9	60.0	34.6	47.9
NWFP												
1975	24.1	5.3	15.3	1.8	0.2	1.1	33.4	9.9	22.3	68.9	22.4	46.4
1980	25.7	6.4	16.6	2.3	0.3	1.4	31.9	8.9	21.2	69.8	20.5	46.1
1985	30.4	8.5	20.1	2.3	0.3	1.3	33.1	9.1	21.0	73.2	21.5	48.3
1990	37.5	12.0	25.4	2.8	0.3	1.6	43.6	12.1	28.6	94.5	28.1	62.5
1995	46.2	17.0	32.1	2.9	0.4	1.7	46.3	17.9	32.7	96.3	41.4	69.9
1997	50.3	19.6	35.3	3.2	0.6	1.9	47.8	20.0	34.4	99.2	46.5	73.8
BALOCHISTAN												
1975	15.0	4.2	10.2	1.2	0.1	0.7	15.0	3.8	10.0	33.6	7.3	20.8
1980	15.2	4.3	10.3	1.9	0.4	1.2	13.6	3.4	9.1	31.5	5.9	19.0
1985	18.6	5.8	12.8	2.5	0.3	1.5	18.9	5.0	12.7	44.4	9.2	27.4
1990	24.1	8.4	16.9	1.7	0.2	1.0	26.1	6.5	17.2	60.6	13.1	38.2
1995	31.1	12.0	22.3	1.9	0.2	1.1	30.3	13.1	22.5	63.5	30.0	48.1
1997	34.5	13.9	25.0	2.5	0.3	1.5	30.6	16.8	24.3	63.6	39.6	52.7
PAKISTAN												
1975	31.8	13.0	23.2	2.0	0.4	1.3	28.9	13.4	21.7	57.0	27.9	43.1
1980	34.8	15.7	25.9	2.4	0.5	1.6	27.2	13.4	20.7	56.2	28.4	42.8
1985	38.1	18.1	29.8	2.9	0.7	1.9	30.6	15.3	23.3	63.7	32.7	48.8
1990	43.9	22.4	34.9	3.0	0.8	1.9	35.8	18.7	27.6	73.9	39.7	57.5
1995	50.5	27.6	40.9	3.3	1.0	2.2	36.0	22.7	29.6	72.9	49.2	61.5
1997	53.4	30.0	43.6	3.8	1.3	2.6	34.6	22.9	29.0	70.2	49.7	60.4

NOTES:
1. Figures for Pakistan represent the four provinces combined
2. Literacy rate is estimated using 1998 population census
3. Primary and secondary school enrolment represents enrolment in the government sector only
4. Tertiary enrolment is the sum of intermediate college, degree college, and university enrolment
5. Degree college enrolment is the sum of general degree college, post graduate college and professional degree college enrolment

DEFINITIONS:
- **Literacy rate:** The number of literate persons as a percentage of population aged 10 and above
- **Mean year of schooling:** Average number of years of schooling received per person aged 25 and above
- **Combined enrolment ratio:** The number of students enrolled in all levels as a percentage of the population aged 5 to 24
- **Enrolment ratio (primary):** The number of students enrolled in primary level classes (I to V) as a percentage of the population aged 5 to 9

SOURCES:
1. Development Statistics of Provincial Governments (various issues)
2. Education Statistics of Provincial Governments (various issues)
3. GOP, Pakistan School Statistics, Central Bureau of Education (various issues)
4. GOP, Pakistan Education Statistics, Central Bureau of Education (various issues)
5. National and Provincial Education Management Information Systems (various issues)
6. GOP, Labour Force Survey, Federal Bureau of Statistics (various issues)
7. GOP, Census Report of Pakistan, Population Census Organization (various issues)

EDUCATION 7

| | Pupil-teacher ratio (primary) ||| Percentage of cohort reaching |||||| Availability of primary schools |||
| | | | | Grade 2 ||| Grade 5 ||| | | |
Year	Male	Female	Total	Male	Female	Total	Male	Female	Total	Male	Female	Total
PUNJAB												
1975	43.4	39.6	42.0	75.7	66.2	72.3	n/a	n/a	n/a	176	258	207
1980	41.5	41.1	41.3	80.3	53.9	68.6	53.2	33.3	44.9	177	251	206
1985	36.1	43.3	38.4	93.5	54.7	75.3	62.0	34.4	49.3	129	257	170
1990	38.6	46.7	41.5	83.3	51.6	68.0	69.5	44.4	58.1	136	199	161
1995	35.9	49.9	40.9	72.0	49.2	60.5	55.5	40.1	48.2	149	221	177
1997	34.5	49.1	39.8	64.8	47.3	56.0	53.0	37.9	45.6	154	226	182
SINDH												
1975	27.9	20.6	25.3	58.4	70.3	61.3	n/a	n/a	n/a	136	658	219
1980	35.3	25.8	31.9	72.3	79.6	74.3	45.2	58.1	48.6	154	802	255
1985	40.2	30.1	36.5	69.7	79.3	72.4	43.1	52.3	45.7	128	624	208
1990	40.4	20.1	32.6	64.9	62.5	64.3	45.2	38.0	43.1	80	509	135
1995	20.9	27.1	23.4	54.1	52.1	53.4	43.2	61.5	47.7	75	410	132
1997	20.3	28.2	22.5	52.5	57.2	54.0	40.5	40.6	40.5	75	381	122
NWFP												
1975	52.5	52.2	52.4	71.9	67.5	70.8	n/a	n/a	n/a	196	509	278
1980	68.8	54.8	65.2	56.6	64.4	58.2	35.5	36.7	35.8	209	547	297
1985	50.9	48.9	50.5	42.6	46.1	43.3	31.1	28.4	30.6	206	540	294
1990	44.7	36.5	42.6	40.4	40.4	40.4	32.7	26.7	31.4	115	355	171
1995	36.8	41.8	38.1	30.3	40.1	32.9	21.9	29.0	23.4	82	286	125
1997	30.0	41.7	32.8	29.9	41.3	33.1	23.9	25.5	24.4	83	242	122
BALOCHISTAN												
1975	35.2	28.6	33.9	46.7	43.4	46.0	n/a	n/a	n/a	146	606	231
1980	38.3	38.6	38.4	56.7	51.8	55.2	28.4	26.0	28.0	192	837	308
1985	40.4	56.3	42.3	46.2	35.4	44.0	28.7	34.4	29.7	120	900	207
1990	23.6	27.2	24.2	25.8	32.6	27.0	19.7	20.5	19.8	92	873	158
1995	24.1	43.3	27.6	29.0	30.2	29.3	19.7	24.1	20.6	86	407	135
1997	24.7	40.2	28.5	28.7	28.1	28.5	18.6	23.9	19.8	89	297	131
PAKISTAN												
1975	39.6	34.2	37.8	69.5	66.6	68.6	n/a	n/a	n/a	165	340	219
1980	42.6	37.2	40.7	72.0	59.4	67.5	46.9	37.7	43.7	176	352	231
1985	39.1	40.1	39.4	72.4	57.6	67.0	48.7	36.9	44.4	136	348	192
1990	38.7	38.5	38.7	63.9	50.9	59.1	51.0	40.3	47.2	111	267	155
1995	30.6	42.7	34.4	53.6	47.5	51.1	40.6	40.5	40.6	107	266	150
1997	28.9	42.5	33.1	50.0	46.7	48.6	40.1	35.9	38.4	109	257	150

DEFINITIONS:
- **Pupil-teacher ratio (primary):** The ratio of pupils enrolled in primary level classes (I to V) to the number of teachers in primary schools
- **Percentage of cohort reaching Grade 2:** The percentage of children starting primary school who reach Grade 2
- **Percentage of cohort reaching Grade 5:** The percentage of children starting primary school who reach Grade 5
- **Availability of primary schools:** The ratio of population aged 5 to 9 to the number of primary schools

SOURCES:
1. Development Statistics of Provincial Governments (various issues)
2. Education Statistics of Provincial Governments (various issues)
3. GOP, Pakistan School Statistics, Central Bureau of Education (various issues)
4. GOP, Pakistan Education Statistics, Central Bureau of Education (various issues)
5. National and Provincial Education Management Information Systems (various issues)

EDUCATION 8

Year	Availability of primary school teachers Male	Female	Total	Ratio of boys to girls (primary)	% of female teachers (primary)	Enrolment ratio (secondary) Male	Female	Total	Pupil-teacher ratio (secondary) Male	Female	Total	Ratio of boys to girls (secondary)	% of female teachers (secondary)
PUNJAB														
1975	75	120	91	1.9	36.0	29.6	10.0	20.8	28.5	8.5	18.9	3.6	48.0
1980	76	120	92	1.7	36.6	26.2	9.9	18.7	24.9	8.2	16.6	3.1	49.5
1985	57	109	74	1.7	32.6	28.3	12.0	20.7	26.7	8.6	17.0	2.7	53.5
1990	52	87	65	1.5	35.7	35.5	18.3	27.4	15.4	14.2	15.0	2.2	33.3
1995	50	84	62	1.3	35.9	39.4	24.1	32.1	14.6	16.6	15.3	1.8	33.2
1997	51	85	63	1.2	36.1	36.4	24.1	30.5	13.0	16.6	14.1	1.6	32.4
SINDH														
1975	53	88	66	2.5	35.6	22.2	14.4	18.8	21.2	14.3	18.2	1.9	43.3
1980	61	101	75	2.4	36.3	24.4	15.4	20.3	24.2	17.2	21.2	1.9	42.7
1985	63	103	78	2.3	36.6	29.5	17.2	23.9	30.3	19.4	25.6	2.0	43.5
1990	63	95	75	3.3	38.1	30.9	17.7	24.8	27.1	17.7	23.1	2.0	42.8
1995	32	79	47	2.0	28.5	27.1	16.9	22.4	24.8	19.5	22.6	1.9	40.4
1997	34	82	47	1.9	27.5	26.6	17.1	22.2	21.0	18.7	20.1	1.8	38.1
NWFP														
1975	76	233	113	3.3	23.4	24.3	3.9	15.1	17.7	16.7	17.6	7.6	12.2
1980	98	267	141	3.7	25.5	20.9	3.4	13.0	14.6	9.1	13.6	7.5	17.6
1985	70	220	104	3.7	22.1	22.0	3.7	13.6	14.0	10.3	13.4	7.0	16.2
1990	47	130	68	3.6	25.3	32.6	6.3	20.3	15.8	13.2	15.4	5.9	16.8
1995	38	101	55	2.5	26.0	41.9	11.5	27.5	18.8	17.9	18.6	4.1	20.7
1997	30	90	44	2.3	23.8	44.3	13.2	29.5	20.9	18.6	20.4	3.7	23.5
BALOCHISTAN														
1975	105	394	163	4.9	20.1	8.8	2.5	6.1	7.0	6.7	6.9	4.8	17.6
1980	122	656	202	5.6	15.1	7.4	2.7	5.4	6.7	5.8	6.5	3.7	23.5
1985	91	610	154	5.2	12.2	9.4	3.9	7.1	5.9	6.7	6.1	3.2	21.5
1990	39	207	63	5.2	14.4	13.3	4.6	9.7	5.7	6.8	5.9	3.9	17.8
1995	38	144	57	2.5	18.3	22.3	7.2	15.9	8.5	10.1	8.8	4.3	16.4
1997	39	101	54	1.9	24.2	21.7	9.1	16.4	8.0	8.7	8.1	3.3	21.5
PAKISTAN														
1975	69	123	88	2.2	34.1	26.3	9.8	18.9	24.0	10.0	18.1	3.3	41.7
1980	76	131	95	2.1	34.9	23.9	9.8	17.5	21.7	10.0	16.7	2.9	42.8
1985	61	123	81	2.1	31.7	26.5	11.5	19.6	23.1	10.6	17.5	2.7	45.0
1990	52	97	67	2.0	33.4	32.7	15.7	24.8	16.3	14.7	15.8	2.4	31.9
1995	42	87	56	1.6	30.9	36.0	19.9	28.4	16.0	17.0	16.3	2.0	31.6
1997	41	85	55	1.5	30.8	34.5	20.3	27.8	14.7	16.8	15.4	1.9	31.5

DEFINITIONS:
- **Availability of primary school teachers:** The ratio of population aged 5 to 9 to the number of primary school teachers
- **Ratio of boys to girls (primary):** The ratio of male students to female students enrolled in primary level classes (I to V)
- **Percentage of female teachers (primary):** The number of female teachers as a percentage of total teachers in primary schools
- **Enrolment ratio (secondary):** The number of students enrolled in secondary level classes (VI to X) as a percentage of the population aged 10 to 14
- **Pupil-teacher ratio (secondary):** The ratio of pupils enrolled in secondary level classes (VI to X) to the number of teachers in secondary schools
- **Ratio of boys to girls (secondary):** The ratio of male students to female students enrolled in secondary level classes (VI to X)
- **Percentage of female teachers (secondary):** The number of female teachers as a percentage of total teachers in secondary schools

SOURCES:
1. Development Statistics of Provincial Governments (various issues)
2. Education Statistics of Provincial Governments (various issues)
3. GOP, Pakistan School Statistics, Central Bureau of Education (various issues)
4. GOP, Pakistan Education Statistics, Central Bureau of Education (various issues)
5. National and Provincial Education Management Information Systems (various issues)

EDUCATION

	Percentage of cohort reaching Grade 6			Percentage of cohort reaching Grade 10			Availability of secondary schools			Availability of secondary school teachers		
Year	Male	Female	Total	Male	Female	Total	Male	Female	Total	Male	Female	Total
PUNJAB												
1975	88.8	75.9	85.6	n/a	n/a	n/a	906	1705	1147	96	85	91
1980	91.8	65.9	83.7	34.0	41.3	35.6	947	1749	1200	95	83	89
1985	95.2	76.3	89.1	40.6	44.6	41.6	861	1575	1092	94	72	82
1990	92.4	87.6	90.7	44.5	51.9	46.6	708	1001	822	43	78	55
1995	93.8	84.2	90.0	44.4	46.5	45.1	648	948	764	37	69	48
1997	88.1	80.7	85.2	40.9	46.1	42.7	558	953	697	36	69	46
SINDH												
1975	59.8	97.2	69.1	n/a	n/a	n/a	938	2056	1234	95	99	97
1980	74.6	89.4	79.4	70.3	60.7	66.8	1059	2474	1432	99	111	104
1985	81.7	90.5	84.5	66.8	58.0	63.7	1010	2630	1407	103	113	107
1990	84.1	95.7	87.6	57.5	54.3	56.4	920	1827	1193	88	100	93
1995	67.8	81.1	71.9	52.9	54.7	53.5	976	1850	1247	91	115	101
1997	65.1	75.1	68.4	60.0	61.9	60.7	806	1722	1067	79	109	91
NWFP												
1975	75.2	26.6	61.8	n/a	n/a	n/a	857	3447	1294	73	430	116
1980	67.3	32.6	59.4	45.6	43.5	45.4	949	3605	1425	70	271	105
1985	77.0	49.4	71.5	46.3	39.5	45.4	897	3521	1365	64	280	99
1990	81.8	79.6	81.4	57.5	48.8	56.2	732	2793	1116	48	211	76
1995	96.1	78.2	91.6	63.3	55.7	61.8	618	1895	908	45	156	68
1997	103.1	77.7	95.8	59.7	52.6	58.3	584	1639	842	47	140	69
BALOCHISTAN												
1975	75.7	64.8	73.6	n/a	n/a	n/a	800	2567	1128	79	272	113
1980	72.9	80.7	74.3	40.7	71.3	45.9	847	3109	1224	90	216	120
1985	72.3	81.9	74.3	51.6	63.5	53.6	766	2649	1097	63	170	86
1990	72.0	82.4	73.8	41.4	36.0	40.1	542	2095	789	43	146	61
1995	81.1	84.7	81.8	55.2	44.9	53.4	557	2126	808	38	141	55
1997	81.6	81.9	81.6	60.9	72.3	62.6	557	1808	784	37	96	49
PAKISTAN												
1975	80.2	73.6	78.5	n/a	n/a	n/a	900	1940	1183	91	102	96
1980	84.0	68.7	79.4	41.7	47.6	43.1	963	2082	1276	91	102	96
1985	88.7	77.8	85.4	47.1	48.9	47.6	889	1942	1186	87	92	89
1990	88.3	88.7	88.4	49.0	52.1	49.9	737	1282	919	50	93	64
1995	88.0	83.0	86.3	48.9	48.8	48.9	690	1196	862	44	85	57
1997	85.2	79.4	83.1	47.7	49.8	48.4	605	1165	783	43	83	55

DEFINITIONS:
- **Percentage of cohort reaching Grade 6:** The percentage of children finishing primary school who reach Grade 6
- **Percentage of cohort reaching Grade 10:** The percentage of children enrolled in Grade 6 who reach Grade 10
- **Availability of secondary schools:** The ratio of population aged 10 to 14 to the number of secondary schools
- **Availability of secondary school teachers:** The ratio of population aged 10 to 14 to the number of secondary school teachers

SOURCES:
1. Development Statistics of Provincial Governments (various issues)
2. Education Statistics of Provincial Governments (various issues)
3. GOP, Pakistan School Statistics, Central Bureau of Education (various issues)
4. GOP, Pakistan Education Statistics, Central Bureau of Education (various issues)
5. National and Provincial Education Management Information Systems (various issues)

HEALTH

Population (in thousands) per

Year	Hospital bed	Doctor (Total)	Doctor (Female)	Nurse	Para-medic	Rural health facility
PUNJAB						
1975	2.3	14.0	57.9	12.1	10.6	413.9
1980	2.1	9.4	41.1	9.3	9.4	218.0
1985	2.1	4.1	18.3	5.6	9.6	92.3
1990	1.8	2.8	11.8	3.8	11.3	61.4
1995	1.7	2.3	8.9	3.3	12.6	62.0
1998	1.7	2.1	7.0	2.7	n/a	65.6
SINDH						
1975	1.5	7.8	25.4	59.0	19.6	338.4
1980	1.2	5.0	16.8	32.9	17.8	199.6
1985	1.2	1.8	6.3	35.5	15.8	179.1
1990	1.1	1.2	4.0	29.4	9.3	93.7
1995	1.1	0.9	3.2	21.9	6.8	70.9
1998	1.1	0.9	2.6	19.3	6.6	68.8
NWFP						
1975	1.4	8.6	54.3	28.9	5.4	435.8
1980	1.4	6.2	39.1	40.2	5.0	255.5
1985	1.3	3.5	21.4	11.4	2.5	75.6
1990	1.3	2.5	13.7	15.7	2.7	64.9
1995	1.3	2.1	10.3	9.1	2.9	63.1
1998	1.3	2.0	8.7	7.6	n/a	61.3
BALOCHISTAN						
1975	1.5	17.2	56.3	22.0	3.8	223.3
1980	1.9	11.1	46.5	40.2	3.7	249.1
1985	1.7	4.7	24.5	30.9	3.0	121.7
1990	1.5	3.5	16.6	23.8	2.2	37.7
1995	1.4	2.8	11.2	24.3	1.8	35.0
1998	1.4	2.4	9.9	16.2	n/a	33.3
PAKISTAN						
1975	1.9	11.1	44.4	16.8	9.6	384.9
1980	1.7	7.4	30.7	13.4	8.6	221.1
1985	1.6	3.1	12.9	8.2	6.8	99.1
1990	1.5	2.1	8.3	5.9	6.6	63.5
1995	1.4	1.7	6.3	4.9	6.4	60.8
1998	1.5	1.5	5.1	4.1	n/a	61.9

NOTES:
1. Number of nurses and paramedics of provincial governments only
2. Number of rural health facilities = [No. of RHCs+(No. of BHUs/5)]
3. Data representing institutions run by armed forces and private sector are not included
4. The ratio of hospital beds, doctors, female doctors, nurses, paramedics per thousand people

SOURCES:
1. Pakistan Statistical Yearbook
2. Pakistan Medical and Dental Council, Islamabad
3. Development Statistics of Provincial Government (various issues)
4. Pakistan Nursing Council, Islamabad

SHELTER 11

Indicators	Unit	1980	1989	1998
RURAL				
Growth rate of housing unit	%		2.0	2.2
Persons per housing unit	No.	6.6	6.7	6.5
Rooms per housing unit	No.	1.8	2.0	2.1
Persons per room	No.	3.6	3.4	n/a
Nature of tenure				
Owned	%	83	91	87
Rented	%	2	2	2
Rent-free	%	15	7	11
Quality of construction				
Pacca (baked bricks/blocks/stone)	%	30	49	45
Semi-pacca (unbaked bricks/earthbound)	%	59	46	45
Katcha (wood/bamboo and others)	%	11	5	9
Housing unit with:				
Electricity	%	15	51	61
Inside piped water	%	3	9	13
Gas piped	%	0	1	2
URBAN				
Growth rate of housing unit	%		3.3	3.1
Persons per housing unit	No.	7.0	6.9	6.6
Rooms per housing unit	No.	2.2	2.3	2.4
Persons per room	No.	3.2	3.0	n/a
Nature of tenure				
Owned	%	68	79	68
Rented	%	22	18	23
Rent-free	%	10	3	9
Quality of construction				
Pacca (baked bricks/blocks/stone)	%	79	89	85
Semi-pacca (unbaked bricks/earthbound)	%	18	10	13
Katcha (wood/bamboo and others)	%	3	1	2
Housing unit with:				
Electricity	%	71	92	93
Inside piped water	%	38	60	58
Gas piped	%	20	42	56
OVERALL				
Growth rate of housing unit	%		2.4	2.5
Persons per housing unit	No.	6.7	6.7	6.5
Rooms per housing unit	No.	1.9	2.0	2.2
Persons per room	No.	3.5	3.3	n/a
Nature of tenure				
Owned	%	78	89	81
Rented	%	8	5	9
Rent-free	%	14	7	10
Quality of construction				
Pacca (baked bricks/blocks/stone)	%	44	61	58
Semi-pacca (unbaked bricks/earthbound)	%	48	35	35
Katcha (wood/bamboo and others)	%	9	4	7
Housing unit with:				
Electricity	%	31	64	71
Inside piped water	%	13	25	27
Gas piped	%	6	14	19

Note: Gas Piped and Gas Cylinder are combined for the year 1980, while for 1989 and 1998 only the term 'gas' is mentioned

SOURCES:
1. GDP Housing Census Report, Population Census Organization (PCO)(1980)
2. GDP Survey of Housing and Housing Facilities in Pakistan, FBS (1989)
3. GDP Census Bulletin of Pakistan, Population and Housing Census, PCO (1998)

PUBLIC FINANCE 12

	Government expenditure (Rs. per capita) on[a]					Public expenditure on social sectors as a percentage of total expenditure				
Year	Education	Health	Physical planning & housing	Other social sectors	Total social sectors	Education	Health	Physical planning & housing	Other social sector	Total social sectors
					PUNJAB					
1975	159	45	58	4	266	21	6	8	1	36
1980	155	60	85	9	309	19	7	11	1	38
1985	240	83	69	12	404	22	8	6	1	37
1990	318	118	73	21	530	24	9	6	2	40
1995	404	97	72	22	594	28	7	5	2	42
1997	425	97	72	21	614	31	7	5	2	45
1999	376	89	80	20	565	29	7	6	2	43
					SINDH					
1975	194	47	72	17	330	22	5	8	2	38
1980	203	44	58	8	313	22	5	6	1	34
1985	255	67	78	10	411	22	6	7	1	35
1990	357	126	77	24	584	22	8	5	1	35
1995	485	116	73	17	691	22	5	3	1	31
1997	420	122	47	16	605	23	7	3	1	33
1999	399	110	41	13	563	24	7	2	1	34
					NWFP					
1975	156	64	37	2	259	18	7	4	0	29
1980	207	91	64	15	377	19	8	6	1	35
1985	360	129	70	9	568	23	8	4	1	36
1990	491	166	84	10	751	23	8	4	0	35
1995	671	193	121	68	1053	29	8	5	3	45
1997	635	163	114	46	958	30	8	5	2	46
1999	644	156	122	59	982	29	7	5	3	44
					BALOCHISTAN					
1975	152	55	37	8	253	10	3	2	1	16
1980	148	52	34	40	274	9	3	2	3	17
1985	324	129	129	54	635	14	6	6	2	28
1990	467	214	226	58	966	15	7	7	2	32
1995	636	281	240	106	1263	19	8	7	3	37
1997	687	225	275	73	1260	23	7	9	2	41
1999	556	212	321	48	1137	20	8	12	2	42
					FEDERAL GOVERNMENT					
1975	29	7	26	0	62	2	0	1	0	4
1980	30	9	4	77	120	1	0	0	4	6
1985	41	11	6	87	145	1	0	0	3	5
1990	47	16	5	122	190	1	0	0	3	5
1995	55	34	6	61	157	2	1	0	2	4
1997	52	43	8	45	149	1	1	0	1	4
1999	46	32	6	31	115	1	1	0	1	3
					PAKISTAN					
1975	189	54	81	7	331	7	2	3	0	13
1980	197	67	75	88	427	7	2	3	3	14
1985	297	96	78	101	571	7	2	2	2	14
1990	395	144	86	143	768	7	3	2	3	14
1995	513	155	91	91	850	9	3	2	2	16
1997	505	158	88	70	821	9	3	2	1	15
1999	461	138	92	56	747	9	3	2	1	14

[a] At constant prices of 1998-99

NOTE: Per capita expenditure is based on 1998 census

DEFINITIONS:
- **Expenditures:** Represents both current and development, combined
- **Physical planning & housing expenditures:** Consists of expenditure on public health services and urban town planning and regulatory services, housing and physical planning

SOURCES:
Annual Budget Statements of Provincial Governments (various issues)
Annual Budget Statements of Federal & Provincial Governments (various issues)

BIBLIOGRAPHY

Ahmed, M., and Q.M. Ahmed.
1995   The Estimation of the Black Economy of Pakistan through the Monetary Approach. *Pakistan Development Review* 34(4).

Ahmed, V., and R. Amjad.
1984   *The Management of the Pakistan Economy: 1947-82.* Karachi: Oxford University Press.

Akhtar, S., and M. Ahmed.
1999   *Modelling Poverty Trends in Pakistan: Some Additional Empirical Evidence.* Research Report No. 27, Poverty and Gender Research Unit. Karachi: Social Policy and Development Centre.

Alauddin, T., and B. Reza.
1981   *Tax Progressivity in Pakistan.* Research Report Series 133. Islamabad: Pakistan Institute of Development Economics.

Amin, R., et al.
1995   Poor Women's Participation in Credit Based Self-Employment: The Impact on their Empowerment, Fertility, Contraceptive Use and Fertility Desire in Rural Bangladesh. *Pakistan Development Review* 34(2).

Ashraf, J.
1998   Earnings in Karachi: Does Gender Make a Difference? *Pakistan Economic and Social Review* 36(1).

Asian Development Bank (ADB).
2000   *Aide Memoire: Proposed Legal and Judicial Reform Program.* Fact-finding mission. Islamabad.

2000   *Asian Development Outlook.* New York: Oxford University Press.

Bardhan, P.
1997   *The Role of Governance in Economic Development: A Political Economy Approach.* Paris: OECD Development Centre Studies.

Bardhan, P., and D. Mookherjee.
1999   *Capture and Governance at Local and National Levels.* University of California at Berkeley: Institute of International Studies; Boston University: Department of Economics.

Barro, R.J.
1991   Economic Growth in a Cross-Section of Countries. *The Quarterly Journal of Economics* 106(2).

Bennett, K.M.
1995   Economic Decline and the Growth of the Informal Sector: The Guyana and Jamaica Experience. *Journal of International Development* 7(2).

Burgess, R.S.A., and N.H. Stern.
1993   Taxation and Development. *Journal of Economic Literature* Vol. 31.

Burki, S.J., et al.
1988   *Pakistan's Development Priorities: Choices for the Future.* Karachi: Oxford University Press.

Commission on Global Governance.
1995   *Our Global Neighborhood.* New York: Oxford University Press.

Datt, G., and M. Ravallion.
1992   *Behavioral Responses to Workforce: Evidence for Rural India.* Washington, D.C.: The World Bank.

DeSoto, H.
1989   *The Other Path: The Invisible Revolutions in the Third World.* New York: Harper and Row.

Easterly, W.
1997   *The Ghost of Financing Gap: How the Harrod Domar Growth Model Still Haunts Development Economics.* Policy Research Working Paper, Development Research Group. Washington, D.C.: The World Bank.

1999   *The Middle-Class Consensus and Economic Development.* Policy Research Working Paper, Development Research Group. Washington, D.C.: The World Bank.

Edirisinghe, N.
1987   *The Food Stamp Scheme in Sri Lanka.* Washington, D.C.: International Food Policy Research Institute (IFPRI).

Ellis, F.
1994   *Agricultural Policies in Developing Countries.* U.K.: Cambridge University Press.

Ercelawn, A.
1991   *Absolute Poverty as Risk of Hunger.* Karachi: Applied Economics Research Centre. Mimeographed.

1992   *Absolute Poverty in the '80s: Rural and Urban Trends in Pakistan.* Discussion Paper No. 161. Karachi: Applied Economics Research Centre.

Ezemenrai, K., and K. Subbarao.
1998   *Jamaica's Food Stamp Program.* Washington, D.C.: The World Bank.

Faruqee, R.
1995   *Structural and Policy Reforms for Agricultural Growth: The Case of Pakistan.* Agriculture and Natural Resource Division, South Asia Department. Washington, D.C.: The World Bank.

Feige, E.L.
1990   Defining and Estimating Underground and Informal Economies: The New Institutional Economic Approach. *World Development* 18(7).

Ghaus, A.
1989   The Incidence of Public Expenditure in Karachi. *Pakistan Journal of Applied Economics,* 8(1). Summer 1989.

Government of Pakistan (GOP).
1985   *Food Composition Table for Pakistan.* Planning and Development Division.

1996-97 *Labour Force Survey.* Statistics Division. Islamabad.

1997   *Household Integrated Economic Survey,* 1996-97.

1997   *Pakistan Integrated Household Survey,* 1996-97.

1997   *Overcoming Poverty.* Report of the Task Force on Poverty Alleviation.

1999-2000 *Economic Survey of Pakistan.* Ministry of Finance. Islamabad.

2000   Budget Speech, 2000-2001. Minister for Finance, Economic Affairs and Statistics, Finance Division. Islamabad.

Gregorio, J.D.
1992   Economic Growth in Latin America. *Journal of Development Economics* 39(1).

Griffin, K., and A.R. Khan, eds.
1972   *Growth and Inequality in Pakistan.* London and Basingstoke: Macmillan Press.

Haq, M.
1983   *The Poverty Curtain: Choices for the Third World.* Lahore: Ferozsons.

1997   *Human Development in South Asia.* Karachi: Oxford University Press and the Human Development Centre.

Hart, K.
1973   Informal Income Opportunities and Urban Employment in Ghana. *The Journal of Modern African Studies,* Vol. 1.

Hasan, P.
1998   *Pakistan's Economy at the Crossroads.* Karachi: Oxford University Press.

Hashemi, S.M., et al.
1996   Rural Credit Programs and Women's Empowerment in Bangladesh. *World Development 24(4).*

Havinga, I.C., et al.
1989   Poverty in Pakistan, 1984-85. *Pakistan Development Review 28(4).*

Heckman.
1976   The Common Structure of Statistical Models of Transaction: Sample Selection, Variables and a Sample Estimation for Such Models. *Annals of Economic and Social Measurement,* Vol. 5.

Human Development Centre (HDC).
1999   *Human Development in South Asia: The Crisis of Governance.* Karachi: Oxford University Press.

Hussain, I.
1999   *Pakistan: The Economy of an Elitist State.* Karachi: Oxford University Press.

Iqbal, Z., and G.M. Zahid.
1998   Macroeconomic Determinants of Economic Growth. *Pakistan Development Review 37(2).*

Ismail, Z.H.
1996   Gender Differentials in the Cost of Primary Education: A Study of Pakistan. *Pakistan Development Review 35(4).*

1998   *Impediments to Improvement of Social Sectors in Pakistan.* Conference Paper No. 27. Karachi: Social Policy and Development Centre.

Ismail, Z.H., M.G. McGarry, et al.
2000   *Alternative Delivery Mechanisms for Social Services: Some Case Studies from Pakistan.* Research Report No. 36. Karachi: Social Policy and Development Centre.

Jacob, Y., et al.
1998   Promoting Efficient Rural Financial Intermediation. *The World Bank Observer* 13(2).

Jafri, S.M.
1999   Assessing Poverty in Pakistan. In A Profile of Poverty in Pakistan, by Mahbubul Haq. Pakistan: Centre for Human Development and UNDP.

Jafri, S.M., and A. Khattak.
1995   Income Inequality and Poverty in Pakistan. *Pakistan Economic and Social Review* 33(1& 2).

Jahan, R.
1996   The Elusive Agenda: Mainstreaming Women in Development. *Pakistan Development Review* 35(4).

Jeetun, A.
1978   *Incidence of Taxes in Pakistan.* Research Report No. 10. Karachi: Applied Economics Research Centre.

Jehle, G.A.
1995   *Zakat* and Inequality: Some Evidence from Pakistan. *Review of Income and Wealth* 40(2).

Kemal, A.R., and R. Amjad.
1997   Macroeconomic Policies and their Impact on Poverty Alleviation in Pakistan. *Pakistan Development Review* 36(1).

Kemal, A.R.
1998   *The Urban Informal Sector of Pakistan: Some Stylized Facts.* Research Report No. 161. Islambad: Pakistan Institute of Development Economics.

Khan, A.
1998   *Female Mobility and Social Barriers to Accessing Health/Family Planning Services: A Qualitative Research Study in Three Punjabi Villages.* Islamabad: Ministry of Population Welfare; London School of Hygiene and Tropical Medicine: Department for International Development.

Khan, M.H.
1998   *Public Policy and the Rural Economy of Pakistan.* Pakistan: Vanguard Books (Pvt.) Ltd.

Khan, S.R.
1999   *Fifty Years of Pakistan's Economy: Traditional Topics and Contemporary Concerns.* Karachi: Oxford University Press.

Khan, S.R., and M. Irfan.
1985 Rates of Return to Education and the Determinants of Earnings in Pakistan. *Pakistan Development Review* 24(3&4).

Khandker, S.R.
1998 *Fighting Poverty with Micro-credit: Experience in Bangladesh.* New York: Oxford University Press for the World Bank.

Klaus, D., and H. Binswanger.
1999 The Evolution of the World Bank's Land Policy. *The World Bank Research Observer* 14(2).

Knight, M., et al.
1993 Testing the Neoclassical Theory of Economic Growth. *International Monetary Fund Staff Papers* 40(3).

Lanjouw, P.
1994 *Regional Poverty in Pakistan: How Robust are Conclusions?* Washington, D.C.: The World Bank. Mimeographed.

Mahmood, M.
1999 Reforming the Agrarian Land Market. In *Strategic Reforms for Agricultural Growth in Pakistan.* WBI Learning Resources Series. Washington, D.C.: The World Bank.

Mahmood, S., et al.
1996 *Sustainable Development: With Special Reference to Pakistan.* Lahore: Laser-soft Composers and Printers.

Malik, M.H.
1988 Some New Evidence on the Incidence of Poverty in Pakistan. *Pakistan Development Review* 27(4).

Malik, M.H., and N. Saqib.
1989 Tax Incidence by Income Classes in Pakistan. *Pakistan Development Review* 28(1).

Malik, S.J., et al.
1994 *Pakistan's Economic Performance, 1947-1993: A Descriptive Analysis.* Lahore: Sure Publishers.

Murdoch, J.
1999 The Microfinance Promise. *Journal of Economic Literature* 37(4).

1999 The Role of Subsidies in Microfinance: Evidence from the Grameen Bank. *Journal of Development Economics* 60(1).

Nabi, I., et al.
1991 *The Agrarian Economy of Pakistan: Issues and Policies.* Karachi: Oxford University Press.

Naseem, S.M.
1973 Mass Poverty in Pakistan: Some Preliminary Findings. *Pakistan Development Review* 13(4).

Noman, O.
1997 *Economic and Social Progress in Asia.* Karachi: Oxford University Press.

North, D.
1991 Institutions. *Journal of Economic Perspectives* 5(1).

Nouriel, R.
1992   Financial Repression and Economic Growth. *Journal of Development Economics* 39(1).

Obasanjo, O.
1994   Corruption, Democracy and Human Rights in Africa. Keynote address to the Africa Leadership Forum on Corruption, Democracy and Human Rights in Africa, Contonou, Benin, September 19-21.

O' Hava, P., ed.
1988   The Informal Sector. *Encyclopedia of Political Economy*. London: Routledge.

Organization for Economic Cooperation and Development (OECD).
1995   Participatory Development and Good Governance. *Development Cooperation Guideline Series*. Paris.

Otsuk, K.
1993   Land Tenure and Rural Poverty. In *Rural Poverty in Asia: Priority Issues and Policy Options. An Introduction*. Hong Kong: Oxford University Press for the Asian Development Bank.

Pasha, H.A.
1997   *Political Economy of Tax Reforms: The Pakistan Experience*. Policy Paper No. 12. Karachi: Social Policy and Development Centre.

2000   *Elements of Good Economic Governance*. Research Report No. 30. Karachi: Social Policy and Development Centre.

Pasha, H.A., et al.
1999   *Social Development in Pakistan: Social Development in Economic Crisis*. Karachi: Oxford University Press.

Pasha, H.A., and A.M. Iqbal.
1994   Taxation Reforms in Pakistan. *Pakistan Journal of Applied Economics* 10(1&2).

Pasha, H.A., and A. Nasar.
2000   *Public-Private Partnerships in the Health Sector*. Research Report No. 34. Karachi: Social Policy and Development Centre.

Pasha, H.A., and S.A. Wasti.
1989   Unemployment and Rates of Return to Education. *Singapore Economic Review* 34(2).

Peattie, L.
1987   An Idea in Good Currency and How it Grew: The Informal Sector. *World Development* 15(7).

Przeworski, A., and F. Limongi.
1993   Political Regimes and Economic Growth. *Journal of Economic Perspectives* 7(3).

Quddus, M.A., et al.
1997   The Livestock Economy of Pakistan: An Agricultural Sector Model Approach. *Pakistan Development Review* 36(2).

Qureshi, M.L.
1984   *Planning and Development In Pakistan: Reviews and Alternatives, 1947-1982*. Lahore: Vanguard Books (Pvt.) Ltd.

Qureshi, S.K.
2000   *Farm Size and Productivity.* Islamabad: Unpublished paper.

Qureshi, S.K., and G.M. Arif.
1999   *Profile of Poverty in Pakistan, 1998-99.* Islamabad: Pakistan Institute of Development Economics. Mimeographed

Rahman, A.
1999   Micro-credit Initiatives for Equitable and Sustainable Development: Who Pays? *World Development* 27(1).

Ravallion, M.
1992   *Poverty Comparisons: A Guide to Concepts and Methods.* LSMS Working Paper No. 88. Washington, D.C.: The World Bank.

Roth, G.
1987   *The Private Provision of Public Services in Developing Countries.* Karachi: Oxford University Press.

Sen, A.K.
1982   *Poverty and Famines: An Essay on Entitlement and Deprivation.* New Delhi: Oxford University Press.

1999   *Development as Freedom.* New York: Oxford University Press.

Social Policy and Development Centre (SPDC).
1994   *Optimal Mix of Health Sector Expenditure.* Research Report No. 5.

1994   *Optimal Enrolment and Cost-Effective Expenditure for Public School System.* Research Report No. 6.

1997   *Review of the Social Action Programme.* Research Report.

1997a *Database Report 1997: Federal Finance Module.* Database Report No. 1.

1997b *Database Report 1997: Provincial Finance Module.* Database Report No. 2.

1998   *Social Development in Pakistan.* Annual Review. Karachi: SPDC and Hamdard Press (Pvt.) Ltd.

1999   *Social Development in Pakistan: Social Development in Economic Crisis.* Annual Review. Karachi: SPDC and Oxford University Press.

Subbarao, K., et al.
1997   *Safety Net Programmes and Poverty Reduction Programmes: Lessons from Cross-Country Experience.* Washington, D.C.: The World Bank.

United Nations Development Programme (UNDP).
1997   *Governance for Sustainable Human Development: A UNDP Policy Document.* Management Development and Governance Division. New York: UNDP and Oxford University Press.

1999   *Fighting to Improve Governance.* Management and Governance Division, Bureau for Development Policy. New York: UNDP.

2000   *Human Development Report 2000.* New York: Oxford University Press.

2000   *Poverty Report 2000: Overcoming Human Poverty.* New York: UNDP.

Waqar, A.J., et al.
1998   Estimating the Production Potential of Major Crops in Pakistan's Agriculture during the 21st Century. *Pakistan Development Review*, Vol. 31.

World Bank (WB).
1994   *Governance: The World Bank's Experience.* Washington, D.C.: The World Bank.

1995   *Pakistan: Poverty Assessment.* Report No. 14397-PAK. Country Operations Division, Country Department, South Asia Region.

1995   *Towards Gender Equality: The Role of Public Policy.*

1998   *A Framework for Civil Service Reform in Pakistan.* Report No. 18386-PAK.

2000   *Multi-Donors Review Mission.* Aide Memoire, SAPP-II, Vol.1 (June 9). Islamabad.

2000   *World Development Indicators 2000.*

2000   *World Development Report 2000/2001: Attacking Poverty.* New York: Oxford University Press.

Zaidi, A.
1999   *Issues in Pakistan's Economy.* Karachi: Oxford University Press.

Zaman, A.
1996   *Wheat Subsidy: An Economic Review to Determine Welfare and Budgetary Effects.* Karachi: Arshad Zaman Associates (Pvt.) Ltd.